CAPITALISM AND COVID-19
VOLUME 1

Studies in Critical Social Sciences Book Series

Haymarket Books is proud to be working with Brill Academic Publishers (www.brill.nl) to republish the *Studies in Critical Social Sciences* book series in paperback editions. This peer-reviewed book series offers insights into our current reality by exploring the content and consequences of power relationships under capitalism, and by considering the spaces of opposition and resistance to these changes that have been defining our new age. Our full catalog of *SCSS* volumes can be viewed at https://www.haymarketbooks .org/series_collections/4-studies-in-critical-social-sciences.

CAPITALISM AND COVID-19

VOLUME I

F/Ailing Capitalism
and the Challenge of COVID-19

NOEL CHELLAN

Haymarket Books
Chicago, IL

First published in 2023 by Brill Academic Publishers, The Netherlands
© 2023 Koninklijke Brill NV, Leiden, The Netherlands

Published in paperback in 2024 by
Haymarket Books
P.O. Box 180165
Chicago, IL 60618
773-583-7884
www.haymarketbooks.org

ISBN: 979-8-88890-227-1

Distributed to the trade in the US through Consortium Book Sales and
Distribution (www.cbsd.com) and internationally through Ingram Publisher
Services International (www.ingramcontent.com).

This book was published with the generous support of Lannan Foundation,
Wallace Action Fund, and the Marguerite Casey Foundation.

Special discounts are available for bulk purchases by organizations and
institutions. Please call 773-583-7884 or email info@haymarketbooks.org for more
information.

Cover design by Jamie Kerry and Ragina Johnson.

Printed in the United States.

Library of Congress Cataloging-in-Publication data is available.

To the many millions who lost their lives in the time of COVID-19

*To the millions of moms, dads, sons, daughters,
husbands, wives, grandmas, granddads, friends, etc.
who lost loved ones in the time of COVID-19*

*To the hundreds of millions of workers on the frontline in the
time of COVID-19, who have sacrificed so much – with both their
lives and their energies – so that the human race can go on*

*To the caring states and leaders in all parts of the world – that
chose lives over the profit economy in the time of COVID-19*

*To the many that gave little and much to the
needy – in the time of COVID-19*

*To family, friends and colleagues who have passed on in
the time of COVID-19. You will be forever remembered*

*To the children of the world – waiting for the adults
to create a better world and a better future*

The Struggle Continues

∵

Contents

Preface

Published in two volumes viz. *F/Ailing Capitalism and the Challenge of* COVID-*19* (Volume I) and *Capitalism and* COVID-*19: Time to Make a Democratic New World Order* (Volume II), these books are about the failings of the capitalist system to effectively, and efficiently, respond to COVID-19. The two volumes present my broad analysis and understanding of the world in the time of COVID-19. Volume I deals with the failure of capitalist countries to respond effectively and efficiently to COVID-19. Volume II deals with a range of themes linked to capitalism, and in the final analysis argues for the democratic remaking of the current world order. The two volumes are underpinned primarily by Karl Marx's analysis of capitalism.

If the 2008 Financial Crisis resurrected "The End of History" debate, then COVID-19 has turned up the heat on the debate quite considerably. It is hoped that these two volumes will serve as a contribution to that discussion and debate – one that will be ongoing for some time to come. I have used a kaleidoscope of views to put together these two volumes, in order to support the central thread of my argument viz. that capitalism engineers society to rationalise profit over people – even during a global pandemic! I have written from a multi-disciplinary perspective. These two volumes are a combination of a broad spectrum of COVID-19 related issues, my opinions and analysis of the political-economy of COVID-19, as well as an argument for moving to a post-capitalist society.

I attempt to make a case against the capitalist system by arguing that where citizens of a country have been infected and died, then it is in the main – due to the prevailing and stubborn capitalist ideologies, and an imperfect understanding and paradigm of liberty, freedom, democracy and human rights in the Western world. My primary aim, through these two volumes, is to attempt to deconstruct the prevailing and stubborn ideological beliefs of capitalism that have been in existence for many centuries. I engage with the phenomena of COVID-19 in the capitalist era through a historical perspective as well – and within the framework of geopolitics in the globalised world. These two volumes are also a mini or micro chronicling of a vast range of views that were aired, articulated and written in all parts of the world in the time of COVID-19. For this I am indeed thankful to the many people in many parts of the world who shared their views, opinions, perspectives and criticisms in the time of COVID-19. In this regard, the views of scholars, writers, journalists, opinion makers, critics etc. were left intact as quotes but integrated in a way that makes for continuous flow of reading. Unfortunately like any book that relies on the vast array of information that is out there, all information of a similar nature could not be assimilated into these two volumes for practical reasons. I assume responsibility for any errors of one sort or another.

These two volumes are only possible because of the ample and varied views on so many aspects of the world that were available at one time in world history. This was only possible because of COVID-19. As COVID-19 unleashed the productive power of people, written material in the form of journal articles, newspaper articles, books, etc. on COVID-19 were produced thick and fast, and within the shortest possible time. COVID-19 had unleashed the ideological and the scientific human. COVID-19 had unleashed the opinionated human. COVID-19 had brought forth the critical human. These two volumes are part and parcel of the burst of information and analysis that COVID-19 had generated. The world became more informed and educated about the workings of capitalism in the one year that COVID-19 struck than it had in the hundreds of years of capitalism's existence! These two volumes are an attempt at understanding capitalism and its real workings through the lens of COVID-19. The work is a no-holds-barred critique of the capitalist system – and the ideological-based economic science that keeps this historical and broken system plodding along.

In the final analysis, I put forward the argument that the capitalist system should be abandoned and abandoned fast. The current Volume I – *F/Ailing Capitalism and the Challenge of COVID-19* – commences with my views and experiences related to COVID-19, followed by the attempt to understand the concept of "ideology", and ends with attempting to understand the origins and make-up of the capitalist system. It sets the arguments and groundwork for volume II – *Capitalism and COVID-19: Time to Make a Democratic New World Order.* People in all countries should contribute to making a better world. The starting point is to understand the workings of capitalism. COVID-19 has given us the opportunity to do so.

Acknowledgements

I am extremely grateful to all of the World's Media – BBC, CGTN, RT, CNN, South African media, internet sources, the presenters, workers and professionals that appeared on TV screens, radio, zoom, YouTube channels, etc. and shared their experiences, views and analysis on COVID-19. I acknowledge the work from all scholars that have been invaluable in my understanding of the various subject matters related to COVID-19 discussed in the two volumes. I am also grateful to family and friends who were sharing via social media in the time of COVID-19. There was a flurry of information that was churned out on a second-by-second basis on COVID-19 and its impact on all spheres of society. One simply could not keep up with the abundance of news, information and analyses. I am especially indebted to the writers and contributors in the print media that carried such large amounts and diverse range of views on COVID-19. These written media views, opinions, analyses and critique form the backbone of the two volumes relating to capitalism and COVID-19. Such views, opinions, analyses and critique provided the material and data for me to critique the capitalist system and its poor handling of a global pandemic. Without the world's print media and its many contributors – these two volumes would not have been possible. I tried to capture as many views and analyses as was practically possible – and in this burst of activity also tried to secure the sources as best as I could.

I am extremely thankful and indeed grateful to David Fasenfest, Series Editor at Brill Publishers, for facilitating the publication of the two volumes. His professional and on-the-mark suggestions on how I could go about improving the initial single manuscript has made possible the two volumes: *F/Ailing Capitalism and the Challenge of COVID-19 – Volume I* and *Capitalism and COVID-19: Time to Make a Democratic New World Order – Volume II*. His expert guidance and timeous feedback were pillars of strength in helping me to sustain and see my work through to completion. It was a real pleasure working with David.

My appreciation is also to Jason Prevost, Senior Acquisitions Editor at Brill Publishers, for initially accepting my book proposal and linking me up with David Fasenfest. I am indeed thankful to the reviewers for constructive feedback on the manuscripts. Many thanks to Judy Pereira, Production Editor at Brill, for her skilful guidance and patience. To the entire team at Brill Publishers, thank you for your guidance and for agreeing to publish the two volumes titled: *F/Ailing Capitalism and the Challenge of COVID-19 – Volume I* and *Capitalism and COVID-19: Time to Make a Democratic New World Order – Volume II*.

To my University (The University of KwaZulu-Natal), partner and family, thank you for your continued support.

Acronyms and Abbreviations

ANC	African National Congress
BBC	British Broadcasting Corporation
BJP	Bharatiya Janata Party
CGTN	Chinese Global Television Network
CNN	Cable News Network
COVID-19	Coronavirus Disease of 2019
EU	European Union
GDP	Gross Domestic Product
PBUH	Peace Be Upon Him
PPE	Personal Protective Equipment
RT	Russia Today
UK	United Kingdom
UN	United Nations
US	United States
USA	United States of America
USSR	Union of Soviet Socialist Republics
WHO	World Health Organisation

Introduction

Normal led to this.
ED YONG

• • •

This pandemic has magnified every existing inequality in our society – like systemic racism, gender inequality, and poverty.
MELINDA GATES

• •
•

I've lost family, friends, colleagues and community members to COVID-19. It was a common experience felt by all of humanity in the early part of the 21st century. Many have never witnessed death and dying on such scale, rate – and with such pain, hopelessness and despair. The luck of the draw under capitalism sometimes saw entire families being wiped out at once. Some lost more than one family member within short spaces of time. Mothers died. Babies died. Fathers died. Grandparents died. Pregnant women died. Husbands died. Wives died. Partners died. Families died. Politicians died. Celebrities died. Nurses died. Doctors died. Policemen and women died. Funeral workers died. Pastors and priests died. Nuns died. Sisters died. Brothers died. Professors died. Students died. More loved ones died in capitalist countries than in communist and or socialist countries. Social media was never short of images and video clips of people from one's immediate and extended communities who succumbed to COVID-19. The images of loved ones being carted away to be buried or cremated without any final goodbyes must surely be a shock to the physiological and psychological systems. The hurt, pain and trauma for those closest will remain – for a long time to come.

There were times when I thought I had contracted COVID-19. My energy levels were low. I felt sick. I called my doctor – he did not think I displayed symptoms of COVID-19. That was in July 2020. I felt sick in May of 2021 again. It is difficult to completely rule out COVID-19. It is easy to become complacent. It is easy to go about life as if everything is normal – until you start to get those headaches, that itchiness in your throat, that increased temperature, etc. You start to trace your whereabouts in your mind – trying to figure where you may have contracted COVID-19, if you did contract COVID-19. You start to think about the many times you let your guard down. You start to think about whether it was worth it to go to the restaurant, whether you should have been more assertive with friends and family members who did not wear a mask in your presence, whether you should have brushed-off the cough that your builder had – which he brushed off as a throat irritant. You start to make comparisons – and think about the relativity of things and phenomena. You start to think about your responsibility to those that live in the same house – especially the vulnerable and the elderly.

For many, having unknowingly infected loved ones resulting in their deaths – the hurt and pain will be many times more severe. Always a curios and questioning species, we thought secretly and sometimes asked openly – how did people become infected which led to their deaths? Behind such thoughts and acts was the uncomfortable question: Were the many who died responsible for their infections and deaths? I've heard sad and painful stories of people unknowingly taking the virus home with them – and in turn wiping out family members. The burden they carry must surely be heavy. How do such members of the human race heal from the turn of events that were mostly not of their own doing? How do such people be comforted? How does a caring society help them to heal – if ever?

But there are also other and bigger questions that have been asked – and have to be asked. How much power do individuals have in society to beat-off a global pandemic? Can an individual be held responsible for a business owner who decided to have a rave party in the middle of a pandemic? Or is it the local government which gave permission for such parties to take place that should be held responsible for COVID-19 infections and deaths reeling out of control? Does one blame the high school students who attended a party in a wealthy district – or the fact that it was legal to do so in the middle of a global pandemic? Are the megachurch events – or the Trump rallies which led to people being infected and dying – culpable for the many infections and deaths? Did the weather contribute to deaths peaking or plateauing? Do we blame the bats or the people eating the bats?

Do we hold god responsible for creating coronaviruses – under the grand plan of Intelligent Design? Or does god have nothing to do with the number of infections and deaths – in the same way that she had nothing to do with the youth's success in turning the tide against climate change, Joe Biden winning the 2020 elections, or Prince Harry falling for Meghan Markle. Is the local government leader responsible for telling people to take loved ones out and shop in the middle of a global pandemic? Is the local hairdresser who refused to close her salon during a lockdown responsible for infections and possible deaths? Is the ideology of wanting to improve Gross Domestic Product (GDP) numbers in the middle of a global pandemic to be blamed for millions getting infected and dying? Are states that failed to put in place adequate and effective public health infrastructure responsible for the many infections and deaths? Is Donald Trump to be held liable for his poor handling of a global pandemic whilst in the White House? Is Boris Johnson to be held accountable for thinking that COVID-19 is similar to chickenpox?

Is Narendra Modi to be blamed for wanting to compete with China – instead of saving Indian lives – during a global pandemic? Is the person who refused to wear a mask responsible for infections and deaths? Is the person who refused to get vaccinated responsible for infections and deaths? Do scientists who provided opposing scientific views about the global pandemic bear huge responsibility for the number of infections and deaths? Are those that called for the unbanning of alcohol responsible for the reckless actions that resulted from drunkenness and loss of capacity in responsible decision-making at the height of a global pandemic? Are the people that demanded their individual freedoms, rights and liberties in the midst of a global pandemic responsible for the infections and deaths of their fellow humans? Are the Black Lives Matter protesters – and the many other protesters that went out and protested during the height of a global pandemic – responsible for the infections and resultant deaths? Are the churches and other religious organisations that demanded the opening of religious organisations during a global pandemic responsible for the deaths of the members of their congregations?

Do those countries that hoarded vaccines for their populations many times over bear responsibility for the deaths of people in developing countries who could have lived – had the vaccines been delivered to them on time? Is China responsible for infecting and killing millions of people in all parts of the world? Are countries in the Western world responsible for the infections and deaths of many hundreds of thousands of their citizens – by not acting timeously, decisively and effectively – when their leaders became aware of COVID-19? Were cruise-ship operators who did not test their passengers responsible for COVID-19 related deaths? Were those who implemented the natural herd-immunity model responsible for the hundreds of thousands of deaths of their citizens? Were ski resorts in Europe – the super-spreaders of COVID-19, thereby resulting in needless deaths? Will history judge that responses by some states fall within the category of "genocide"?

If the people needed food – was it the state or the capitalist market that controlled the supply of food during a global pandemic? If people needed monies – was it the state or the capitalist market that controlled the supply of monies? If people needed medicines – was it the state or the capitalist market that controlled the supply of medicines? If people needed vaccines – was it the state or the capitalist market that controlled the supply of vaccines? Did the

United States (US) enable the many painful deaths in India – by banning the export of raw materials required for manufacturing vaccines? If people needed hospital beds – was it the state or the capitalist market that controlled the supply of hospital beds? If people needed oxygen – was it the state or the capitalist market that controlled the supply of oxygen? Did the state enable the deaths of health care workers – by not providing personal protective equipment (PPE) to them in time and in sufficient quantities? And if they did – were the PPEs suitable to do battle with an invisible enemy known as COVID-19?

With the increasing number of lawsuits and class actions related to COVID-19 infections and deaths, it is clear that people are demanding accountability and sometimes compensation – in one form or another – for the infections and deaths of their loved ones. Through such lawsuits and class actions they are saying that entities in society – usually those in and with power – were responsible and enablers for the infections and deaths of their loved ones.

Families and communities were torn apart – not knowing how to manage livelihoods in the midst of an invisible but known enemy. Where I could, I had to restrict my movements lest I got infected – or infected my elderly 78-year-old mom or younger brother who is diabetic and live with me. There were times when I was responsible. There were times when I was reckless. There were times when I had little or no power as an individual, to reduce the risk of contracting COVID-19. If an owner of a crowded store did not have a policy of social distancing in his store, then there was little one could do on one's own, to maintain social distancing. There were times when I – on my own – dropped my guard in the war against COVID-19.

Also, social and cultural pressures worked against science – and left family members exposed to COVID-19. At a family funeral which was not COVID-19 related, family members broke COVID-19 protocols – and succumbed to cultural practices to mourn the death of a loved one. I felt the tribal contempt when I tried to intervene, to suggest social distancing of sorts. I found myself trying very hard to explain myself. I felt like a tribal outcast. In time science overcame understandable and predictable emotions during mourning – but the experience left one walking on eggshells – when having to choose between ingrained culture and public health science. Fortunately for the tribe, the luck of the draw prevented infections and deaths of family members from COVID-19, at least from that particular gathering. A family wedding also witnessed COVID-19 protocols being violated. There too, cultural practises prevailed – and public health science was pushed to the side. With ingrained cultural practises, neoliberal ideologies and capitalism sitting side by side, it was never going to be easy to navigate one's way through a global pandemic. At least this was becoming evident as the days, weeks and months dragged on.

Capitalism has come a long way to Africa since the Western world learnt about the richness of Africa. My tribal ancestors were coerced by the British to leave India around the 1850s and seek their fortunes in Africa. My mom used to tell me that her grandfather and others were told by the British that the "streets of South Africa were paved with gold". This was part of the cache of capitalist ideologies that also motivated Indian lovers of gold – to leave their land and arrive on the shores of Africa. In actual fact they were 'brought' as cheap labourers to work on sugar cane plantations in the tropical regions of KwaZulu-Natal on the east-coast of South Africa. They were slave-like workers on the frontline of capitalism's early development in South Africa.

That the white man was superior to the black man – and any other colour man for that matter – was another ideological influence of capitalism – which informed the stratification of South African society for a very long time – and subsequently gave us another fearful, violent and evil system that came to be known as apartheid. The apartheid state was a formidable state. Together with formidable states in the West, it enforced the development and growth of race-based capitalism in South Africa. There was no free market or invisible hand that saw to it that whites become owners of the means of production – and blacks – very cheap labourers. Ever since apartheid in South Africa – and the half-baked transition to democracy in 1994 – I wanted to understand the work-ings of society in general – and of human exploitation in particular. My type fell into the category of the exploited. I stumbled upon the concepts of capi-talism, socialism and communism. We were already well-versed in the concept and painful workings of racism.

The fall of the Berlin Wall and the break-up of the Union of Soviet Socialist Republics (USSR) underpinned by communist ideologies witnessed capitalist ideologies assuming hegemonic dominance in world affairs in the early 1990s. With the 1994 democratic breakthrough in South Africa, the democratic but capitalist-biased state embarked on the ideology of black economic empow-erment. In reality, only a minority of blacks became like their white counter-parts – wealthy and some extremely wealthy. South Africa's white capitalist economy was lawfully commanded by the state – to absorb some blacks into the commanding heights of the capitalist economy. After the ideology of black economic empowerment, some blacks live large, proud and in charge in impoverished South Africa. But the term white monopoly capital still sticks – when one talks about the unjust economy in the country.

Primitive capitalism shed its apartheid ideologies – and modernised into non-racial capitalism. But capitalist ideologies prevailed; any talk of a develop-mental state was laid to rest. A developmental state falls into the category of socialist and communist ideologies. The national narrative would allow none of this nonsense! Black capitalists mushroomed overnight in South Africa – the so-called Rainbow Nation of Nelson Mandela. The new South Africa was certainly different from the dark days of apartheid. Living under the authoritarian and draconian state overseen by white settlers from the West – lockdowns of sorts were the order of the day for the majority of South Africa's peoples.

We could not go to schools, universities, beaches, places of leisure, etc. that whites had freedom to go to. Our freedoms and human rights were taken away by the state. Being a settler from the East – I and my kind were relegated to the economic category of "coolies" – hired or unskilled Indian labourers. The colonial mother states set about reorganising and re-engineering South Africa through violent means – the land was first seized and thereafter its natural resources. The indigenous peoples of this vast rich and beautiful land were subsequently turned into wage-labourers. The central ideology which was used to justify the appropriation of land and livelihoods was that the Westerners were superior, civilised and educated – and the southern and Eastern peoples were inferior, uncivilised and uneducated.

The natives were to be civilised through Western and Christian ideologies. All the while, the ideology of white supremacy translated in practice into military rule over the economy, the land, the politics, the cultural space, the educational sphere, the sporting sphere, and the means of production. The subsequent ideology that justified and masked the seizure and capture of the choice chunks of the country was one of "good neighbourliness". Such an ideology was conceptualised and violently imposed by Dr Hendrik Verwoerd, an applied psychology and sociology professor and subsequent ruler over apartheid South Africa. Education in South Africa served as a key ideological tool in the hands of the oppressor. Some saw through Verwoerd's racist ideology – and violently acted on it. Dr Hendrik Verwoerd was assassinated in 1966 by Dimitri Tsafendas, a parliamentary aide with supposed leanings toward communist ideologies. Apartheid was race-based primitive capitalism in its most evil form.

We in South Africa are relatively new to the world of human rights, freedoms and democracy. We have lived under a white totalitarian state for most of our lives. We are also acutely aware that human rights, freedoms and democracy have not delivered the good life to tens of millions of South Africans. We now live in a capitalist market tyranny – with very little agency for the state to address the three main social ills of South African society: unemployment, inequality and poverty. Besides the real fear of crime, we also live with the ideology of fear under capitalism viz. any state involvement in the capitalist market economy is bound to lead to South Africa being another basket case in Africa. At least this is the fear that is dished out by mainstream economic scientists – favouring the capitalist mode of production and consumption in all parts of the world. Three hundred and fifty years of colonialism, apartheid and capitalism has delivered to us a broken South Africa. Against such odds, it was never going to be easy to do battle with COVID-19.

When one looked across the Atlantic Ocean at the violent rioting that took place during a global pandemic in the US – we witnessed a country at breaking-point as well. We are all too aware that the entire of the Middle East is also a troubled and broken region. The tens of thousands that are left to die in our oceans – as they attempt to seek a better life in the developed world – is testimony to the deficient morality of the countries which deny them entry. The Western world continually bomb these countries – and they then expect the people of those countries to live happily-ever-after amongst the ruin, rubble and rubbish. The clumsy, reckless and irresponsible responses by many countries – especially in the Western world to COVID-19, is an indication that we live in a broken world with broken ideologies. In a world overpowered with Western and capitalist ideologies – can it even be fathomed that socialism and communism are superior systems to capitalism? If not, then how do we explain to our children, our students and future generations – the needless loss of lives in the Western capitalist world – a world saturated with wealth, power, state of the art technologies, enviable science and untold experiences in waging wars?

For example, *The Guardian* in the UK carried the following headline on 27 May 2021: "Tens of thousands of of people died who didn't need to die." How do we explain to future generations – that one year later – more than a billion people were 'free' – and at liberty to celebrate the Lunar New Year in communist China – whilst the rest of the Western world – except for New Zealand – were on lockdown of sorts – and still losing their citizens in the tens of thousands? In the face of such overwhelming evidence, can capitalist ideologues and mainstream economists still continue brainwashing the world with ease – about the wonders of capitalism and the capitalist market economy? These are uncomfortable and inconvenient but necessary questions that COVID-19 has thrown up.

The world has gone through many major upheavals since the beginning of history. Earth has witnessed societies form and die – and form again. There is a general feeling – and one that is expressed in all parts of the globe – that the world will never be the same again – after COVID-19. If this is the general sentiment being expressed by many – all over the world – then it is prudent for us all to attempt to understand the world we currently inhabit, the ideologies that keep the broken world stumbling along, and how it came it be. More importantly, the challenge for us all is to explore ideas and processes with which to democratically make and build a better and happier world. It is possible. After all, capitalism was possible post-feudalism, and feudalism was possible after slavery. There is life after capitalism – in the similar manner that there is life after apartheid – for both blacks and whites.

From a wealth perspective, capitalism has been both a success and a failure. Capitalism is a tremendous success – for those that have made it to the top of the economic and financial world. Capitalism is an abysmal failure for the many thousands of millions who feel that they are swimming against the tide of life – on a daily basis in order to acquire and sustain a livelihood. For the many hundreds of millions that fall into the economic category of capitalism's labour reserve army, they have to rely on hand-outs from so-called nanny states – and the quantity and quality of such hand-outs are dependent on the shape, form, financial strength and ideological underpinnings of such states. From a humanistic, ethical, and moral perspective – capitalism is a failed system. It resorted to violently killing-off the indigenous peoples of the world – and seizing their natural environments and land – in order to set itself up as an apparently legitimate free market economic system. Can it therefore be deduced that private property laws under capitalism are constructed upon the theft of lands and natural environments in many parts of the world?

From a technological point of view, capitalism is tremendously successful. But from a distributional point of view – capitalism is a failed system. Only the well-off children of the world were able to continue with their education – through remote learning from home in the time of COVID-19. From a nature or ecological point of view, capitalism is an unspeakable failure. Planet earth is a garbage dump for capitalism's waste. In other words – capitalism is shitting on Mother Earth. Insofar as capitalism has not been able to reach its Gross Domestic Product (GDP) nirvana in recent decades means that capitalism is not up to it any longer. Insofar as capitalism is dependent on the nanny state to rescue it – or bail it out when it goes into an existential crisis mode – means that capitalism is a continually failing system, underpinned by failed economic ideologies dressed up as Nobel award-winning economic science.

Whilst neoliberal economic scientists wish to argue otherwise, capitalism is a planned economy – a planned economy serving only the narrow and selfish interests of the rich and powerful in capitalist society. Whereas socialism and communism are planned economies for the many – capitalism is a planned economy for the few. COVID-19 is forcing one to ask the question – whether a democratically planned economy for a new world order is not a better option than the planned capitalist dictatorship that is foisted upon humankind and the natural environment by neoliberal ideologies? I attempt to argue that the beneficiaries of capitalism – the rich and the powerful, and their accompanying economic scientists – have a tool-box of ideologies by which they uphold the exploitative, inhumane and destructive system – that has come to be known as capitalism.

The politics at the beginning of the 21st century – as was the case for most of the 20th century – is bound up within two competing historical systems viz. capitalism and communism. In the 20th century, the contest for geopolitical supremacy was between the capitalist West and communist Russia. In the 21st century, the contest seems to be between the West and China. Political systems and ideologies are also at the heart of the rivalry – as it was during the Cold War. With the fall of communism in the Soviet Union, one is guarded against making a case for a communist future. But this in no way means that capitalism is therefore the ideal and happy socio-economic and cultural system for humankind and the natural environment. The reigning ideology of capitalism is profit. People and planet are merely fodder for such profit. People and planet are the means – profit is the end of all forms of capitalist economic planning and execution. People needlessly died in capitalist countries in the time of COVID-19, because capitalism does not favour life. Capitalism favours profit above all else. We were witnesses to states choosing to save people first – and the economy later. We were also witnesses to states choosing to save the economy first – and the people later – if at all. The latter occurred mostly in the Western world.

The economy is very important. So are human rights, liberties, freedoms and democracy. But nothing is more important than life itself! For the millions that lost loved ones and for the millions that were infected, only they can meaningfully identify with the statement that, nothing is more important than life itself! The moral question for a post-COVID-19 society is: what would a post-COVID-19 society be willing to trade life for? COVID-19 has been hard on everyone and continues to be – presidents and citizens alike. It's been hard on both public health scientists as well as economic scientists. It's been hard on capitalist as well as communist believers. But COVID-19 has been devastatingly hard on workers, people of colour and the poor.

Never has there been a time in history when a creature from nature threw up so much data and information about the real world we live in. COVID-19 exposed the real and factual world – the one that lay hidden for centuries under layers of Western, capitalist and economic ideologies appearing as scientific truth and Western values. Science too can fall into ideological camps. Science which once argued for racial supremacy is one such example. COVID-19 has made the task of exposing the workings of capitalist ideologies that much easier. Capitalist ideologies have condemned man to live in a "fool's paradise" all these centuries. COVID-19 has disrupted and exposed the ideological architecture and foundation of the capitalist system. COVID-19 has not only reformed our thinking about how the world actually works, it may actually have revolutionised the way we think about the world – and to embark on democratically remaking the world. In the same way that Marx turned Hegel on his head, COVID-19 has turned capitalist ideologies on their heads.

What would you do in order to get a loved one back? Would you give up some of your freedoms, liberties and individual human rights? Would you agree to using a tracking app that tells you that one of the persons in your immediate vicinity is COVID-19 positive? Would you agree to being tested and your test results captured onto a national COVID-19 data base? Would you agree to being vaccinated? Would you agree to possess a vaccine passport? Would you trust the state or an "invisible hand" to take full control over a global pandemic to protect you and your loved ones from infections and deaths? Would you trust the state or an "invisible hand" to protect you and your loved ones in times of war? COVID-19 has forced humankind to confront the prevailing and stubborn ideologies in our time. It has resulted in the levelling out of the ideological field – by which to attempt to understand the real and factual workings of the world in general – and the capitalist world order in particular.

Nature is in charge. But the capitalist system made it that much harder and more challenging for man to survive against man's enemies in nature – such as coronaviruses. After capitalism's dismal performance in the time of COVID-19, humankind is compelled to democratically plan and make a new world order. Only then will future pandemics not be as disastrous and devastating – as was COVID-19 in the capitalist era.

COVID-19 showed us how people behave in uncertain times. It showed us how effective or ineffective 21st century world leaders are. It showed us how capitalism works. It showed us how socialist and communist systems work. COVID-19 provided a universal education on how the world really works – not how we were told and promised for so long as to how it works. Under capitalism we live in two worlds – the one world that we continually are told that we live in – and the other – the real world that we inhabit. The former is the ideological world that we live in – the latter is the real world. In the time of COVID-19, the ideological world of capitalism slowly dissolved – and gave us all a jolt – as to the real world we live in. It is time to make sense of the ideological world of capitalism and the dominant ideas that keep it going – in order to understand the real world that we live in. It is time to unmask the ideas and ideologies which have propped-up capitalism for so long – still does – and will continue to do so – unless capitalism is unmasked and finally done away with. COVID-19 has provided us with a historical window of opportunity to do so. It is now up to us all – in all parts of the world – to decide how to use this historical window of opportunity – to democratically make a better and happier world than the current world of sickness, stress, strife and suffering viz. the world of capitalism that weighs heavily on so many of us.

CHAPTER 1

Unravelling Ideas and Ideologies Which Prop Up the Capitalist System

The general population doesn't know what's happening, and it doesn't even know that it doesn't know.

NOAM CHOMSKY

∙∙∙

The ideas of the ruling class are in every epoch the ruling ideas, i.e., the class which is the ruling material force of society, is at the same time its ruling intellectual force.

KARL MARX

∙∙
∙

1 The Word Ideology in the Time of COVID-19

Just when COVID-19 was wreaking havoc across the world in general – and in the United States in particular – the word "ideology" or "ideological" made its presence felt. In South Africa, the word cropped up more often than not. The South African state was accused of too often using "the lockdown to pursue their own particular ideological objectives" (Editor, 2020: 16). In another media write-up Silke (2020: 18) states:

> The lack of clarity over economic policy and political philosophy is what has held back the country in recent years. We don't need more of this. In these ways, SA has a choice. It can rise from the ashes to enhance its citizenry and restore its name in the world. Or it can fall into *ideologically* induced despair.

The writer was implying that the African National Congress (ANC)-led government in South Africa was using COVID-19 to move away from the apparently tried and tested ideas of the capitalist market economy. For the tens of millions still waiting for the better life promised by Nelson Mandela and his African National Congress, they are in the best position to know and feel what being held back means – as a result of capitalist and neoliberal ideologies that have taken root and flourished in South Africa.

Mthombothi (2020: 15) writes on the state's handling of the capitalist economy in the time of COVID-19:

> When Ebrahim Patel, as trade, industry and competition minister, whose portfolio is at the heart of driving economic activity, looks at a range of policy options, which *ideological* inclination takes precedence? Does he seek to grow the economy or does he see things through his class-war prism?

It is refreshing to see that the writer has acknowledged that aiming for economic growth is indeed *ideological*. Working towards a classless society is a noble goal in a land of vast inequities. Imagine the backlash from the Black Lives Matter movement – if Nelson Mandela was accused of seeing things through his race-war prism – and then decided to leave racist South Africa (SA) intact! On its criticisms of the economic ANC proposal document in the land of huge inequality, massive unemployment and extensive poverty, Business Unity SA stated:

> The document resurfaces old *ideology* and dogma of a significantly increased role in the economy for the state. We remain convinced that the private sector is best placed to stimulate such economic growth, provided the state creates an enabling environment and business and labour reach a constructive compact.
>
> JOFFE, 2020: 2

It is indeed perplexing for any thinking person to be confronted at the same time with the words: "resurfaces old *ideology* and dogma of a significantly increased role in the economy for the state" and "provided the state creates an enabling environment". On the one hand the state is threateningly advised to stay out of the capitalist market economy, and on the other, there is a welcoming request and appeal for the state to involve itself in the capitalist market economy. One can be forgiven for thinking that we are living in a schizophrenic world under capitalism. But then again, we live in two worlds under capitalism: the ideological world – and the real world. Big and powerful businesses, it seems, want to have their cake and eat it!

Persons that call for state intervention in the capitalist market economy are easily accused of being socialists and communists – in other words *ideologues*. Apparently, capitalists and believers in capitalism are never *ideological* – and can never be accused of being *ideological*! A capitalist economy means that the capitalist market is best placed to distribute needs and wants to humankind. In other words, the state should not get in the way of capitalist market functioning. For example, the state has no business trying to stop people from smoking – even when cigarette smoking is scientifically proven to cause millions of deaths. In time people may realise that smoking causes deaths and – may of their own accord – decide to stop smoking. Under the umbrella of capitalist ideologies, it's known as "the freedom to choose".

It seemed many leaders – as heads of states in the Western world – transformed into socialists and communists in the time of COVID-19. They pushed for the state to get involved in the capitalist market economy – but to save capitalism! Persons that argue for no state intervention in the economy belong to the economic category called neoliberalism. Margaret Thatcher, Ronald Reagan, Milton Friedman and Ayn Rand, are neoliberal purists – in a similar manner that Hitler was a purist in racial supremacy and Stalin a purist in dictatorial communism – they all believed passionately and strongly in their respective *ideologies*. The capitalist economy would be kaput – had not the state intervened in the capitalist economy in the time of COVID-19.

When should the state involve itself in the capitalist market economy – and when should it not? That is the question that is now confronting all fair-minded people in the 21st century – more so after experiencing the devastating impacts of COVID-19 on lives and livelihoods under capitalism. Many called for practical and pragmatic functioning in the time of a global pandemic – instead of succumbing to questionable Western *ideologies*. What was actually being demanded was more of the same: more capitalism – but by other means necessary than that of the capitalist market itself:

> We have been presented with a multitude of plans, but little sense that anyone is in charge. Debates are often stuck between competing *ideological* positions rather than developing and driving real practical ideas to grow the economy, improve productivity and provide jobs.
>
> JONAS, 2020: 19

COVID-19 resurrected memories of the tussle between the capitalist West and the Union of Soviet Socialist Republics (USSR):

It would seem the world is becoming increasingly subjective. Within that subjectivity, old and familiar points of reference are being replaced by new paradigms. As during the Cold War, proxy wars were fought between the two superpowers in third world countries due to *ideology*, the proxy wars of the modern world are now fought in Internet chatrooms, on Facebook, Twitter and many other sites besides.

ALDEN, 2020: 13

The Cold War between the West and the USSR impacted heavily on the economics, politics and narratives of South Africa in the 20th century. Cold War sentiments seemed to continue into the 21st century in the time of COVID-19. Professor Themba Sono critiqued the Western ideological slant of journalism in South Africa:

Chris Barron is my favourite scribe, a meticulous researcher and writer. Solly Mapaila is a politico, a unionist nonpareil, an *ideologue* par excellence. But last Sunday an *ideologue* reduced a seasoned columnist to an incoherent babble. Never did I believe that Mapaila would upend Barron in a one-on-one exchange. Barron asked the *ideologue* if he was not endangering our people by "preferring" Russian and Chinese vaccines, presumably over those of the West. Mapaila responded: "No. The Russians are people, the Chinese are people, and they are using the same vaccines and they are living. All we are saying is that scientific data is available". Yet Barron remained impervious to this very common-sense statement. After Mapaila informed Barron that "all vaccines should be explored", Barron inanely asked: "including from Russia and China?" As if the word "all" somehow miraculously excludes China and Russia. Who is the super-*ideologue* now? Certainly not Mapaila. The notion that Westerners are not *ideological* because of being more scientific is fallacious. Look at the US Democrats after whipping the erratic, narcissist Donald Trump. They remain obsessed with their age-old Russophobia. Barron falls into this Western paranoia of Russo/Sinophobia. He too holds the view that COVID can only be contained by Western medicine, as if Sino-Russo scientific methodology is inferior, when their astrophysics and astronomy operate at the same level as that of the West. Who is more *ideological* now?.

Sunday Times, 2021: 18

Common sense was required in the time of a global pandemic but Western *ideologies* prevailed. And all this while, left-leaning citizens are told to have

common sense when it comes to the economy! The learned professor discovered and pointed out that modern journalism sits on an *ideological* scale –
which tilts to the West. In fact, the entire modern world sits on an *ideological*
scale – which tilts to the West – in favour of the capitalist system. Prevalent but
covert *ideologies* in capitalist society were certainly made visible in the time of
COVID-19.

The word *ideology* was not restricted to South Africa's borders. In Canada:

> In February, a 17-year-old man allegedly stabbed two women in their
> Toronto workplace, killing one. The *ideology* that their investigation
> asserts incited the attack. Involuntary celibacy, or the "incel movement"
> – a loose collection of people, primarily men, who interact online and
> share their frustrations about a lack of access to sex, relationships,
> women and social status.
>
> DAVIS, 2020: 11

We are beginning to realise that *ideology* refers to sets and sub-sets of specific
beliefs – which in turn influences particular types of attitudes and behaviours.
In neighbouring United States of America (USA), Bernie Sanders opted out
of the race for the nomination of president of the United States (US) when
COVID-19 began gradually removing the cobweb of capitalist *ideologies* – built
over many decades – from the hearts and minds of people in all parts of the
world. In his exit speech – Bernie Sanders stated:

> Together, we have transformed American consciousness as to what kind
> of country we can become. Few would deny that over the course of the
> past five years our movement has won the *ideological* struggle. In other
> words, the future of this country is with our ideas.
>
> PAZ, 2020

If Bernie Sanders has ideas for America, then what ideas should the rest of us
have for a future world? We are also learning that politics means the struggle of
ideas and belief systems. The Ku Klux Klan subscribed to the idea and *ideology*
of white supremacy. Owing to this belief-system or ideology, they could therefore easily hang and burn black people. By "our ideas" Bernie Sanders meant
the ideas of "democratic socialism" – which he was trying very hard to implement in the United States of America – the world's most capitalistic country,
i.e., until he dropped out of the presidential nomination.

Should a post-COVID-19 world subscribe to the ideas of democratic socialism? If yes – then what are the ideas informing democratic socialism? About

a month after Bernie Sanders' exit speech – and in a letter to the editor of the *Washington Times* – Berkert (2020) wrote:

> The left's anti-gun agenda is fuelled by a powerful motivator that has nothing to do with gun safety and everything to do with *ideology*.

To think that gun safety is a common sense, practical and pragmatic approach to solving the mass killings in the US! So, we have those on the left speaking of the right as being immersed in *ideology* – and those on the right accusing the left of clinging to *ideology*. In Australia:

> There is a conspiracy theory within the Coalition that universities are hotbeds of left-wing *ideological* fervour. Some *ideological* warriors like to attack our institutions for accepting funding from abroad.
>
> ONSELEN, 2020: 22

China was obviously not left out of any direct talk relating to *ideology*:

> The crisis may well present Beijing with an opportunity to gain inroads in poorer countries from the Middle East to South and East Asia, Africa and Latin America, even countries that otherwise may have viewed China's offers of aid and infrastructure financing with *ideological* or economic suspicion.
>
> TAYLOR, 2020: 11

I guess the writer is suggesting that China intends to impose Chinese ideas on other nations. Should we also view the West with *ideological* suspicion – when the West offers aid to other countries? Should we view Non-Governmental Organisations from the West – operating in foreign countries – with *ideological* suspicion? The Russian news channel RT, for example, was registered as a foreign agent in the US in 2017. Still, staying with Australia:

> The nation needs to expand consumption taxes and reduce reliance on income taxes. But Labour's apparently frozen *ideological* opposition makes this almost insurmountable without a compact from the premiers and that's unlikely.
>
> KELLY, 2020

It is well known that taxing the rich is *ideologically* frowned upon, meaning capitalists and capitalist sympathisers believe that it is a bad idea to tax big businesses. This fundamental capitalist *ideology* of the mega-rich not needing to pay tax therefore explains why: "60 of America's biggest companies paid no federal income tax in 2018" (Cerullo, 2019). Ideas and *ideologies* prop up the capitalist system in all parts of the world – like the extremely rich not needing to pay their fair share of tax. This is one of the reigning *ideologies* of capitalism – an *ideology* that the rest of the world has come to accept as normal – and might it be said – good for society! That's the thing about capitalist *ideologies* – they have become so naturalised – and we have become so used to it – that we have accepted it as the natural order of things!

Whilst China, South Korea, etc. used 21st century technology to do formidable battle with a 21st century pandemic, a writer points out that human rights in the West are *ideologically* driven:

> Instead of letting *ideologically* driven human rights campaigners destroy hope for the rest of us, let's embrace the technology, thank the people who have made it possible and look forward to a future where we defeat COVID-19.
>
> POLLARD, 2020

One would have thought that the important subjects of human rights, democracy and freedom are not contaminated by capitalist *ideologies*. But then again, how else do we explain the West's attraction to Saudi Arabia – and repulsion to North Korea – if the important subjects of human rights, democracy and freedom are not contaminated by capitalist *ideologies*? We are beginning to learn that for the West, the important subjects of human rights, democracy and freedom are not fundamental values in and of themselves – but also *ideological* tools – with which to harass, shout down and discipline economic rivals and perceived enemies. It's why the US was "firmly opposed and deeply disappointed" when the United Nations Human Rights Council (UNHRC) decided to investigate Israel for war crimes in the Gaza Strip. Western ideas and ideologies – even if they trounce human rights, democracy, freedom, etc. – are primarily about hegemony, power and empire. It is why the US has a history of overthrowing democratic regimes favouring socialism, and propping up dictators and authoritarian leaders favouring capitalism.

2   Attempting to Make Sense of Ideas and Ideologies

We all have ideas about ourselves, about others, about other races and nationalities. We have ideas about the opposite sex and ideas about sex itself. The idea that two people of the same sex cannot be in a relationship may be described as homophobic *ideology*. Ideas float around in society and into and out of our minds like the air we breathe. Bad ideas may prove to be detrimental to one's physical and mental health – as bad air can be. Breathing in air saturated with contaminants – as is the case in many cities such as Ghaziabad in India and Beijing in China – has proven to be detrimental to its citizens' physical and mental health. The idea that I should inject myself with disinfectant in order to cleanse my body of COVID-19 is an idea – but a very bad idea – even though such an idea came from the brain and mouth of the world's most powerful man – Donald Trump – in a world of about 7 billion people.

Leaders are influential people – the masses are known to hold on to what they say. There's also the idea that if a pandemic is sweeping through society – as a caring state – you should allow it to take its course – the strong will survive and the weak will die off. I've learnt that this idea is called "natural herd immunity". Whether natural herd immunity should fall into the swollen category of capitalist *ideologies* is a matter for society to discuss and debate. But hundreds of thousands of people did die as a result of the *ideology* of natural herd immunity. This is what some leaders and some prominent scientists in the Western world believed. They held onto this *ideology* – until the reality of COVID-19 knocked sense and science into their thick Western *ideological* skulls. Who would have thought that humankind would be thrown back into the animal kingdom – to be part of the many other animal herd species from whose stock he was derived from! Nonetheless, it is an *ideology* – and a real one at that – as was evidenced in some parts of the globe in the time of COVID-19.

Many in powerful positions in the Western world believed that by not wearing a mask, they would be sending the intended idea to the masses – the idea that COVID-19 was not really a threat to life and limb – and kith and kin. The idea of whether to wear a mask or not during a pandemic was not an easy one to settle – but it was an idea that finally gained traction as COVID-19 went on its merry way – in and out of communities:

> Whether to wear masks has become a political issue, rather than merely a public health one.
> DENNIS ET AL., 2020

In many parts of the US, wearing a mask was seen as un-American:

> The act of donning a simple piece of fabric over the mouth has become a symbol of our new and dangerous reality – and an expression of people's deeply held political views and beliefs.
> ZHAO ET AL., 2020

Beliefs matter – but do what we believe really explain the world we live in? As the pandemic maimed and killed, the idea of not wearing a mask slowly fizzled away. But for the most powerful man in the world – Donald J. Trump – wearing a mask would be sending the wrong *ideological* message to the American people. He therefore stuck to his *ideology* of "strong man" and "the capitalist economy is most important" – and went about his ways naked-faced:

> Instead, Trump who publicly prizes strength and symbols of masculinity including height, firm handshakes and deep voices suggested he considers it unseemly or un-presidential to be seen in a mask. Masks have become emblematic of a cultural and increasingly political divide over restrictions meant to slow the spread of the coronavirus. Screaming mask-less protesters, some armed, faced off with masked law enforcement officers inside the Michigan Capitol last month. A confrontation between a calm Costco employee and a shopper in Colorado who refused to wear a mask 'because I woke up in a free country' went viral online this week.
>
> GEARAN ET AL., 2020: 11

Refusing to wear a mask symbolised Trump's deep disdain for science: "Mr Trump has resisted wearing a mask himself and has not put one on in public" (*The Straits Times*, 2020). To think that the practical and common-sense idea of wearing a mask during a global pandemic would take on an *ideological* shape and form! This is in the mainstay of the Western world – that part of the world that dishes out civilisation and apparent values to all and sundry. But then again, we live in a capitalist society – where not much seems to make sense any longer – like countries agreeing to slow down and halt climate change – but still continuing on the centuries' old activity of coal-mining and coal-burning! We live in two worlds under capitalism: capitalism's ideological world – and the real world! We live in a world of make-believe and in the real, harsh and brutal world of capitalism.

The idea or *ideology* that America is the greatest nation on earth is not without truth – unless one takes into consideration the number of mass shootings that takes place in the US – or how badly the US handled the COVID-19 pandemic – or that the president of the most powerful country would threaten to set the world's most powerful army on his own people – just because they chose to remind America that "Black Lives Matter". In relation to such phenomena, America is indeed exceptional! Then there was the *ideology* that if the Free World got rid of Muammar Gaddafi, they would be bringing peace and freedom to Libya. Eleven years later, Libya is more dangerous, more corrupt, deadlier and much more in siege than it ever was under Gaddafi. But such *ideology* of the Free World has not stopped those in and with power from attempting to export Western notions of freedom, democracy and liberty to other countries in the Middle East and Latin America.

Western and capitalist *ideologies* prevail in the early part of the 21st century – as it has done for a good few centuries before. In the time of COVID-19 Western and capitalist *ideologies* went viral, in response to the practical, pragmatic and common-sense approaches that were taken by countries – in varying degrees – in different parts of the world. For a long time and up to and including today – and will still go on into the near future – communism has been denounced as an *ideology* – and one that is always doomed to fail. Communism proved to be a failed system as demonstrated by the breakup of the Soviet Union in the latter part of the 20th century. Communist *ideology* and its propagators were relegated to the dustbin of history when the Soviet Union collapsed. But of late, capitalist *ideologies* have also been taking a beating. One is therefore at pains to understand the meaning, content and goals of communist and capitalist *ideologies*. What is *ideology*? Is *ideology* based on evidence and science? Is *ideology* rooted in reality? Is *ideology* an outdated mode of thinking? Is *ideology* a set of abstract ideas – which cannot be implemented in the real world? Is humankind tricked into believing in communist *ideologies*? Is humankind swamped and duped by capitalist *ideologies*? Is *ideology* fake news? Is *ideology* a form of brainwashing? Is *ideology* a form of indoctrination? Is *ideology* the "opium of the masses"? Is *ideology* utopian thinking? Is *ideology* meant to distract humankind – from the real conditions in which humans live? Does *ideology* serve particular and narrow interests? Is *ideology* meant to preserve the status quo? That god will save us from COVID-19; is this scientific or *ideological* thinking? Is the use of the word *ideology* meant to instill fear into people about the others' intentions?

Free speech and freedom of thought is seemingly almost lifeless in the Western world. Any discussions or debates seeking to improve one's understanding of socio-economic systems is shot down due to being accused of having *ideological* leanings:

> Even to-day open, frank, and 'objective' inquiry into the most sacred and cherished institutions and beliefs is more or less seriously restricted in every country of the world. It is virtually impossible, for instance, even in England and America, to inquire into the actual facts regarding communism, no matter how disinterestedly, without running the risk of being labelled a communist.
>
> MANNHEIM, 1953: xvii

This was said in 1953! The intolerance to alternate forms of belief systems in the US is seemingly low in 2020 as well – and *ideological* accusations are glaringly implicit:

> In transforming U.S. schools and colleges into socialist indoctrination centres, the left has created a whole generation of uncompromising young voters who believe anything short of Bernie's radicalism is intolerable and even corrupt.
>
> HASKENS, 2020: 8

In the UK – the US's sister, brother or mother country – *ideological* bashing continued:

> A clue as to the political philosophy of Dr Mary Bousted, the teachers' union leader trying to sabotage next month's return to school, can be found in her passion for communist Cuba.
>
> PIERCE, 2020: 7

So much for the right to freedom of thought and conscience in the Western world! It's why a Latin American poet once said: "In America – liberty is a statue"! *Ideologies* are meant to inform and keep different types of societies intact. The apartheid regime in South Africa wanted to keep the status quo intact at all costs. The set of ideas that they dreamt up and implemented were that blacks were meant to be labourers – and whites were meant to be rulers. We hence had the *ideology* of apartheid in South Africa. The bible was also used as a powerful *ideological* tool to keep the apartheid system intact:

> It is a well-known fact that the Bible was used in some Reformed circles to justify the policy and practice of apartheid.
>
> VOSLOO, 2015: 1

Hence one view of the concept of *ideologies* is that they are:

> Those complexes of ideas which direct activity toward the maintenance of the existing order.
>
> MANNHEIM, 1953: xxiii

The ideas and *ideologies* of capitalism are what props up capitalism and keeps the system going – despite its despicable record in the spheres of unemployment, inequality, poverty, continuous wars and environmental catastrophes. It always seems to be a conundrum in capitalist society as to when one is being pragmatic – and when one is being *ideological*. For example, is the state being *ideological* when it gives out monies to unemployed workers in the time of a global pandemic? What type of *ideology* is the state following when it hands out large sums of monies to the capitalist class in the time of a global pandemic? Was it capitalist market *ideology* or socialist *ideology*? What *ideology* did the state follow when it handed over trillions of taxpayers' dollars to big businesses and corporations when there is no global pandemic – as was the case during the 2008 Great Financial Crisis? Was it capitalist market *ideology* or socialist *ideology*?

The scholar who wrote the best-selling book, *Capital in the 21st Century,* had this thought on *ideology* and the use of it:

> I am of course well aware that the word *ideology* can be used pejoratively, sometimes with good reason. Dogmatic ideas divorced from facts are frequently characterised as *ideological*. Yet often it is those who claim to be purely pragmatic who are in fact most *ideological* (in the pejorative sense): their claim to be *post-ideological* barely conceals their disdain for evidence, historical ignorance, distorting biases, and class interests.
>
> PIKETTY, 2020: 9

Evidence of this view was witnessed in the time of COVID-19, when the Western world cast aside all evidence of a global pandemic – and acted as if life could go on as normal. None were so blind and beholden to *ideologies* as was the Western world in the time of a global pandemic! So, from Piketty (2020: 9), we get a more extensive understanding of the concept of *ideology*: "dogmatic ideas divorced of facts" and those in denial in the face of "evidence" could be said to be *ideological*. Interestingly those with "class interests" also succumb to *ideology* – maybe to preserve their class interests?

In modern times, the two main competing *ideologies* in society that have squared-up to each other in order to inform the economic, political, social, cultural and psychological fabric of global society – since the break-up of feudalism – is that of capitalism and communism. Gray (2008) cited in Petri (2018: 13):

> Observes that in intellectual terms the Cold War was a competition between two *ideologies*, Marxism and Liberalism, which had a great deal in common. Many in the west "tend to believe their philosophical, religious, and ethical thought to be particularly profound and of unlimited value, whereas the ideas and notions of others are downgraded to

'beliefs' or *'ideologies.'*" It is commonplace in history for an excess of power to cause blindness.

PETRI, 2018: 14

The world witnessed how the belief systems of the West let its citizens down in the time of COVID-19. According to Gamble (2006): cited in Petri, 2018: i): "The West was originally a European concept" but then "migrated to America". We are beginning to learn that there is also such a thing as Western *ideology*. It seems that Western *ideology* is also associated with the concept of propaganda: Petri (2018: 12) states further:

> When you tune into the television news and you hear a political leader talk about 'advanced' countries, and a geopolitical pundit suggests armed 'humanitarian' intervention, and the sober presenter qualifies a murder as 'barbaric', you know that coarse undertones of *Western ideology* truly exist. It is not immediately dismissed as propaganda by the public because the underlying *ideology* has swamped minds over the centuries thanks to a hypnotic repetition of concepts not necessarily invented, but surely consecrated, by the founding works of Western culture.
>
> PETRI, 2018: 12

Is Petri (2018) even suggesting that people are hypnotised, misled, under a spell, indoctrinated, brainwashed, programmed, conditioned, moulded, prepared, trained, automated, coached, instructed, disciplined, coerced, etc. by Western *ideologies*? Is this what Noam Chomsky meant when he stated:

> The general population doesn't know what's happening, and it doesn't even know that it doesn't know.

Around 1800 the French liberal Destutt de Tracy used the term [*ideology*] to denote an objectifying 'science of ideas' (Petri, 2018: 3), but Napoleon had already assigned two predominantly negative meanings to *ideology*: as theory devoid of practical relevance and as a set of untrustworthy dogmas. For Karl Marx, however, *ideology* was not simply a false consciousness of reality; as he pointed out, it:

> Can mislead even when nothing in its claims is strictly speaking false; it might, for instance, misdirect critical attention by concentrating on a part rather than the whole of a truth.
>
> LEOPOLD, 2013: 24

For Karl Popper and others:

> *Ideology* involves a systematically organised presentation of reality.
> KRESS and HODGE, 1979: 15

Up until COVID-19, much of society had a false consciousness of capitalism. What has been presented to people about capitalism all of these years does not correlate with the lived experiences of people under capitalism. Apparently, all of us are influenced by *ideologies*:

> Political cognition of an individual, the way we see the world of politics around us—no matter whether this person is a president of a country, an accountant, or a college professor—is affected by *ideology*, specific political beliefs, and pure pragmatic considerations of the day.
> SHLAPENTOKH ET AL., 2008: xiii

For Francis Fukuyama, fascism and communism are *ideologies*. Apparently, capitalism – for this 'false prophet' – does not seem to fall into the scholarly category of *ideologies*:

> Liberal democracy was challenged by two major rival *ideologies*—fascism and communism—which offered radically different visions of a good society
> FUKUYAMA, 1992: 7

But COVID-19 unravelled the *ideological* make-up of capitalism. COVID-19 taught us what capitalism is really about. And it certainly was not about saving lives!

3   Toward the Unravelling of Neoliberal and Capitalist Ideas and Ideologies

Karl Marx was a German scholar and economist – but kicked out of his native Germany – because his ideas counter-posed with the ideas that were dominant in his time. In *The German Ideology* (1932) Marx viewed the dominant ideas and *ideologies* of society as serving the interests of the dominant class in society:

The ideas of the ruling class are in every epoch the ruling ideas, i.e. the class which is the ruling material force of society, is at the same time its ruling intellectual force. The class which has the means of material production at its disposal, has control at the same time over the means of mental production, so that thereby, generally speaking, the ideas of those who lack the means of mental production are subject to it. The ruling ideas are nothing more than the ideal expression of the dominant material relationships, the dominant material relationships grasped as ideas (1998 [1845]).

The ruling class in the historical era that we now occupy is that of the capitalist class. Capitalism is the overwhelmingly dominant economic system in the world. So, for Marx, the ideas of a capitalist society are not ideas that have been democratically informed – but ideas of the class that own the means of production as well i.e., the capitalist class. As to how one class of humankind came to own large quantities of private property and the means of production – this is a subject that I will attempt at some point in both volumes I and II.

According to Marx, the ideas that are dominant in capitalist society are the ideas that are conceived, distributed and consolidated throughout society – by the capitalist class and its' loyal representatives – mostly in the form of economic scientists. So, what are some of the ideas and *ideologies* that are dominant under the capitalist system? That the capitalist market is the best social mechanism to achieving a prosperous society is one dominant *ideology* in capitalist society. That the state should not involve itself in the capitalist market is a dominant *ideology* in capitalist society. That climate change can only be solved through the capitalist market is another dominant *ideology* in capitalist society. That man is greedy by nature is a dominant *ideology* of capitalist society. That a profit economy is the only economy that can serve the needs of humanity is a dominant *ideology* in capitalist society. That the capitalist market is the only social mechanism that can meet the needs and wants of humans is a pervasive *ideology* in capitalist society. The state, for example, should not provide free education, health care, housing, etc. That socialism and communism are evil and must be destroyed by all means necessary is an overarching *ideology* of capitalist society. It's why the US bombed the 'living daylights' out of Vietnam in the 1960s – and why Cuba and Venezuela are forever bullied, harassed and sanctioned by the US.

That to believe in socialism and communism is to be *ideological* and utopic in thinking is a dominant *ideology* in capitalist society. To believe that the state should involve itself in the economy is viewed as being *ideological* in capitalist society. That the reason for one's lot in life is due to one's individual free choice is a dominant *ideology* in capitalist society. That one's inner world determines one's outer world is a super-dominant *ideology* in capitalist society. In other words, just think good thoughts – and your entire world around you will transform into wholesome goodness!

That Gross Domestic Product (GDP) is the only measure for success, progress and well-being for humankind is a reigning *ideology* that cannot be tampered with under capitalism. In fact, if one does question the necessity of economic growth, then one is opening up oneself to being labelled an *ideologue*! That continuous shopping and consuming is one of the hallmarks of success is a persistent *ideology* in capitalist society. That civilisation is associated with the West is an inescapable *ideology* of capitalist society. That capitalism is the only civilised system for humankind is a conclusive *ideology* of capitalist society. It's why Francis Fukuyama's book – *The End of History and the Last Man* – was a best seller. It was a powerful *ideological* book used as a 'weapon' against communism.

One may also associate the concept of *ideology* with that of fake news – a concept that was coined by Donald Trump – in protest at the information and apparent misinformation that was put out to the world – through mainstream media. The many more related *ideologies* that are pervasive in capitalist society are: That America is the greatest nation on earth. That owning guns keeps one safe. That Iraq had weapons of mass destruction. That wars are between good (the West) and evil (the rest). That only foreign direct investments and low wages create jobs. That you have to "get back to work" during a global pandemic – in order to survive. That human rights are absolute – and exist independently of responsibility and accountability to others in society. That "there's no such thing as society". That all men are born equal. That wealth will trickle down to the masses – and eventually take them out of poverty. That capitalism is the end of history. That war is necessary for peace. That if the US did not drop atom bombs on the people of Japan – then the war would not have ended. That god and prayer – and not gun control – is that which will solve the problems of mass shootings in the US. That the coronavirus was manufactured in a lab in China. That 5G masts in the UK were responsible for the transmission of the coronavirus. That COVID-19 was god's punishment to humankind – for they have strayed in their ways. That the rebellions taking place in the time of COVID-19 were race-riots and not symptomatic of a class war. That the Chinese state is an authoritarian state and the Saudi Arabian state is not. That Alexei Navalny's 30-day imprisonment in Russia requires constant global media coverage – and Jamal Khashoggi's killing in the Saudi Arabian embassy in Turkey does not.

Any ideas that seek to challenge the dominant ideas and *ideologies* of capitalism are met with contempt, ridicule, vitriol and sometimes violence. Ironically this is another idea that dominates in the capitalist system – that it is a system which values, cherishes and nurtures democracy – both within its borders and in the rest of the world. So cherished is the ideological idea of democracy in the Western world, that it sometimes feels the need to export such democracy through the enforcement of colossal quantities of violence.

The war against COVID-19 was taking on different forms and shapes in different countries. But there was also an *ideological* war going on – between China and the Western world – a war between capitalist *ideology* and communist pragmatism and realism – what the West would term communist *ideology*.

Twenty-first-century society always had an idea that the world is an interconnected place. Globalisation has been much spoken about, but since the 2008 Financial Crisis, countries have opted to be inward looking. However, it took a microscopic creature called the novel coronavirus – later termed COVID-19 – to reveal to 21st century society as to how globalised the world really is. Ever since the virus was identified in Wuhan, China, sycophants of Western and capitalist *ideologies* seized onto the impending disaster to denounce China as the new "axis of evil". For a while, it was to be used as another weapon in the arsenal of the trade war with China – which has been going on since China's economic rise under the Chinese brand of communist ideas and *ideologies*.

As other countries such as Italy and Spain had to finally resort to what in the West would normally be regarded as totalitarian measures to try and contain the devastating impacts of COVID-19, human rights were being coloured with new meanings and interpretations in the developed world. Against the *ideological* capitalist gospel of no state intervention, the state had to assume centre stage in order to try and contain the virus, as well as to guide human affairs – at least for a brief moment in capitalist time. To quote Marx: "all that was solid melted into the air". All that humanity was made to believe about capitalism was met with the stark reality of how capitalist societies and capitalist states really function. In other words, the *ideologies* of capitalism – carefully crafted and constructed over centuries – met face to face with the harsh realities of capitalism's real nature, shape and form.

COVID-19 made transparent capitalism's *ideological* DNA sequence or code. COVID-19 forced humankind into a space with which to confront fact or fiction, evidence or hearsay, science or superstition, people or profit, pragmatism or *ideology*. COVID-19 made possible what capitalist *ideologies* have programmed modern humans into believing was impossible. The capitalist system is held up by neoliberal and capitalist *ideologies* – a set of values which makes the masses believe that the capitalist system is acting in everyone's interest. In fact, capitalist *ideologies* have the implicit and explicit purpose of benefitting a select few in capitalist society – the 1% at the expense of the 99% and the natural environment. COVID-19 has provided 21st century society with the material evidence against which neoliberal and capitalist *ideologies* and values can be squared-up and measured.

Up until now, the primary default position of capitalist society was that everything that has to do with socialism and communism is *ideological*. The globalisation of a crisis revealed the crisis of globalisation – under a capitalist neoliberal agenda. As COVID-19 was eating away at life and living, states in most parts of the world had to appropriate socialist principles – or what the antagonists of socialism would call socialist *ideologies* – in order to get a handle on COVID-19. This is not the first time that socialist ideas and *ideologies* were used to deal with the failures of capitalism. There are many other times in history where this was the pattern – to save capitalism from itself. The challenge for a post-COVID-19 society is to decide whether 21st century society will allow the scaremongers, the sycophants, the praise-singers, the cheerleaders, the advocates, the *ideologues*, the prophets, the lobbyists, the neoliberal economic scientists of capitalism to once again fill humankind's brain with myths, fake news, *ideologies* and values about capitalism – and its supposed virtues for humankind and the natural environment?

COVID-19 has forced Western civilisation into the global spotlight. COVID-19 has transformed the world into a global laboratory; the real operations and functioning of the world came face to face with the dominant *ideological* system viz. neoliberal capitalism. COVID-19 began diluting all of the *ideologies* that were heaped mountain high on modern society – since its entry as a world historical system. COVID-19 has once again placed the controversial and much heated topic of capitalism versus communism or socialism on the discussion and debating table of 21st society. It has put to the test the ideas constructed around capitalism versus the ideas constructed around socialism and communism. What first started as China's problem – and a public health issue at that – gradually transformed into a political, cultural and *ideological* battle – stopping short of any military warfare. Many commentators concluded that the US was in a Cold War with China – a term that has all the memories to do with the USSR and the Iron Curtain – that guarded the communist experiment for much of the 20th century.

Neoliberal and capitalist *ideologies* became undone with the naked exposure of Western civilisation's inept ability to contain a virus that was contaminating and killing off its citizens in the millions. The gatekeepers of capitalism and neoliberal *ideologies* were becoming agitated – as the virus not only killed-off the men, women and children of their civilised countries but was posing a huge threat to their profit, power and prestige – and their neoliberal capitalist and Western ideologies as well. Instead of utilising their colossal quantities of material and financial resources to fight and defend what many in the West referred to as an invisible enemy, capitalist countries instead sent out their *ideological* commanders, generals, and foot-soldiers to defend the profit economy, to defend capitalism, to defend neoliberalism, to defend Western *ideologies* and to defend Western hegemony. There was little evidence of countries with mega quantities of money and resources attempting to really defend its citizens from COVID-19. The *ideological* battle was heating up.

Ideological war sets the stage – and prepares the supposed moral highground to destroy the other – by violent means if necessary. In terms of its politics – the US is primarily a two-party state. In so far as its *ideology* is concerned, the US is a one-party state – a neoliberal state and country with the highest form of capitalism in the world. COVID-19 provided the material evidence for how political systems really function. COVID-19 forced open the *ideological* ringfence guarding the capitalist enterprise for the entirety of its existence. It showed cracks in capitalism's *ideological* firewall and peeled away capitalism's *ideological* layers. COVID-19 exposed the *ideological* fault-lines of Western civilisation.

The capitalist system is set on a default position for profit maximisation – and not for meeting the needs of people – the main need being that of securing life in the time of a global pandemic. The *ideologies* of profit-making and maximisation – and individual liberties devoid of responsibility and accountability to one's fellow men and women – prevented countries from functioning efficiently and effectively to prevent the spread of COVID-19. The ensuing consequence of such dominant *ideologies* were the needless deaths of millions of people in the 21st century. Western, neoliberal and capitalist *ideologies* enabled and ensured death by design.

The primary aim of capitalist neoliberal *ideology* is to control the body of the human-being. It does this by controlling his or her mind. The notion of free choice under capitalism is just that – a notion – not a lived reality. The secondary aim of capitalist *ideology* is to control nature and subject nature to the *ideology* of unlimited growth and wealth accumulation. COVID-19 has confronted humankind to ask the following uncomfortable questions: which system saved its citizens in the time of COVID-19 – communism or capitalism? Which system placed people before profit – capitalism or communism? Which system was more scientific in its approach and response to COVID-19 – capitalism or communism? Which system was more *ideological* in its approach and response – capitalism or communism? Which system went to the aid of other countries in the time of COVID-19 – capitalism or communism? Which system absolved its responsibilities – capitalism or communism? Which system went into scapegoating mode – capitalism or communism? Which system fiddled and farted – whilst its people were infected and dying – capitalism or communism? Which system accused the other system of being *ideological* – communism or capitalism?

What is it about the current dominant *ideologies* that pitted lives against livelihoods in the time of COVID-19? Why did the current dominant *ideologies* gradually but forcefully coerce man to set aside the major risk to his life in the face of a global pandemic? How extensive and intensive are human rights and freedoms in capitalist societies? How is it that after 27 years in prison and 30 years of black and democratic governance, in Nelson Mandela's South Africa people did not have easy access to water – to wash their hands – and to thereby reduce the risk of infecting themselves with COVID-19? How is it that after centuries of the goodness of capitalism – people in many parts of the world still go hungry in a planet of plenty? What about the fear factor – which is at times used as an *ideological* weapon to entrench Western and capitalist *ideologies*? Should we fear contracting COVID-19? Should we fear going hungry and homeless? Should we fear losing our privacy? Should we fear the Chinese? Should we fear the Russians? Should we fear the police and army of the US? Should we fear communism? Should we fear capitalism? Should we fear the state? Should we fear being unemployed in the capitalist market? Should we fear not having investors in the capitalist economy? How does the ruling class tap into people's fear – and use it for its own selfish *ideological* interests? Is it true that we are merely individuals – and that there is no such thing as society? Is it true that under capitalism – that we are truly free to choose? Is it true that the state – even though it is the most powerful institution and force in modern society – should not be there for the people? Is the media communicating to us facts – or feeding us with Western and capitalist *ideologies*? Has socialism and communism completely failed? Has COVID-19 made humankind conscious of a world of "which humankind had hitherto always hidden from itself with the greatest tenacity" (Mannheim, 1953: 37)? How long can capitalism rely on its cache of *ideologies* to uphold its increasingly fragmented make-up and structure:

> The concept *ideology* reflects the one discovery which emerged from political conflict, namely, that ruling groups can in their thinking become so intensively interest-bound to a situation that they are simply no longer able to see certain facts which would undermine their sense of domination. There is implicit in the word '*ideology*' the insight that in certain

situations the collective unconscious of certain groups obscures the real condition of society both to itself and to others and thereby stabilises it.

MANNHEIM, 1953: 36

In order to unravel and understand the history, *ideologies* and workings of capitalism – it may help to understand the history, workings and *ideologies* of communism and socialism.

CHAPTER 2

Communism – the End of History

A spectre is haunting Europe, the spectre of Communism.
KARL MARX

• • •

What is to be done?
VLADIMIR ILYICH LENIN

• •
•

Socialists and communists existed before Karl Marx – known to many as the father of communism. There are some who think that Jesus Christ was a socialist – from whose ideas about wealth, poverty and society many critics of capitalism have been influenced – Pope Francis being one of them (Dreier, 2016). For thousands of years, sections of humankind have fought – and many have died in their quest for a more just, fair and equitable society. Many have also dreamed and theorised about what a just, fair and equitable society would or should look like. The fact that we do not live in a slave or feudal society any longer means that humankind has succeeded in eradicating the unfair, unjust and inequitable societies of the past. Nevertheless, we currently still live in an unfair, unjust and a highly inequitable society – capitalist society. Many in the developing world could only watch and wonder when their turn will come – when the Western world were vaccinating their citizens in their hundreds of millions!

Many have tried to eradicate capitalism – but none have thus far succeeded. Some are on a never-ending battle with capitalism. Examples are Cuba, Venezuela, North Korea and Kerala in India. Instead of trying to kill-off capitalism, China has decided to tame and ride the capitalist tiger. It seems to be working. The evidence is there for all to see – even if what they see hurts their ideological eyes and brains. It's why Donald Trump can't stop saying: China, China, China, China! It's why Western ideologues also can't stop saying China, China, China, China!

In his book *Utopia* – published in 1516 – Thomas Moore imagined a future society where all of humankind will live in peace and harmony. Like Jesus who was executed for not relinquishing on his principles, Moore was tried for high treason and executed in July of 1535 – about 1500 years after the death of Christ. This was the time of feudal society – the precursor to capitalist society. Communism has often been termed as utopia – an ideology, an imaginary world, idealism at its best, an unattainable dream. But men, women and sometimes children continue to pine, fight and die for utopia. Millions have died in their quest for a communist future. Ernesto Che Guevara and Rosa Luxemburg are just two of the many millions. Like Chris Hani in South Africa, they were taken-out by capitalist ideologues and capitalist sympathisers. They were killed violently like so many others – who dared to challenge the capitalist order.

But Homo sapiens always hope for a better future – for themselves and for their children – for those who have children. It's what Homo sapiens are preoccupied with – for most of the day of life under capitalism. We always want a better future – since capitalism keeps us mostly in a state of constant anxiety, financial insecurity and fear. Constant anxiety, financial insecurity, and fear are what the capitalist market generates – for the thousands of millions without access to the means of production. Living for the moment seems to be a non-negotiable in capitalist society. Escaping from the clutches of capitalism through meditation and yoga for brief episodes of capitalist time may give one the nirvana of living in the moment – but then capitalism forcibly draws you back into its harsh and alienating reality. You cannot escape from the iron clutches of capitalism, you can only withdraw into subjective worlds and imagined utopias for brief periods of time – or numb yourself with stuffs – from the onslaught of capitalism on your senses. But with the arrival of Karl Marx, it seemed that hope was on the horizon – to finally escape from the brutal stranglehold of capitalism's tentacles. It would require some work though – and one would have to be patient – whilst giving capitalism permission to undergo its supposed destiny of the exploitation of labour and the natural environment.

According to Marx (1848) – history will end when communism is the system by which children, women and men will live their lives – and conduct their livelihoods in peace, harmony – and without fear and violence. Marx's mumbojumbo seemed more realistic than the back-cover of the Jehovah's Witness magazine – which shows a family sitting happily in the company of lions. I think it is called The Watchtower magazine. In any event, people in a communist world will look out for each other, protect each other and live happily ever after! Those who do not think so accuse Marxists, socialists, communists, the Left, Bernie Sanders and Jeremy Corbyn of being ideologues, utopians and idealists – in other words dreamers! John Lennon was also a dreamer – as is evident in his song *Imagine*. He once put his foot in it – when he remarked that the Beatles were more popular than Jesus! Although Jesus turned water into wine – he couldn't really sing. I can't imagine Jesus Christ singing *Imagine*! On the other hand – maybe I can! The two men had something in common: they both hated the established orders of their times. Being a dreamer and an ideal- ist, John Lennon also wrote and sang *Give Peace a Chance*. However, bombings by the Western world have not stopped – especially in the Middle East. The US only got out of Afghanistan in 2021 – after waging war for 20 years in this impoverished land. The West is hardly-ever interested in giving peace a chance. Their hegemony – and a large part of their capitalist economy – depend on the war economy. In any event, John Lennon's more realistic outlook of how capi- talism functions, was evident in his song *Working Class Hero*.

For well over 150 years since modern capitalism, sections of global society attempted to build the communist dream – or communist utopia on planet earth. The most recent utopian project was Capitol Hill Occupied Protest (Chop) later named Capitol Hill Autonomous Zone (Chaz) – slap-bang in the middle of capitalist USA! This happened in the time of COVID-19, when the Black Lives Matter movement gained social and political traction for their cause. Like the Union of Soviet Socialist Republics (USSR) – it collapsed dis- mally! Unlike the USSR it did not have a state, it lasted for about 2 months – and it did not send a man into space. Unlike Chop or Chaz – Russia is still around – but in a highly capitalistic form. A visit to current-day Russia can- not take place without a visit to Red Square. Here lies the embalmed body of Vladimir Ilyich Ulyanov – who later came to be known as Vladimir Lenin. It's as if he's taking an afternoon nap – but his body has lain there since January 1924, the year he died at the age of 54 of a stroke. He had once survived an assassi- nation attempt on his life – when two bullets were propelled into his chest by a woman assassin a few years earlier.

If Karl Marx was the theorist suggesting that communism was the end of his- tory, then Vladimir Lenin was the practitioner chosen by Russian history – to implement "the end of history" hypothesis: "Russia was the world's first social- ist state" (Service, 2000: 5). That Russia would relinquish socialism after about 70 years – and embrace full-blown capitalism – would have been unthinkable to Lenin. This, after all, was the man who had given his entire life to creating, witnessing, and presiding over the socialist revolution in Russia. His brother was earlier hanged by Tsar Alexander III for his activities of a would-be assas- sin. Historical change became personal for Lenin. But it seems history has a way of disappointing men and their dreams. Hitler never did achieve his dream of European and possibly world domination. The European Union (EU) project came apart in 2016 after the United Kingdom cut off ties with the EU. Trump never did get a second term as president of the US. Adam Smith's self-interest theory has not resulted in the world becoming a better place – even after centuries of capitalism and empty promises masquerading as economic science.

For the entire four years of his presidency, the Democrats in the US tried to pin Trump's election win in 2016 on Russian interference. It shows Russia's importance in the world – since its time as a backwater country – before the socialist revolution of 1917. Russia had come a long way in 100 years. Trump's revenge for the questioning of his election to the presidency was to question Biden's election to the presidency in 2020. This line of questioning finally resulted in the storming of Capitol Hill on 6 January 2021. Democratic elections are one thing – political systems quite another! If Trump and Biden were at odds over democratic outcomes, they were united under the banner of capitalism – against communism and socialism. The divided political classes stand ideologically united in the US. In order to fully understand communist systems – their ideological as well as pragmatic shape, form and function – we have to dig a little deeper into history.

Russia was the first country in the world to consciously plan and apply socialist ideas – in order to inform its way of life and living. Before 1917 Russia was ruled by an authoritarian tsar, and the masses of Russia were kept in subservience – or subjection by the ruling class ideology that the tsars – like the kings and queens of the world – were god's chosen leaders on planet earth. If the tsar was made in god's image, then god has much to answer for – for the types of leaders he has chosen – as his representatives on earth. They tend to do a bad job of taking care of god's creation.

In any event, the consequence of such ideological people-programming was that the masses toiled hard and did not see much of the rewards of their toil – whilst the rulers of the land enjoyed material life to the hilt on planet earth. The masses were promised a better life in the afterlife. This is not dissimilar to the current capitalist system – whereby thousands of millions of workers toil everyday – but with most of the value generated from the productive activity of labour going to the capitalists and ruling classes. The middle class gets a little more value than the working class. Very little value generated by the superb productivity of capitalism finds its way to the working class. They too are promised by religious teachings of a heaven in waiting. But only after they make huge sacrifices to capitalism on planet earth. Some in Russian society saw through the ideological layers blinding the masses – and decided to revolt against tsarist Russia. Karl Marx would be the one to awaken the consciousness of persons like Lenin.

Marx's central thought on historical, economic and social change of societies over thousands of years can be found in the first page of the *Communist
Manifesto* (1848):

> The history of all hitherto existing society is the history of class struggles.
> Freeman and slave, patrician and plebeian, lord and serf, guild-master
> and journeyman, in a word, oppressor and oppressed, stood in constant
> opposition to one another, carried on an uninterrupted, now hidden,
> now open fight, a fight that each time ended, either in a revolutionary
> reconstitution of society at large, or in the common ruin of the contend-
> ing classes.

History for Marx is as a result of class struggle over the ages. Capitalism is a
class society – and we were all witnesses to how COVID-19 exposed the vast
disparities between the different classes making up capitalist society – and its
impacts thereof. Marx was unequivocally committing himself to a supposed
iron law of historical economic development: that capitalism – just like the
class societies of the past – was doomed. With these words, he gave those who
were looking for reasons and ways to change their material conditions the
theoretical ammunition to embark on social change – sometimes violently. In
Russia, Marx's thought on historical and societal change was the perceived scientific foundation on which the new society was to be conceived and made. At
least a misreading of Marx was the spur for the socialist revolution in Russia.
For Marx, history moves from communalism to slave society to feudalism to
capitalism to communism – with socialism guided by the state – to help medi-
ate society from capitalism to communism. The last stage of history would be
communism. It came to be known as Marx's "End of History" thesis. This is
the stage in world history when peace would descend upon earth – and all of
humankind would live in eternal happiness. It is possible that Marx was thinking of the Second Coming – or smoked something really strong – to have the
audacity to suggest love, peace and happiness amongst humankind. There's no
way that Donald Trump is going to hug and kiss Hillary Clinton. There's no way
that the National Rifle Association (NRA) is going to advocate for gun control –
just because it will stop mass killings in the US. So, Vladimir Lenin would hear
none of this Marxist nonsense! He and his enthusiastic band of revolutionaries decided to take tsarist Russia straight out of feudalism, short-circuit Marx's
idea of the historical process, bypass the young but immature phase of capitalism in Russia – and move headstrong towards a communist future:

When the Bolsheviks announced the formation of a government of sovi-
ets of workers' and soldiers' deputies on 25 October 1917, they believed
they were inaugurating a new stage in human history, namely, the beginning of the transition from capitalism, a system they believed was based
on exploitation, inequality, and war, to communism. Communism, in
their eyes, would be a society without a state or social classes, characterised by radical equality, peace, and all-round human development.

SMITH, 2014: 2.

Like neoliberal ideologues, communists did not – in the final analysis – want
a state to rule over them. Unlike neoliberal ideologues, they recognised the
reality and role of the state in transitioning from one society to the next. Even
though arch neoliberal ideologues like Margaret Thatcher and Ronald Reagan
abhorred the state, they were both comfortably embedded at the highest level
of the organs of the state. Nothing can be more powerful than being a president or a prime minister of the state!

Lenin commenced the socialist project in Russia almost 70 years after Marx
wrote the *Communist Manifesto*. However, Russia in 1917 was never capitalist
like the United Kingdom (UK) or the US – but mostly feudal with capitalist
beginnings:

It was true that Russia in 1917 was a predominantly peasant country. But
the proletariat had at least been numerous enough to provide the spear-
head of the revolution.

CARR, 1990: 652

In Russia in October of 1917 – the socialist revolution had begun. It was also
the time of World War 1 – a war that started on 24 July 1914 and ended on
11 November 1918. By the end of World War 1 – 1918 – the entire world was
impacted by the Spanish Flu pandemic. It was a global pandemic that started
in Kansas in the US. Soldiers from the US were loaded onto American ships
to fight in World War 1. Wherever they went – the virus went with them. The
name Spanish Flu was given – after the pandemic hit Spain – and then the
press got to know about the devastation being wrought by the disease. In a
matter of two years, it is thought that 50 million people died of the Spanish
Flu world-wide. Death seems to come easily to the human race – death by pandemics, death by war, death by genocide and death by revolutions. The Soviet
Union is known for the many deaths that it inflicted on its citizens in its grand
plan for a better future.

Mao Tse Tung is also well known for the many deaths that he caused – in his grand plan for a better China. The West is well known for the grand scale of deaths – which it had inflicted on its soldiers – through countless wars – and on others through constant wars and colonial conquests. After killing the representative head and his family of feudal subservient ideology in Russia, Vladimir Lenin went about building his communist utopia. It was like killing the king and queen of France during the French Revolution of 1789 – and building a France of liberty, equality and fraternity.

France is a country where liberty, equality and fraternity have been taken seriously ever since the French Revolution of 1789. Once the Bolsheviks took power in Russia, Lenin introduced the New Economic Policy in 1921. It was an economic policy that favoured the many and not the few. When the ANC – under Nelson Mandela – took power in South Africa in 1994 – they drew up economic policies that still favoured white monopoly capital – and a minority of politically-connected blacks. Russia's economic policy under Lenin was socialist in form. The economic policy under Nelson Mandela was capitalist in form. It is clear that since the days of the Romanovs, Russia under communism had undergone social, scientific and economic changes in leaps and bounds. Nonetheless it seems that there was and is unhappiness about the way the Russian state ruled the USSR:

> Millions of people perished in the Soviet Union; they were killed by deliberate state terror, collectivisation, and several wars.
> SHLAPENTOKH ET AL., 2008: 11

As if one world war was sufficient to learn the lessons of the preciousness of life – Europe decided to embark on World War II – on 1 September 1939. If there is one thing for which the entire world is thankful to the first communist country in history and in the world – it is the sacrifice that communist Russia made in defeating Hitler and the ideology of German supremacy:

> Despite grave military setbacks in 1941–1942, the Soviet Union has defeated the Nazi military machine in 1945. The Communists undeniably modernised the country turning it into a powerful industrial and welfare state with a strong military and an expansionist foreign policy.
> SHLAPENTOKH ET AL., 2008: 24

The Soviet Union under communism developed Russia and its people more in 70 years than the Tsars of Russia had ever done in its many hundreds of years of authoritarian rule – under the ideology of god's supreme representative on earth:

> Many social changes were taking place in the Soviet Union – rapid urbanisation, modernisation, mass education, and rising living standards—all these were obvious changes apparent in the 1960s in comparison with the 1930s.
>
> SHLAPENTOKH ET AL., 2008: 28

Whereas the capitalist West kept much of the world in servitude and subjection through its colonial conquests and programmes, the Soviet Union set about assisting the oppressed of the world – to regain their freedoms and countries seized by capitalist forces from the West. After the Russian revolution of 1917 and the commencement of the building of communism in Russia, many countries – especially in the colonised world – comprised revolutionary movements attempting to embark on a similar trajectory as that of Russia. Such countries wanted to escape the clutches of primitive accumulation – the beginnings of the capitalist mode of production in many parts of the world. They too wanted to enter utopia – the communist future – after being brutalised by the West through colonialism and the exportation of capitalism. The result was many failed experiments in Africa – and in many parts of the world. Since then, much of the developing world has been firmly in the iron grip of capitalism.

In South Africa the colonialists or importers of capitalism stayed – the term coined for such a phenomenon is "colonialism of a special type". Thanks to colonialism and apartheid underpinned by ruthless capitalism, South Africa is now the most unequal and about the most crime-violent country in the world! Depressingly, the cover of the 13 May 2019 edition of *Time Magazine* revealed South Africa to be "the world's most unequal country". It is the wealthiest country on the African continent – but the vast majority of its people are poor and black. Wealth and poverty are still racialised in the Rainbow Nation – 28 years into its democracy.

In other parts of the world such as India, the colonialists went back to their mother country – after dividing the Indian landmass into India and Pakistan. The current world order is founded on the divide and rule ideology of the West. Divide and rule is a dominant ideology of the West. It is how the West exerts its hegemony over much of the world. The matriarchal Queen of England was the ultimate symbol of colonialism – overseeing the exporting of capitalism through violent means – and subsequent empire-building. Her statue still sits in India, as a reminder of the ambitious mother – who wanted to bring up other peoples' children – but thrashed them in the process. In South Africa whilst the West propped up apartheid capitalism, the Soviet Union and communism were formidable partners in the fight against the evil projects of colonialism and apartheid:

> In fact, Moscow provided assistance to the anti-colonial struggle in different parts of the world during the entire Soviet period of Russian history. Supporting the struggle of people for national liberation and social progress was confirmed as one of the aims of Soviet foreign policy in the 1977 USSR Constitution. It was the USSR that at the UN General Assembly session in 1960 proposed to adopt the Declaration on Granting Independence to Colonial Countries and Peoples.
>
> SHUBIN, 2008: 2

Communism – unlike capitalism – was not built on the ideology of self-interest. It sought to give a hand-up to countries that were destroyed – through Western ideologies of greed, power and empire-building:

> The Soviet Union had long proclaimed decolonisation, social rights and labour movements worldwide as communist causes.
>
> FURST ET AL., 2017: 4

With big brother assistance from Eastern Europe, much of the decolonised world – contrary to building their countries after Marx's capitalist image of history – sought to build their countries after the perceived image of communism:

> In 1917 communism had established itself as the creed of the most revolutionary and radical party – the Bolsheviks, victors in the Russian Revolution. Half a century later, communist parties had seized power in countries ranging across Eastern Europe, Asia, Africa and Latin America, with robust communist parties vying for power in many other countries.
>
> FURST ET AL., 2017: 4

In South Africa the following slogan reflected the pining for a better future: "socialism is the future – let's build it now"! In Europe the ideology separating communism from capitalism took on a material form – in the same way that the ideology of apartheid has taken on a material form through the wall separating Israel from Palestine. The wall in Israel is meant to maintain apartheid. The Berlin Wall was meant to keep out capitalism and to maintain communism:

During its existence from 1961 to 1989, the Berlin Wall became the emblem of the Cold War separating socialism to the East from capitalism to the West. Its builders' aim was to stabilise East Germany economically and politically, protect socialist East Germany from fascist and capitalist infiltration, and define the political status of Germany as part of the Soviet alliance.

LEUENBERGER, 2011: 62

The Russia of the 1970s was a far cry from the Russia of 1917. Capitalism started in Western Europe – but it was communist Russia that sent the first human into space. When the socialist revolution of 1917 commenced, Russia was grossly undeveloped in comparison to the West in general – and the US in particular. In 1917 America was already surging ahead in terms of industrialisation. The 1776 American Revolution gave the world the Rights of Man. The 1789 French Revolution gave France the Bill of Rights. The 1917 October Revolution gave Russians a way out of tsarist Russia and feudalism. Before the October Revolution of 1917, Russia was ruled by a government of absolute autocratic power. After 1917, Russia became a republic. Power was vested in an elected constituent assembly. Communist Russia was leap years ahead of tsarist Russia. But for Lenin and his Bolshevik Party, freedom was much more than the virtues of democracy. Freedom entailed freedom from class rule. They installed a communist dictatorship in Russia. Communist Russia was utopia – when compared to Tsarist Russia. For about 70 years, the communist dream was built on planet earth. For 70 years, the peasants and workers of communist Russia were living in utopia. For 70 years, planet earth had experienced "The End of History" – as theorised by Karl Marx – and as put into motion by the likes of Vladimir Lenin and those that came after him. For 70 years, communism was "The End of History". Marx was right – capitalism would one day come to an end and communist Russia was proof of Marx's "The End of History" thesis.

The Fall of the Berlin Wall and the End of History

What we may be witnessing is not just the end of the Cold War, or the passing of a particular period of post-war history, but the end of history as such.

FRANCIS FUKUYAMA

• • •

It is now easier to imagine the end of the world than to imagine the end of capitalism.

FREDRIC JAMESON

• •
•

1   Capitalism – the End of History

Historical events disappoint or reward – depending on whether one is a beneficiary or victim of such historical events. It appears to be the case with the fall of the Berlin Wall separating the East from the West:

> On Thursday, November 9, 1989, the Berlin Wall fell after having divided East and West Germany for 28 years. On that day at 6:57 p.m., Günther Schabowski, a leading member of the ruling communist party in East Germany, had casually announced to a stunned audience during a live televised press conference that all East Germans were immediately allowed to travel freely to wherever they wanted.
>
> BOHN ET AL., 2007: 565

The socialist or communist dream came crushing down with the fall of the Berlin Wall: "communism was dismantled in Eastern Europe in 1989 and in the USSR at the end of 1991" (Service, 2000: 1). The West celebrated the triumph of capitalism and the immediate death of communism. The break-up of the Soviet Union also witnessed the dissolution of the communist dream and the death of Marxist philosophy – or what believers in capitalism would refer to as the death of Marxist ideology and utopian thinking about a communist world. Marxism was no longer a science of society and history – but belonged to the garbage heap of failed ideologies. For believers in the capitalist system, communism was a failed ideology – a utopian dream that had no place in the real, pragmatic and common-sense world. Their criticisms of Marxism and communism were vindicated by the fall of the Berlin Wall and the break-up of the USSR. For the ardent followers of Karl Marx, the crumbling of the communist empire was a bitter pill to swallow:

> Even if it [Marxism] had not been abruptly dropped in the academy, it would have been hard to sustain after the collapse of Eastern Europe had revealed that illusions about socialism's ultimate appeal were precisely that. State socialism did not have the economic success its founders anticipated.
>
> BRENNAN, 1993: 19

Thirty-three years after the end of communism in the USSR, COVID-19 had ignited deeply held views on the matter in far-away South Africa:

> The SACP [South African Communist Party], with its discredited policies, behaves as though the Berlin Wall is still intact. It hasn't learnt the lessons of that epoch. If it had, it would, like its counterparts in the Soviet bloc, have disbanded long ago. It is afraid to submit itself to the will of the people through elections because it knows it will be rejected decisively and that would be curtains for it. It won't take that risk.
>
> MTHOMBOTHI, 2020: 15

It is clear that any mention of the word "communism" is bound to instil fear in people – learned people alike. Whilst many pronounced communism as a failed ideology resulting in the dismantling of the USSR, some believed that it was the fault of Mikhail Gorbachev – the then leader of the Soviet Union:

> Gorbachev appeared to unintentionally instigate political collapse in the Soviet Union and the Soviet economy went into free fall.
>
> FURST ET AL., 2017: 8

In any event Russia is now a capitalist country – it no longer suits communism – and communism no longer suits Russia. The communist experiment – USSR style – was a failure. It seemed Jehovah's Witnesses had better luck living amongst lions than Russians living in a communist utopia! The end of communism in the USSR witnessed the triumph of capitalism – and the "mass privatisation of the former Soviet economies" (Klein, 2014: 24). With the fall of the Berlin Wall and the break-up of the Soviet Union, Marxism was declared dead – a dead duck. You could not get more dead than a dead Marxist ideology:

> Until the 1980s, for instance, the British Labour Party and French Socialists favoured programs of nationalisation, but after the fall of the Berlin Wall and the collapse of communism they abruptly gave up on redistribution altogether.
> PIKETTY, 2020: 34

The communist and socialist dreamers and utopians of the world got a rude and shock-awakening from their ideological slumber – about living happily ever after in paradise on earth:

> Because the working-class movement had been so battered and blood-ied, and the political left so robustly rolled back, the future seemed to have vanished without trace. For some on the left, the fall of the Soviet bloc in the late 1980s served to deepen the disenchantment.
> EAGLETON, 2018: 6

Didn't the communists in the USSR know that communism was a planned economy and that planned economies don't ever work? The notion of a planned economy raises the ire of any neoliberal-inclined person, political party or institution. State or government planning of the economy are dirty words in capitalist economies – and the dirt stuck like glue to communism since the fall of the Berlin Wall.

Francis Fukuyama was a relative unknown in world affairs before the break-up of the USSR. He was once a deputy director in the US Department of Policy Planning – in a country that apparently approves policy planning for a capi-talist economy – but not policy planning for a communist economy! With the collapse of the Soviet Union, he penned the best seller – *The End of History and the Last Man (1992)*. It was an instant success! In it he stated:

> Virtually everyone professionally engaged in the study of politics and for-eign policy believed in the permanence of communism; its worldwide collapse in the late 1980s was therefore almost totally unanticipated. This failure was not simply a matter of ideological dogma interfering with a dispassionate view of events. It affected people across the political spec-trum, right, left, and centre, journalists as well as scholars, and politicians

both East and West. The roots of a blindness so pervasive were much more profound than mere partisanship, and lay in the extraordinary historical pessimism engendered by the events of this century.

FUKUYAMA, 1992: 8

He went on:

As we reach the 1990s, the world as a whole has not revealed new evils, but has gotten better in certain distinct ways. Chief among the surprises that have occurred in the recent past was the totally unexpected collapse of communism throughout much of the world in the late 1980s.

FUKUYAMA, 1992: 12

Enabling the deaths of almost a million people in the time of a global pandemic, in the most resourced and most capitalist country in the world must surely qualify as an evil doing!

According to Fukuyama there is nothing after capitalism. By declaring capitalism, "The End of History", he trounced Marx – the greatest thinker of the last 1000 years! Marx and Marxism were discredited. Marx's view that history would end with communism was given the death knell. Capitalism was declared "The End of History". Capitalist man was the last man on planet earth – none would come after capitalist man. There was no better system than capitalism. Nothing comes after capitalism. Men, women and children are best served under capitalism – and will be best served under capitalism. That millions died in capitalist countries in the time of COVID-19, must be excluded from the grand ideological framework of capitalism – being the last, only and suitable socio-economic system for humankind!

The pursuit of happiness can only take place under capitalism. Man's peace, safety, security and destiny lay with capitalism. Capitalist man is the highest form of human development. Capitalist man is the purest form that man can take – just like Elon Musk, Jeff Bezos, Frederick Hayek, Ayn Rand, Ronald Reagan, Margaret Thatcher and Donald Trump. Freedom lay with capitalism. Free choice lay with capitalism. Liberty lay with capitalism. Fraternity lay with capitalism. Even terrorists are guaranteed freedoms under capitalism. Nelson Mandela gained his freedom when capitalism was declared "The End of History" in the late part of the 20th century.

The capitalist state is the highest and purest form of state development in world history. At least this is the view of a Western state ideologist:

Madeleine Albright, declared the United States the 'one indispensable nation-state'.

GERSTENBERGER ET AL., 2011: 3

It is the same indispensable state that Donald Trump's supporters challenged on 6 January 2021. It is the same indispensable state that demonstrated that US lives are dispensable and tradeable – as was evident in the time of COVID-19. There was one problem with capitalist man though – he would always require a working and unemployed man and woman in order to exist – and unregulated access to nature and energy to exploit!

2   The New World Order under the Mighty Capitalism

The collapse of Soviet-styled communism reverberated throughout the world and its impacts reached as far as the distant land called South Africa – a country in the grip of colonial and apartheid rule for approximately 350 years. No longer fearing a socialist and communist take-over by the ANC, the last colonial and apartheid president of South Africa, F.W. de Klerk, felt that the coast was clear to release one of the world's most feared terrorists – Nelson Mandela – now affectionately known as Madiba – The Father of the Nation. Why should a man imprisoned for 27 years be feared any longer when evidence of his socialist or communist ideology is crumbling all around him! Nelson Mandela was released on 11 February 1990 – three months after the fall of the Berlin Wall. With his newly-given freedom, communist Cuba was the first country that Nelson Mandela visited – when he was released from prison after 27 long and painful years!

Even the United Nations (UN) celebrates Mandela Day on 13 December of each year – since the passing of this once-feared terrorist. Such was the ideological heaviness of the West – that the US had Nelson Mandela on its terrorist watch-list as recent as 2008 (Dewey, 2013) – thirteen years after Nelson Mandela received the Nobel Peace Prize on the world's stage! Mandela would go on to become the darling of the neoliberal and capitalist world – wined and dined by its best and finest. It was no fault of his that Marx and Marxists would prove to be flawed in their understanding of history and world affairs. Mandela had to let go of any revolutionary ideas of a socialist or communist South Africa he may have built-up over 27 years in prison – and dance to the tune of capitalism. When Mandela danced – the entire capitalist market and capitalist world danced with him!

It is 33 years since the fall of the Berlin Wall – and capitalism declared "The End of History". Ever since, we have been living in what has come to be known as the New World Order. It simply means communism – evil; capitalism – good! The end of communism in the USSR between 1989 and 1992 heralded:

> The triumph of capital in the 'New World Order,' as Bush Senior heralded – stealing the words right out of the mouth of Gorbachev himself.
>
> GERSTENBERGER ET AL., 2011: 3

Even the Berlin Wall itself had become a precious commodity post-communism. Many visitors to Germany could buy a piece of the Berlin Wall that once stood long, tall and mighty to keep capitalism out and communism in. I bought a piece of the Berlin Wall myself – when I visited Germany in 2005. It cost me a few euros for a piece that was about a centimetre in size. In its fallen form, it is no longer the common property of the communist state – but the private property of the capitalist market. The New World Order demands that all and sundry must be subjected to the capitalist market. For example, in the US:

> Trump's policy initiatives were now, all of a sudden, strikingly and explicitly neoliberal on any number of fronts across the policy spectrum, from charter schools, to privatising Social Security and Medicare, to tax cuts for the rich, to enforcing personal responsibility on the poor to be market compliant actors who overcame their adversity by being successful in the deregulated economy. Neoliberalism was not evidently ever in retreat, and now it appears to be ever ascendant.
>
> SCHRAM ET AL., 2018: xvii

This singular statement explains The New World Order in a nutshell. The New World Order is apparently made up of East Germans – who seem worse-off than they were under communist rule. If communism failed the USSR in the past, then it seems that capitalism is failing the residents of the former USSR in the present:

> In 1990, Chancellor Helmut Kohl famously promised East Germans "blossoming landscapes" within five years. However, this vision was not realised, as economic restructuring and marketisation in reunified Germany led to plant closings, extensive deindustrialisation, and widespread unemployment.
>
> KUBICEK, 2011: 87

Those who feel it know it. We cannot leave it to the West in general – and the US in particular – to educate and inform the world on the failures of communism. After all, they were the ones who convinced the world that Saddam Hussein had weapons of mass destruction. They were the ones who convinced the world that applying sanctions to apartheid South Africa will only hurt the black majority and not big Western businesses. They are the ones who continually tell the world that Israel is merely defending itself. In South Africa blacks in general – and Africans in particular – are best placed to decide whether apartheid was better than the democratic system we currently have. Likewise, East Germans are best placed to decide whether communism was better than the capitalism that they are now exposed to:

> Surveys as early as 1993, for instance, found that a majority of former East Germans believed that in many domains (job security, child care, crime prevention, gender equality, and social justice) the policies of the former GDR were superior to those in West Germany.
>
> KUBICEK, 2011: 88–89

For many who lived under communism, they were now best placed to judge the merits of both systems. Many were beginning to miss the benefits that came with the communist system:

> In the words of Harvey Greisman, Ostalgie is not the product of massive denial but a painful accurate realisation that life for many is tougher under freedom than it was in a dictatorship.
>
> KUBICEK, 2011: 89

If women have broken through the glass ceiling under capitalism, then it seems there was not much of a glass ceiling for women under communism:

> Some studies singled out women as especially hard-hit, since many of the benefits they had under the old system, including generous maternity leave, funds for expectant mothers, and state-provided child care, were lost. The socialist order put great rhetorical emphasis on a woman's role in the workforce and guaranteed women pay equality: 98 percent of East German women worked outside the home. In reunified Germany, many women in the Eastern Länder found themselves out of work and experienced great difficulties getting new jobs as employers viewed women with children as a liability. In the first two years after reunification, women's unemployment increased to 23 percent. In many other

respects—gender-specific advertising for vacancies, discrimination in employment, exposure to sexual harassment, a gender gap in earnings, repeals of liberal divorce and abortion statutes—women fared poorly after 1990.

KUBICEK, 2011: 89

Hindsight provides 20/20 vision. If capitalism was perceived to be a superior system and brought down the Berlin Wall, then the reality of living under capitalism after the fall put paid to such an ideology:

In 1990 the GDR was judged superior in three of the nine categories (predictably those of social security, gender equality, and maintenance of order), by 1995 the GDR was judged superior in seven of the nine categories, including, perhaps surprisingly, health and housing.

KUBICEK, 2011: 90

Beneath the ideology of the New World Order and the triumph of capitalism, the facts revealed a whole different picture:

If the euphoria of 1989 led us to believe, even momentarily, that we were entering into a 'New World Order' defined by peace and prosperity, history should have disabused us of this idea throughout the conflict-rife 1990s.

GERSTENBERGER ET AL., 2011: 3

Conflict and discontent continued into 21st century capitalist society. On 11 September 2001, two aeroplanes flew into the two iconic towers of the World Trade Center in the US. It was clear that there were some in the world who did not agree with or subscribe to the ideology of the New World Order coming from the West. Many innocent Americans lost their lives in this cruel and heinous act. Those who had committed this evil act – probably under the spell of religious ideology – had sought to disturb a giant. The US would go on to abdicate any opportunities for dialogue and evidence – and mobilised all physical, human and ideological resources to declare war on Iraq. Lies and deceit served a huge part of the Western ideological cache – in order to force the US military onto the Iraqi people. I recall attending an anti-war protest in the city of Durban in South Africa in 2003. Our protest song was something along the lines of: "one, two, three, four – we don't want a bloody war!" The angrier amongst us sang: "one, two, three, four – we don't want a fucking war!" Our idealism about war did not stop the US from invading Iraq under its scorched earth policy – and obliterating almost everything in sight. This was happening under Fukuyama's triumphant capitalism – and Bush's New World Order. We live in two worlds under capitalism: in the ideological world constructed around and about capitalism – and in the real world of capitalism. In 2003, the Iraqis learnt first-hand about how the New World Order really works!

The Berlin Wall may have fallen with the crumbling of communism – but the invisible walls protecting capitalism became visible in the time of COVID-19. We witnessed how the financial walls of capitalism protected the rich – and left the poor exposed in the time of COVID-19. We witnessed how the technological walls of capitalism protected the children with easy access to education – and exposed those without. We witnessed how the walls of nationalism went up during the production, pricing and distribution of vaccines in the time of COVID-19. We witnessed the walls of patent protection – and how this wall under capitalism kept out billions from accessing the scientific marvels of humankind. We witnessed how the walls of the inner circles ensured that the politically-connected get state tenders worth billions of dollars and pounds. We witnessed how the class walls of capitalist society kept the well-off safe and secure – and left the rest exposed to a deadly and menacing virus. Fukuyama was right when he spoke about the triumph of capitalism. We witnessed the triumph of capitalism in placing profits before people during a global pandemic in the Western world. In the communist worlds – where these still exist – we witnessed the power of communism to place people before profits.

Since the fall of communism in the USSR, the information on communism in Russia since the 1917 October revolution has been released into the world through different ideological lenses. Like so much of the information of the world currently, most of it has been through the ideological prism of the West. On a YouTube page for example – "hoodvadhoo" wrote on the topic: Does Socialism Work? Soviet Citizens Speak About Their Lives in the USSR – Nov 15, 2019:

> I was born in socialist Czechoslovakia, I was 11 when it fell. Life was good, simpler and a bit spartan, but we had everything most people need – family, friends, jobs for everyone, good cheap flats. Now, everyone is in debt, worried all the time about work, housing, health care. People have to leave family and friends to find jobs hundreds of kilometres away from home. Socialism worked well, this regime doesn't (31 May 2021).

"Super Trini Gamer" had this to say:

Next time someone says the USSR failed, I'm sending them this. Whenever they say about food shortages, they're talking about the 90s, which was the capitalist reform, so in reality, they're blaming the ideology they're trying to defend, without realising it!! (31 May 2021).

Kristine Smith had this to say:

As an American I can definitely say we've been lied to. When the second lady says that 'things became worse because everyone was only looking out for their own interests' (like capitalism promotes an individualistic society like the US) it really makes you wonder how much evil stems from capitalism. They all have such nice things to say about the relationships and quality of life. Such a shame Americans refuse to look into anything other than the propaganda we're fed at a young age about the USSR (31 May 2021).

However, whatever the criticisms of the West's reporting, analysis and propaganda of Russia under communism or communism under Russia – no left leaning ideologue or objective social scientist can get up one morning and speak of Putin ruling over a Soviet Union or USSR or communist Russia or a Marxist utopia. Lenin's and Stalin's Russia is no more. But the Tsar's Russia is also no more. With the collapse of the USSR, the state was rolled-back and the neoliberal capitalist market moved with lightning-speed into the former USSR. But it seemed that with the fall of the Berlin Wall, not all bought into Fukuyama's ideology of "The End of History" hypothesis – as I will argue in the following two chapters.

CHAPTER 4

Capitalism in Communist China – or Vice Versa

What we need is an enthusiastic but calm state of mind and intense but orderly work.

MAO ZEDONG

• • •

It doesn't matter whether a cat is white or black, as long as it catches mice.

DENG XIAOPING

• •
•

1   Colonialism and the Taking of Hong Kong

Hong Kong was finally handed back to China by the United Kingdom (UK) in 1997. The million-dollar question is: How did it come to be that Hong Kong – a very Chinese name – was finally given back to China – its mother country? Why was it taken from China in the first place? Continuing with its foreign policy of taking and keeping what does not belong to it:

> Britain has defied an order by the United Nations to return control of an overseas territory to the island nation of Mauritius.
>
> MEREDITH, 2019

It was a democratic vote in the United Nations (UN) – and the UK decided to dismiss the democratic majority vote of an internationally-recognised body. The US voted against the resolution. The world's oldest democracy did not bother to take the UK to task for its anti-democratic stance. Maybe when Mauritius becomes as mighty as China, then its Chagos Island might be returned to its rightful owner. Or Britain might decide to do the right thing – and return what does not belong to it in the first place. One does – or should have – huge expectations of the civilised Western world. After all, we keep hearing about Western values – and how important they are in the world that we live in. A brief history of Britain in China will enlighten us on the real and most times covert values so cherished by Western powers.

In the time of feudalism in Europe, merchant trade and the enforcement of Western civilisation was practised with and on countries that were already doing well before the dawn of capitalism. For example:

> After the arrival of the first Portuguese ships in 1516 and the establish-ment of Macao as a Portuguese trading post on the south Eastern coast of China in 1557, other Europeans came to trade, and with the traders came missionaries determined to spread Christianity to China and other parts of the Far East.
>
> HOOBLER ET AL., 2009: 111

With the development of capitalism in the West, Europe and the US were on the hunt for more and bigger markets for their goods. Having been self-sufficient through its own economic model, China had little use for foreign goods. The British:

> Hit on a product that had wide appeal – opium. After British ships began to bring opium from their colony in India, China became flooded with the drug and a serious addiction problem developed.
>
> HOOBLER ET AL., 2009: 117

If "religion is the opium of the masses" –European missionaries decided to give the Chinese people the real thing as well. China responded by forbidding the use of opium and dumped cargoes of opium into the sea. This:

> Action brought on the Opium War (1839–42) between China and Great Britain. It was a one-sided conflict. British warships sank the smaller, lightly armed Chinese ships and took control of the coast. When British troops landed and marched toward Beijing, the emperor asked for peace terms. The Chinese defeat brought about a revolution in China's relation-ships with foreign countries. More ports were opened to foreign trade, and the island of Hong Kong was ceded to Britain. Christian missionaries were free to roam the country to try to make converts.
>
> HOOBLER ET AL., 2009: 119

China – for a long time – was informed by the ideologies and teachings of Confucius. Since losing the Opium War and Hong Kong to the British Empire, China underwent "the century of shame and humiliation". It would not allow this to happen – ever again. China decided to do something about its perceived shameful standing in the world.

2   The Land of Confucius Looks to Karl Marx

If the fall of the Berlin Wall and the collapse of the Soviet Union were historical phenomena used to pronounce the death of Marxism, then developments in China would prove this to not be the case. In March of 2018, twenty-nine years after the fall of the Berlin Wall and the death of Marx's teachings, China celebrated the 200th birthday of Karl Marx. In July of 2021, China celebrated one hundred years of the Chinese Communist Party (CCP). It became clear that China does not subscribe to Francis Fukuyama's "The End of History" ideology. One has to go back in time to look at how and why China chose Marxism to inform its socio-economic policies and functioning in the world.

In July of 1912, five years before spearheading the Russian Revolution in 1917:

> Vladimir Lenin – described China as a 'semi-feudal country', where feudalism was still the main source of oppression and exploitation.
>
> CARR, 1990: 698

But under Marx's teachings, Mao would change the course of China's history:

> Mao was but the foremost of a generation of Chinese intellectuals and activists known as the May Fourth generation (for the patriotic anti-imperialist movement centering on the demonstrations in Beijing on 4 May 1919 that protested against the transfer of some Chinese territory to the Japanese in the Treaty of Versailles). This generation wrestled with a confusing array of Western ideas—from anarchism to pragmatism to social Darwinism and finally, after 1917, Marxism—as a way to explain the failures of the Chinese government to resist the inroads of European and Japanese imperialism. The CCP was officially founded in Shanghai in July 1921, and Mao attended the First Congress as a regional delegate from Hunan.
>
> CHEEK, 2013: 3

The development of communism in China was greatly influenced by the 1917 revolution in Russia:

The Chinese Communist Party at its congress in July 1922 announced its intention to lead the workers to support the democratic revolution, and forge a democratic united front of workers, poor peasants and petty bourgeois.

CARR, 1990: 655

But China approached the capitalist conundrum differently to that of Russia:

Despite many similarities, communist policy as well as communist experience in China, were always distinct from those of the Soviet Union or Eastern Europe. China's revolution emerged from protracted guerrilla warfare centered in revolutionary base areas and, with the subsequent Great Leap Forward and Cultural Revolution, it embarked on its own distinctive path long before the final decades of communism in Europe.

FURST ET AL., 2017: 7

We live in an age of relativity, comparisons and contradictions. One may have come across the saying, "don't judge a man by only the bad that he has done". After all, F.W. de Klerk was a leader that oversaw apartheid in South Africa yet he won a Nobel Peace Prize! Apartheid was declared a crime against humanity by the United Nations. Whilst Mao is known to have taken China from strength to strength – he is also known to have caused the deaths of millions of Chinese. His comrades in the Chinese Communist Party rationalised Mao's crimes against humanity as follows:

The 1981 CCP Central Committee resolution on 'Some Questions in the History of our Party' codified this assessment with the famous formula: Mao's contributions were 70 per cent; his errors 30 per cent.

CHEEK, 2013: 7.

Mao himself once assessed Stalin in a similar manner:

Mao had by then decided that the ratio of Stalin's virtues to his mistakes was 70 to 30, or, as he liked to put it figuratively, of Stalin's ten fingers only three were rotten.

RADCHENKO, 2013: 188

If Hitler is to be assessed in this way, would he be a man with ten rotten fingers and ten rotten toes? How would the neo-Nazi and architect of grand apartheid in South Africa, Professor Hendrik Verwoerd, fare? How would Churchill and

Nixon fare? If Mao's and Stalin's contributions were 70% contributions and 30% errors, how should President Truman be assessed – after having dropped atom bombs on the Japanese people? 50% contributions and 50% errors? 50% for stopping the war and 50% for killing many Japanese? A man with ten rotten fingers and ten rotten toes like Hitler? What about George W. Bush and Tony Blair for their illegal and deceitful war in Iraq: men with 3 rotten fingers like Stalin and Mao? It is a challenging task to try and scientifically assess history and the men and women who made history!

Who would have imagined that Chairman Mao would one day be quoted in the UK parliament in the 21st century – and that his Little Red Book would be given as a gift to the UK Chancellor to read? The Shadow Chancellor John McDonnell said to Chancellor George Osborne:

> Let's quote from Mao, rarely done in this chamber. We must learn to do economic work from all who know how, no matter who they are, we must esteem them as teachers, learning from them respectfully and conscientiously, but we must not pretend to know what we do not know.
>
> GRACE, 2015

It was meant to embarrass the Chancellor – but the move seemed to have backfired! If there is one person that the conservative ruling party in the UK did not want to learn economics from – that was Mao Zedong. The writer John Grace (2015) hinted: "why not go the whole hog and quote from Marx and Lenin, too?"

3   Riding the Capitalist Tiger Using a Marxist GPS

I have a stationary exercise bike at home – it says "made in China". I checked my Dell notebook battery – it also said "made in China". My Dell notebook itself says "made in China". My Microsoft mouse says "made in China". My Wi-Fi router says "made in China". My Telefunken flat screen television says "made in China". I checked my underwear – it also said "made in China". I had had enough! I did not have to check anymore. It was clear that I was living on the cheap labour and economic might of the once impoverished and humiliated China! Just to make sure once more that all things in my home are not made in China – I checked the writing on the box that contained the garbage bags. Thank god! It said "made in South Africa".

In any event a Chinese mall that is relatively close to me is a shopper's paradise for cheap and a variety of goods that are made in China. The Chinese know how to do economics – they leave their homes and conduct businesses in faraway lands. After my shopping spree to the Chinese City about 30 minutes-drive away, I go home with bags of cheap Chinese-made stuff. In my most recent shopping trip to Chinese City, I asked the owner of the store about COVID-19 in China. I was surprised when he answered: "There is no more corona in China". His child – who seemed about 15 years – continued: "No one is wearing masks in China any longer". I wanted to continue my discussions with them – a rare opportunity in a Chinese shop – but there were customers behind me – and they did not come to engage in discussions about China. In any event, it is a good thing that China is the factory of the world – South Africa paid a heavy price when Great Britain was the factory of the world. But China was an economic backwater just a few decades ago:

> For instance, Shanghai was poor, messy, and corrupt in the 1980s, but by the 2010s it approximated the modern, developmental states of East Asia. In 1980 China's GDP per capita was only US\$193, lower than that of Bangladesh, Chad, and Malawi, 24 present-day 'bottom-billion' countries.
> ANG, 2016: 3

China provides a conundrum for the predominantly capitalist world in general – and the scholars of different political systems in particular. It is a challenge to pigeon-hole China into either a communist or capitalist ideological paradigm. However, guided by Marx's theory of historical development, China seemed to have developed the country and its people that are beyond Western comprehension:

> Larry Summers, of Harvard University, observes that when America was growing fastest, it doubled living standards roughly every 30 years. China has been doubling living standards roughly every decade for the past 30 years. In just two years China has extended pension coverage to an extra 240m rural dwellers, for example – far more than the total number of people covered by America's public-pension system.
> DELAIBATIKI, 2021

Following Mao's death, the Chinese leader that took China into the world of market capitalism was Deng Xiaoping, who was described as "The great pragmatist" by *The Guardian* (18 December 2008). He was no longer the communist or socialist ideologue that abhorred the making of wealth. Furst, et al., (2017: 8) described the shape and form of capitalism since Deng Xiaoping's rise as "state capitalism with Chinese characteristics". It is an interesting model of the state's planning of the Chinese economy. With its new-found economic power, China has been able to extend its development hand to much of the former colonised and developing world through its Belt and Road Initiative:

> The Belt and Road Initiative is a loosely defined catchall term for pre-dominantly China-financed, and usually China-built, projects that have pumped billions of dollars into infrastructure in more than 60 countries in recent years. Chinese money has helped finance port projects in Sri Lanka, Greece and Pakistan, new railroad lines in Kenya and Indonesia, and airports in Djibouti and the Maldives.
>
> TAYLOR, 2020: 11

Unlike the Soviet Union, which finally collapsed – through its centrally planned economy, China has been able to move from a feudal economy to the second largest economy in the world in a space of 100 years! In the time of COVID-19, whilst citizens in the Western and capitalist countries were getting relatively poorer, China overwhelmingly won the war on COVID-19 in so far as preventing the needless deaths of its citizens, kept its economy stable, and also took millions out of poverty. How's that for a country that in recent history had its people stoned on opium, its ships sunk, Hong Kong taken away from it and underwent a century of humiliation:

> Meanwhile, in China, the socialist project has abolished absolute poverty during the pandemic. In November 2020, the authorities in Guizhou Province in southwest China announced that the last nine impoverished counties were removed from the poverty list, which means that all 832 poor counties in the country have now been lifted out of poverty. In seven years, the policies in China allowed 80 million people (roughly the entire population of Germany) to depart from poverty; in total, around 850 million Chinese people have lifted themselves out of poverty in the decades since the 1949 Revolution. There have been three metrics for this transformation: first, that every Chinese family would no longer be below the rural poverty line; second, that the communist project would end the 'two worries' of hunger and clothing; third, that the Chinese state would ensure the 'three guarantees' of education, health care, and housing. All of this occurred during the pandemic.
>
> PRASHAD, 2020

On 5 May 2018 in the Great Hall of the People in Beijing, China, the 200th birthday of Karl Marx was celebrated by the Chinese Communist Party. In his opening speech President Xi Jinping said:

Writing Marxism onto the flag of the Chinese Communist Party was totally correct. Unceasingly promoting the sinification and modernisation of Marxism is totally correct.

SHEPHERD, 2018

If the many in the West believe Marxism to be a dead duck, many in the East in general and China in particular believe Marxism to be alive and kicking.

4   Waging War on COVID-19 in a Country of 1.4 Billion People

The 2019 population estimate of China is about 1.4 billion. The official name of China is the People's Republic of China (PRC). Covering approximately 9.6 million square kilometres (3.7 million square miles) comprising 23 provinces, it is the world's third largest country by land area after Russia and Canada. China is one of the world's first civilisations (Wikipedia, 2021). I have never been to Wuhan – the capital city of Hubei Province – let alone to China. Since December 2019, the city of Wuhan has become a household name – for reasons of deadly fear as well as ideological warfare. Wuhan city itself is 8,494 km² in size and comprises a population of 11.8 million people as of 2018 (Wikipedia, 2020).

In December of 2019, a doctor in Wuhan observed a severe respiratory illness which supposedly did not fall into the category of known illnesses. At the local level, the Chinese communist state reacted with heavy-handedness and attempted to suppress crucial public health information, as well as punish the bearer of such information:

The story begins from Li Wenliang, 34, an ophthalmologist, who single-handedly blew the lid of the growing coronavirus epidemic in Wuhan in central China's Hubei province. He revealed in WeChat group on December 30, 2019, that seven patients showing SARS-like symptoms and had been admitted to Wuhan Central Hospital where he worked. The city police detained him for fear-mongering, and forced him to make a confession in an orchestrated move with the media to name and shame Li and other 'rumour mongers.' Later he died of coronavirus in the same hospital. Li's social media information turned into fact within the span of a few weeks when the deadly pneumonic virus began to infect people in Wuhan and other provinces of China.

JAVED, 2020

The "pneumonia of unknown cause first detected in the city of Wuhan", was reported to the World Health Organisation (WHO) Country Office in China on 31 December 2019 (WHO, 2019). The WHO called the coronavirus an emergency in China but stopped short of declaring it of international concern (Groves and Ledwith, 2020). A month later the global ramifications of the disease was recognised. On 30 January 2020 the WHO declared the outbreak of the disease as a "Public Health Emergency of International Concern" (WHO, 2020). In other words what was initially thought of as an epidemic turned out to be a pandemic. On 12 February 2020, the World Health Organisation (WHO) named the illness – Coronavirus Disease 2019, COVID-19 for short. Donald Trump named it the Chinese Virus and sometimes referred to it as the Kung flu Virus. Anti-China social media pundits also called it the Wuhan Virus.

It took the death of Dr Li Wenliang for the communist state of China to remove the veil over its denial of the severity of COVID-19. But once realising the pandemic and deadly nature of the virus, China responded and reacted with precision, efficiency, resourcefulness, commitment and dedication. Wuhan, which covers an area five times the size of Greater London, was put into total lockdown (Groves and Ledwith, 2020: 14). A vast hospital with beds for 1,000 patients was built from scratch in China in a desperate attempt to cope with the coronavirus outbreak – and it was scheduled to be completed in just 10 days. When the UK finally decided to provide a credible response to COVID-19, it converted one of its stadiums to a make-shift hospital in 9 days. Was it Western efficiency or Western ideological posturing? In any event there was no or not much earth-moving equipment in the second feat.

When Wuhan was shut down the world was stunned. One's temperature taken every 300m (Al Jazeera Television News Network, 2020) is a clear indication that China was committed to doing full-on battle with COVID-19. China declared all-out war and threw as much of its resources as it could in fighting COVID-19. The country's pragmatic approach to dealing with COVID-19 seemed to have worked. COVID-19 started in China, but China has also been responsible in giving the world hope when on 7 April 2020 China reported "zero deaths" from COVID-19. The entire world breathed a sigh of relief – China provided hope that the virus could be beaten. The country also embarked on "Aid for a Shared Future". Whether it had done this out of real concern or for ideological manoeuvring – is dependent on how one views China's standing in world affairs. Either way, the end result is that many countries benefitted from China's pragmatic philanthropy in the time of COVID-19. By 2 April 2020, China had hosted more than 40 conferences in order to share information on COVID-19 (CGTN, 2 April 2020). By the end of May 2020 China had sent aid to about

150 countries. China also contributed to other forms of material assistance to countries to help deal with COVID-19:

> Chinese leaders also publicly signed on to a collective pledge by the Group of 20 industrial and emerging-market nations to suspend the collection of interest payments on loans to those borrowers. The move was touted as the equivalent to freeing up some $20 billion for poorer nations to respond to the pandemic.
>
> TAYLOR, 2020: 11

By the end of the first quarter of 2020, China had overwhelmingly won the war on COVID-19. Much of the developed world – even though advanced in the science of viruses – behaved as if the enemy was that of China's and China's alone. They were to get a first-hand lesson on the globalised formation of the world we live in – and how inefficient capitalism's social, political, economic and health systems are, in dealing with a global pandemic such as COVID-19. Saving lives was China's first priority. Saving its market economy was its second. It seemed to have accomplished both. In the meantime, in the Western world one year later – neither the people nor the capitalist economy seemed to be doing well at all.

5   Western Ideologies on the Offensive in the Time of COVID-19

The world is used to being told about the failures of communism – not about its successes. With the response to COVID-19 in China, the world got to witness first-hand the planned response by an efficient state. This would raise the ire of the Western world in the main. Countries in the West went all out to prove that the capitalist, liberal system premised on Western definitions and descriptions of rights, freedom, liberty and values were far superior to that of communist ideologies – even whilst scientific evidence was pointing to the fact that their citizens were in harm's way in the Western world. It seemed like one big social experiment – whereby citizens were apparently used as 'guinea pigs' to prove to the world that a strong state, amongst other Western ideologies, is not good for society. People died in their millions in the Western world – as a result of this apparent social experiment and ideological perversion. If the Western world chose capitalist and neoliberal ideologies over pragmatism and common sense to deal with a global pandemic, there was simultaneously a full-on focus and ideological offensive on China:

The coronavirus was deliberately engineered as a bio-weapon in a Chinese lab! That's the bombshell claim of a criminal complaint filed by former U.S. Justice Department prosecutor Larry Klayman at the International Criminal Court in The Hague, Netherlands! He's also filed a lawsuit against the People's Republic of China, its president, Xi Jinping, and other government officials seeking trillions of dollars in damages, The National Enquirer has learned. It comes as COVID-19 has infected more than 2.6 million people worldwide and claimed the lives of over 183,000 as it brought economies around the world to a near standstill.

National Enquirer, May 11, 2020

It seemed that the real war against COVID-19 was lost sight of – as the ideological contenders engaged in a war of words as to which political and ideological systems were best equipped to respond to the pandemic. There was both an aggressive and a subtle war, an information war fought through the media – both establishment media as well as social media. When Western mainstream media speak about China, the term "draconian" is commonly used. President Trump used the language of war and the word "attack" to describe the pandemic that originated in China. The narrative that China had declared war on the US gained momentum. A so-called terror expert Dr Jim Garrow told *The Enquirer*:

They loaded infected people on planes and sent them to America. It wasn't solely to kill lots of people. It was designed to create economic havoc – and it worked very well.

COVID-19 News, 2020: 6

The Chinese – and not the Americans – were the first people to be infected and whom died from COVID-19. These people were contained in Wuhan city – not first on a plane to New York. Still the ideological warmongering picked up momentum. Mike Pence, the Vice President of the US – like his boss Donald Trump – also blamed China. You can only blame China for so long. At some point, as the most powerful and most resourced country and state in the world, you are going to have to take responsibility for whether the people of your country will live or die – during a global pandemic. Even in trying their very best to denigrate China – some in the West revealed in their statements how successful China was in containing COVID-19:

> Tom Cotton of Arkansas noted China's 'deceit and dishonesty' when tell-
> ing the world about the virus and cited 'the extreme draconian measures
> taken' to contain it showed just how serious it really was.
>
> COVID-19 News, 2020: 6

Donald Trump did not stop at blaming China; he turned his focus to blaming
the Centre for Disease Control (CDC) in the US as well – for not forewarning
the US state about the pandemic. In fact, anyone and any organisation that did
not align oneself or itself with taking ideological sides with the West were pun-
ished in one form or the other. Anyone or any organisation that stood alongside
science and evidence over Western ideologies were victimised in one form or
another. In the time of a global health emergency – Western ideologies dominated. The focus seemed to be on everything else – but on effectively defeating
COVID-19, that was eating away at lives and livelihoods in the Western world in
general, and in the capitalist world in particular:

> Few doubt that the pandemic has created an inflection point in the battle
> for global influence between China and the West, and some warn that
> Washington should be more wary of Beijing's desire to replace the U.S.
> as the world's most go-to economic partner. China's leaders are eager
> to exploit the coronavirus-induced global economic crisis to expand
> Beijing's already ambitious Belt and Road investment campaign through
> a flood of loans to the growing number of nations in need around the
> world. Pro-capitalism and democracy advocates including Canberra,
> Australia; New Delhi; and Tokyo fear the Belt and Road Initiative's real
> goal is to build a China-centred sphere of influence that undermines
> Western free market ideals by pulling developing nations into "debt
> traps" that give Beijing economic sway, and perhaps even authoritarian
> political control, over expanding territory around the world.
>
> TAYLOR, 2020: 11

Whilst the temptation was ever present to fabricate the evidence that the virus
had managed to escape from a Wuhan laboratory, the intelligence sector in the
US was mindful of its poor reputation in the arena of intelligence gathering:

> U.S. officials have said that Mr. Trump, increasingly desperate to deflect
> attention from his dismal handling of the crisis, put pressure on the U.S.
> intelligence community to find evidence for his theory. This raises the
> spectre of the fiasco that took place when George W. Bush invaded Iraq
> based on "slam-dunk" intelligence that a program to build weapons of

mass destruction was under way. Subsequent investigations showed that the intelligence 'evidence' was largely fabricated or the result of deliberately skewed analysis of facts that could have been interpreted in various ways. The intelligence community is now determined to avoid this kind of pressure and to base its analyses on unbiased and factual reporting, and we are seeing this play out. In the final analysis, all countries need to focus on working together to find solutions. First, China did try to cover up the emergence of the threat for a crucial period when it might have been better contained, and the country has lied about it since. No country deserves a perfect mark for its handling of the crisis and all should be held accountable when the dust has settled and the time comes to learn lessons.

FADDEN and JONES, 2020: 11

In its proxy war and Cold War with China – showing its evil side – capitalist USA withdrew 400 million dollars of funding from the World Health Organisation – the time when the WHO and the people of the world needed it the most – to go to war with a global pandemic. This wicked deed revealed the true nature of US reigning ideologies and values under Donald Trump – as opposed to the ideology dished out by its secretary of state, ideologue Mike Pompeo – when he proclaimed in the time of COVID-19 at a press conference on 31 March 2020: "we are a generous and noble people". This from a capitalist state that exited the Paris Climate Change agreement – and allowed the planet to burn. This from a capitalist state that withdrew from the world-Iran nuclear deal and left the world a much more dangerous place – even after the experiences of Hiroshima and Nagasaki! This from a capitalist state that has a migrant family separation policy – whereby children are forcibly separated from their parents! This from a capitalist state that enables its citizens to be mowed down by the 2nd amendment!

China was also accused of wanting to "sabotage" the vaccine programme in the US (Safi, 2020). When asked if China had manufactured the coronavirus in a laboratory, a doctor on the British Broadcasting Corporation (BBC) stated that there was no material evidence for that hypothesis – and went on to say that nature is a laboratory for viruses (Peter Daszak of Ecohealth, CNN). A professor from the London School of Economics stated that the West thought that the breakout of the pandemic in Wuhan, China was a "Chernobyl moment" (BBC 23 May 2020). In reference to the verbal attacks on China, a fireman stated on international television that "we should not be fighting each other when a house is on fire" (CGTN – 20 May 2020). The heaviness of Western ideological offensive against China failed to shift the evidence-based position of the WHO on the origin of COVID-19:

> A day after Trump said he had seen evidence that suggested the virus leaked from a virology laboratory in Wuhan, China, the World Health Organisation underscored its view that the virus is not man-made but that it is still working to understand how the virus jumped to humans. 'We have listened again and again to numerous scientists who have looked at the sequences and looked at this virus. We are assured that this virus is natural in origin,' said Mike Ryan, WHO emergencies chief.
>
> GEARAN ET AL., 2020

6   Containing China

It made sense to contain Hitler and his Nazi army. In fact, this is what the Red Army – under communism in the Soviet Union – had been able to achieve – and got rid of an evil menace that sought to wipe out other countries and races in Europe. It made sense to contain Islamic State of Iraq and Syria (ISIS). This is what some countries in general – and Russia in particular – were able to achieve – and got rid of an evil menace that sought to wipe out other religions and cultures in parts of the world. It made sense to contain the supporters of Donald Trump – during the inauguration ceremony of Joe Biden, the 46th President of the United States. This was achieved by the US army. It made sense to contain COVID-19. This was achieved by countries like China, Vietnam, Cuba, etc. The Western world in the main failed in their containment of COVID-19. It makes sense to contain global warming and subsequent climate change. This seems impossible to do under capitalism – the dominant economic system of the current world order.

It will make sense to contain China – if China is selling a program similar to the Washington Consensus to developing countries – but there is no evidence of China doing this. All China is doing is trying to sell to the world stuff that is made in China – in the same way that the rest of the world is trying to sell to China stuff made in their countries. If there are ideological influences of sorts accompanying China's trading practices, then one has to look at the ideological influences of sorts that are accompanying the West's trading practices as well.

If China has its military ships in the Atlantic Ocean in the same way that the US has its military ships in the South China Sea, then it will make sense to try and contain China. But the entire Western world is hell-bent on containing

China. Ever since the economic rise of China and its ability to continue with its economic development using the brand of Marxist communism with Chinese characteristics – China has been on the West's radar. Actually, China is not the only one that is or was on the US's surveillance radar – Angela Merkel, the former chancellor of Germany, was as well at one time and so are many millions of Americans too. But the red flag is always raised on the West's radar when it comes to China:

> Meanwhile, Western elites driven by Mackinderian nightmares are working hard, and more profanely, on the geopolitical frontline to reinforce their position and obtain China's strategic containment and encirclement. Functional to this effort would be a stronger negative characterisation of that country, but things appear not to work out so easily.
> PETRI, 2018: 14

COVID-19 has not only made visible the West's hostility to China's economic rise, it has also heightened that hostility. The West has ruled the world for a long time. Most of this rule has been destructive and depressing for the ruled. With the rise of China – and the dilution of Western hegemony – the question is: What type of world order should emerge when the world wins the war against COVID-19? The leaders of the US got off lightly for their dismal response to COVID-19. Whereas over a million Americans lost their lives, Donald Trump and the Republican Party merely lost the 2020 US elections. If China underwent a century of humiliation from 1839 to 1949, then under Marx's thought, it appears to be the case that the 21st century will be a century of pride and honor for China and the Chinese people – and maybe for the developing world as well.

CHAPTER 5

Socialisms and Communisms in a Capitalist World

I find capitalism repugnant. It is filthy, it is gross, it is alienating ...
because it causes war, hypocrisy and competition.

FIDEL CASTRO

• • •

Democratic socialism means that we must create an economy that
works for all, not just the very wealthy.

BERNIE SANDERS

• •
•

1 Toward Deconstructing the Celebrated Ideology of Capitalism as the End of History

If socialism and communism are really extinct socio-economic systems of yes-
teryear – then it seems quite extraordinary that so much was said about these
systems in the time of COVID-19. That an invisible virus could trigger vitriolic
attacks against the systems of communism and socialism must really be a sign
of their persistent presence within the global capitalist system – even after the
fall of the Berlin Wall and talk of The End of History. The ideological attacks
were fast and furious in the time of COVID-19:

> The speeches delivered by Pompeo, national security adviser Robert C.
> O'Brien, Attorney General William P. Barr and FBI Director Christopher
> A. Wray are laden with early Cold War red-scare rhetoric. 'America,
> under President Trump's leadership, has finally awoken to the threat the
> Communist Party's actions pose to our very way of life,' O'brien declared
> in the first of the speeches. Xi, he said, 'sees himself as Joseph Stalin's
> successor.' 'If there's one thing I learned' from the Cold War, said Pompeo,
> it's that 'communists almost always lie'.
>
> DIEHL, 2020

Whilst he made this statement in front of the world's press, his boss – arch capitalist Donald J. Trump – boasted that the US had everything under control and that the US was doing a great job in the war against COVID-19. At that time in early 2020, 150 000 US citizens – the highest in the world – had died from COVID-19. Pompeo's boss also lied to the world that he – and not Joe Biden – had won the 2020 US elections. History also recalls how capitalist ideologues at the highest level of the US state lied to the entire world – when they appeared in front of the international press and convinced the world under the spell of Western values that Iraq had weapons of mass destruction. Many innocent men, women and children died in Iraq at the hands of the lying ideologues and fake news pundits – with George W. Bush, Tony Blair and Colin Powell leading the pack of Western liars.

Like so much that was transformed in the time of COVID-19, it seems Adam Smith's "invisible hand" had also transformed into the "hidden hand" of China: "Beijing's hidden hand – how the Chinese Communist Party is reshaping the world" (Hamilton et al., 2020). In the Philippines, the mayor of Gabaldon stated:

> I am also appealing to the public to support our government, the military, and the police on their quest to end local communists in the community. Let us protect our government troops.
> REYES, 2020

In holy and pious India:

> The Congress in Kerala is trying hard to dislodge the Communist Party of India (Marxist) government in the state over the issue of gold smuggling allegedly in a diplomatic cargo from a Gulf country.
> MALANKAR, 2020

But it was in capitalist US that the ideological attack on socialism and communism took on the form of religious fanaticism:

> One of the reasons that the Russian Revolution lasted seven decades, and the Black Lives Matter upheaval will not likely last past the first frost is that the Communists had a coherent agenda based on the philosophy—however misguided—of Karl Marx. By allowing the radicals to become the face of the movement, BLM activists have alienated many middle-road people who could help them attain their goals if they could ever articulate them coherently.
> ANDERSON, 2020

Having a go at the US secretary of state – Mr. Mike Pompeo – a writer in the print media stated:

> A new height of CIA intelligence gathering is that through deep analysis, perhaps use of supercomputers, it has discovered that China is Marxist-Leninist – something that could never have been worked out from the fact it is led by a Communist Party.
>
> ROSS, 2020

Many socialist and communist countries were rattled with the end of communism in the USSR. But many also did not buy into Fukuyama's ideology, propaganda and fake news of *"The End of History and the Last Man"* – although the temptation to do so was overwhelming and extremely coercive. If the Jews are best placed to understand and pronounce on the horrors of Nazi Germany – and black South Africans are best placed to understand the horrors of apartheid South Africa – then Russians are best placed to understand the horrors of communist or socialist Russia. Astonishingly after the fall of the Berlin Wall it seems that many Russians do not see capitalism as the system chosen by history – by which to conduct their lives and livelihoods – but continue to strive for a communist future. Capitalist ideologues may wish to brush it off as merely nostalgia – but black South Africans are not nostalgic for apartheid, nor are blacks nostalgic for slavery nor the Jews for Nazi Germany. Many Russians are not only nostalgic for the past but it seems they wish to do something concrete about it as well – in the form of the Communist Party of the Russian Federation (KPRF)! Actually, it has been the case since the fall of the Berlin Wall. The Communist Party of the Russian Federation (KPRF) is the main opposition party in Russia (Gel'man, 2011). With all of the propaganda coming from the West, who would have thought that this was even possible and happening in the former Soviet Union!

Contrary to the overbearing weight of Western and capitalist ideologies, communism is not dead in Russia but lives on – even in an embryonic form – as the material opposition to capitalist Russia. Communism and socialism live on amongst the biggest populace of the world as well. Thirty-three years since the dissolution of the communist state in the USSR – the communist state in China is still looking solid. Whilst the US is the embodiment of capitalism and the capitalist idea – China as a rising superpower continues to embody communism and the communist idea – whilst attempting to co-exist with the contradictions of dominant capitalism:

As the twenty-first century advances, it may come to seem that the Chinese revolution was the great revolution of the twentieth century, deeper in its mobilisation of society, more ambitious in its projects, more far-reaching in its achievements, and in some ways more enduring than its Soviet counterpart. Certainly, more people lived – and still do today— under communist states in East Asia than ever did in post-war Europe.

SMITH, 2014: 4

Thirty-three years after the break-up of the Soviet Union, socialism and communism continue to live on in other parts of the world and in different shapes, forms and practices – despite what Fukuyama and his ideological backers would like the world to believe. It seems as long as capitalism exists and prescribes to man that his life and livelihood should be left to an "invisible hand" – then it seems that capitalism will be continually challenged. And this challenge to capitalism has become and is becoming more pronounced after the 2008 Financial Crisis, and more so in the time of COVID-19.

There are different types of interpretations and practices of communism and socialism – in the same way that there are different interpretations and practices of capitalism in the world today. Capitalism in the US could be said to be more ruthless than the capitalism in the UK. Capitalism as practised in South Africa – is different to the capitalism practised in Singapore. Communism as practised in China is different to the communism once practised in the USSR. Socialism in Cuba may be said to be different to the socialism or communism of North Korea. Socialism in Venezuela could be said to be different to that of socialism in the state of Kerala in India. The socialisms we have witnessed in the last 100 years grew out of specific socio-historical, cultural and economic conditions. Hence, China has what is known as socialism with Chinese characteristics.

In South Africa the myth and ideology of capitalism being The End of History and a people-friendly and nature-friendly system was strongly challenged in the time of COVID-19:

Capitalism has proved to be more resilient (and more barbaric) than communists in the 1920s had foreseen. Through plunder of natural resources, through socialising debt and privatising profit (see the public bailout of banks in the US after the 2008 financial crisis), through manipulating racial and gendered oppressions, through expropriation of peasants in the periphery and through endless warfare, it has delayed its own demise.

CRONIN, 2020

In Nepal, the communist party called for peace and not conflict:

Reacting to Oli's remarks, Spokesperson of Communist Party of Nepal (CPN) and member of the powerful Central Secretariat Narayankaji Shrestha described the PM's statements as undiplomatic. PM KP Sharma Oli has committed a blunder by making irritating remarks against India, at a time when there is a need for resolving the border issue through dialogue with the southern neighbor.

Mail Today, 2020

Arguably it seems that communists are relatively peaceful – when compared to their capitalist counterparts. In the Philippines – apparently: "President Duterte is willing to give the coronavirus vaccines free to communist rebels but not to the rich, drug pushers, and drug addicts" (Kabiling, 2020). It appears that communists and socialists are everywhere – even though the collapse of the USSR muted a fair amount of people's dream for a communist utopia. Homo sapiens being resilient creatures – continued and continue to dream and to build their utopias. These dreamers seemed to have done better than their capitalist counterparts in the war against COVID-19. When we set aside the capitalist ideology that capitalism is the natural state of affairs for humankind, we then are able to see the world for what it really is – a world of dominant capitalism – but persisting communisms and socialisms as well. The world still seems to be divided along capitalist and communist ideological lines in the main. All those countries that have capitalism as their underlying ideology – even if they are authoritarian and antidemocratic like Saudi Arabia, Egypt, etc. – seem to be friends, allies and buddies of the West. All those countries that are socialist or communist – even though they have excellent health care and welfare systems for its citizens – such as Cuba and China are considered enemies of the West. Such is the overwhelming but bizarre and perverse ideological world foisted by the West upon much of humankind in the modern age.

As the West continued to do battle with phantom threats from China, Russia, Iran, Venezuela, etc., socialist and communist countries took to waging war against COVID-19 with efficiency, timeliness, precision and science. COVID-19 demonstrated that socialists and communist countries were practical in their response – whilst the Western world in general – and the capitalist world in particular – were largely ideological in their war against COVID-19.

2   COVID-19 and the Socialist or Communist Response

Capitalist US did not send its doctors to help other countries in the time of COVID-19. Capitalist UK did not send its doctors to other countries to help out the less fortunate in the world. Capitalist India did not send its doctors to help out the sick and the needy. Neither did capitalist Brazil not capitalist South Africa. But socialist or communist Cuba did! COVID-19 demonstrated that the socialist and communist world was more caring and more people-centered than the capitalist world. In an address to the nation – the South African president nominated Cuban Doctors for the Nobel Peace Prize, 2021: "South Africa must be congratulated for summoning the courage to nominate Cuba" (*The Guardian*, 2021). The president is one of the richest men in South Africa through his capitalist ties – but yet he chose to nominate a socialist or communist country. Many knew that this would not go down well with the Western school of thought:

> Let us not forget that very few countries in the West are going to be dancing to the United Nations headquarters in September to support South Africa's nomination.
>
> *The Guardian*, 2021

It is expected that one would move away from ideology in a world that requires pragmatic and practical functioning – especially in the time of a global pandemic! Instead, capitalist ideologues came out of their woodwork in the time of COVID-19 to uphold capitalist and Western ideologies:

> The president has nominated the Cuban doctors for the Nobel Peace Prize. This is madness.
>
> *The Citizen*, 2021

Cuba is the socialist David that dared to take on the capitalist US Goliath – and succeeded. Cuba is a small island on the doorstep of the US. The US hates dictators as dictators go against American values and the American way of life – but not if such dictators oppress their own people and serve American capitalist interests. Fulgencio Batista was a "U.S.-backed dictator from 1952 to 1959" (Wikipedia) – until the Cuban Revolution overthrew him and installed a socialist state and a humane way of life. Ever since, Cuba has been the target of the US in more ways than one. The then president of the US, John F. Kennedy, and his insurgents suffered a humiliating defeat in the Bay of Pigs Invasion in Cuba. Fidel Castro survived countless assassination attempts by the US and US-backed forces. There is even a documentary titled *638 Ways to Kill Castro*. The attempts were made mainly by the Central Intelligence Agency (CIA). The assassins failed in their many attempts to kill Fidel Castro. Fidel Castro died of natural causes at the age of 90 in 2016!

Economic sanctions on Cuba intensified under the presidency of Donald Trump. When previous American presidents – before Barack Obama – instituted sanctions against Cuba – Castro instructed Cuba to be self-sufficient in many things – one of them being immunology. Thirty years later Cuba is testing its COVID-19 vaccine to be approved (BBC, 2021). For the entire of 2020, Cuba was all-hands-on-deck in its war against COVID-19:

> Just 10 days ago, Cuba registered zero new coronavirus cases for the first time since the start of its outbreak, burnishing its reputation for a textbook handling of disasters like hurricanes and now the fearsome pandemic. Cuba is one of a handful of Latin American countries that have managed to contain the new coronavirus, which continues to devastate regional powers like Brazil and Mexico. The country's free community-based health system has been credited, along with measures such as strict isolation of the sick and their contacts, allowing it to keep the number of cases under 2,600 with 87 deaths – and no new deaths in the past 18 days.
>
> Bangkok Post, 2020

Unlike its mighty and egotistical neighbour and bully – the US – Cuba declared all-out war on COVID-19:

> Desperate for tourist revenue, Cuba closed its border later than most other countries in the region. But ever since the communist-ruled island shut out the outside world in late March it has thrown everything at the virus. The state has commanded tens of thousands of family doctors, nurses and medical students to 'actively screen' all homes on the island for cases of COVID-19 – every single day. That means that from Monday to Sunday, Caballero and her medical students must walk for miles, monitoring the 328 families on her beat. 'There's no other country in the hemisphere that does anything approaching this,' said William Leo Grande, professor of government at American University in Washington DC. 'The whole organisation of their healthcare system is to be in close touch with the population, identify health problems as they emerge, and deal with them immediately. We know scientifically that quick identification of cases, contact tracing and quarantine are the only way to contain the virus in the absence of a vaccine – and because it begins with prevention, the Cuban health system is perfectly suited to carry out that containment strategy.' Cuba has so far reported 2,173 confirmed cases of coronavirus and 83 deaths from it. Everybody who tests positive on the island is admitted to hospital. People suspected of carrying the virus are put

into state-run isolation centers, usually for 14 days. This tracing and isolation regime is made possible by human resources. Cuba has the highest
doctor-to-patient ratio in the world, and the island spends a higher proportion of its GDP on healthcare than any other country in the region.
While 30% of the 630 million people in Latin America and the Caribbean
have 'no access to healthcare for financial reasons', according to the Pan
American Health Organization, everybody in Cuba is covered.

> AUGUSTIN, 2020: 25

Cuba managed the COVID-19 pandemic excellently for most of 2020. However,
the intensified economic sanctions by capitalist US gave Cuba little to no
choice but to open its borders to international tourists for income generation
to meet the basic needs of its citizens. The country experienced surges in early
2021 which continued through most part of the year. According to the Johns
Hopkins University and Medicine Coronavirus Resource Center as of 17 June
2022 Cuba registered 1,105,681 COVID-19 infections and 8,529 deaths.

In a part of India, the communist response was glaringly superior to that
of the capitalist response of the mother country. Kerala is one of 29 states in
India and the only state with a communist government. The response by the
communist state was quick and fast:

> On 20 January, KK Shailaja phoned one of her medically trained deputies.
> She had read online about a dangerous new virus spreading in China.
> 'Will it come to us?' she asked. 'Definitely, Madam,' he replied. And so the
> health minister of the Indian state of Kerala began her preparations. Four
> months later, Kerala has reported only 524 cases of COVID-19, four deaths
> and – according to Shailaja – no community transmission. The state has
> a population of about 35 million and a GDP per capita of only £2,200. By
> contrast, the UK (double the population, GDP per capita of £33,100) has
> reported more than 40,000 deaths, while the US (10 times the population,
> GDP per capita of £51,000) has reported more than 82,000 deaths; both
> countries have rampant community transmission.
>
> *Fiji Sun*, 16 May 2020: 46

This was in May 2020. By December 2020 the number of infected and dead in
the capitalist world had increased tremendously. The writer on the communist
state's response continued:

> The Communist Party of India (Marxist), of which she is a member, has
> been prominent in Kerala's governments since 1957, the year after her

birth. (It was part of the Communist Party of India until 1964, when it broke away). Kerala enjoys the highest life expectancy and the lowest infant mortality of any state in India; it is also the most literate state.

Fiji Sun, 16 May 2020: 46

Scholars who have studied Kerala's response to COVID-19 are of the view that:

Kerala's COVID-19 success is an offshoot of years of investment in health-care and its people-centered development strategy. Kerala tops the human development index, compared to other states in India, and in sharp contrast to the state of Gujarat that is sold as the model of neolib-eral growth and development. Over the years, the Communist Party of India-Marxist-led government has tremendously invested in education and in the healthcare system.

DUTTA ET AL., 2020: 6

However, the state of Kerala did lose control of the situation towards the end of 2020 and the COVID-19 infections and death numbers did increase consid-erably. But when compared to other states in India the death toll in the Marxist and communist state of Kerala was amongst the lowest.

Communist USSR collapsed in the 1990s but communist North Korea is still with the world in the 2020s. North Korea seemed to have been insulated from COVID-19, in the same way that it seems insulated from the rest of the world in all manner of speaking. Not much was said about North Korea in the mainstream media – except that "Rocket Man" was firing missiles across South Korea and Japan. Much of the world breathed somewhat of a sigh of relief when it was discovered that they were short-range missiles. There was also plenty of excitement in the Western mainstream media that Kim Jong Un was ill and on his death bed. There was even talk about his successor. Towards the end of April 2020, Kim Jong Un was once again seen in public. The idea from the Western world floating about before his appearance, was that he went into hiding from COVID-19. The ideological spat between North Korea and South Korea did not stop in the time of COVID-19:

North Korea announced what it claimed was its 'first suspected case' of COVID-19 last week. It said the virus had been brought into the country by a recently returned defector, who'd crossed the militarised border with South Korea illegally. But Seoul said the man, who had been resident in the South for three years, did not have the virus. There is speculation that the virus is creating havoc in North Korea, and that Pyongyang is trying to divert blame for it away from the regime.

The Week, 2020

"Havoc" seems more a description of the capitalist world than the communist world in the time of COVID-19. Whether it is the Republican Party or the Democratic Party, the US is still intent on pushing for state change in socialist countries – even in the time of a global pandemic – with an outcome which obviously favours US selfish interests. With regards to socialist Venezuela:

Biden has been careful to say he does not support "regime change" for Venezuela, the phrase used to describe the George W. Bush administration's approach to Iraq. But he has come close to endorsing the concept in substance. As he told the Americas Quarterly in March, Maduro is a dictator, plain and simple, but the overriding goal in Venezuela must be to press for a democratic outcome through free and fair elections, and to help the Venezuelan people rebuild their country.

LAKE, 2020

Abiding by its foreign policy of "the end justifies the means" the US reactionary response to the 2020 Venezuelan elections was:

In our view the constitutional president of Venezuela today and after January 5, 2021 is Juan Guaidó.

Daily Observer, 2020

Instead of focusing its time, energy and ample resources on saving its citizens in the time of a global pandemic, the US apparently resorted to its favourite past time – actively destabilising countries that are not in its neoliberal ideological camp:

A Venezuelan court has sentenced two former U.S. special forces soldiers to 20 years in prison for their part in a failed beach attack aimed at overthrowing President Nicolas Maduro, prosecutors announced. Guaido blames Maduro for the once wealthy nation's economic and social collapse, while the socialist leader says Washington is manipulating Guaido to steal the nation's vast oil wealth.

The Atlanta Journal-Constitution, 2020

According to the Johns Hopkins University and Medicine Coronavirus Resource Center, as of 19 June 2022, socialist Venezuela registered 524,718 COVID-19 infections and 5,724 deaths. In a country with a population of about 30 million people, this figure is amongst the lowest in the world.

Forget about the collapse of the USSR; long before capitalism was declared The End of History, the Western world in general – and the US and France in particular – mobilised all of their resources to stop communism in its tracks. It may be the case that no other country had more bombs dropped on it than Vietnam. According to Heller (2011: 34):

> Capitalism was deeply challenged by the Vietnam War, which sparked global revolt including revolutionary upheavals in France and Italy. Anti-imperialist revolution reached its zenith in the under-developed countries in the 1970s.

Compared to the country that rained bombs on it because the US believed that Western and capitalist society is most civilised and most superior – Vietnam proved formidable and unbeatable in the wars against France and the US in the 60s and 70s. Unlike the US and France, Vietnam also proved formidable and unbeatable in its war against COVID-19:

> The communist nation was applauded earlier this year for controlling COVID-19 with strict restrictions, quarantines and robust tracing regime. But an outbreak in the beach resort of Danang recently, near Hoi An, has put the country back on high alert. Health officials yesterday also announced the highest single daily caseload since the pandemic began.
> *New Straits Times*, 2020.

The superiority of the communist response – to that of the inferior capitalist response – regarding the war on COVID-19 is concisely captured in the following view:

> Vietnam, a country whose 96 million citizens had a gross domestic product per capita of $2,715 last year, has been able to control the outbreak because of the government's laser-like antivirus focus, a one-party political system and a population that didn't need convincing as a result of past disease outbreaks. The US, with a gross domestic product per capita of $65,280 in 2019, has not. Vietnam's success has been globally lauded. The US, meanwhile, has surpassed 4.3 million cases and 149,000 deaths while President Donald Trump has consistently downplayed the spread

of the virus. Rather than following the advice of the experts, in July he retweeted a post claiming the CDC was lying about the virus. There have been dramatic differences between how Vietnam and US approached the contagion crisis. Within weeks of Vietnam's first reported cases in late January, the government closed schools. The Trump administration continues to resist school shutdowns, and has even threatened to withhold federal funding from schools that don't bring back students. Hanoi quickly deploys tests to anyone suspected of exposure to the virus, while the US continues to face testing shortcomings. Danang's authorities shut down two hospitals where two victims visited and ordered patients, medical staff, caregivers and family members—about 8,800 people in total—to be quarantined for 14 days at centralised bases, hospitals and homes, according to the city's health department. A third hospital also was closed. Vietnam has some key advantages the US doesn't in combating the virus. The Communist Party controlled government dominates a society with a culture of collectivism, and its tough measures, like willingness to put in place lockdowns when needed, has been met with little resistance from the population. This comes despite the fact that its quarantine regime is uncompromising and one of the strictest in the region. The government has placed Vietnamese and even foreigners seen at high risk of infection into isolation, sometimes at remote military camps. Still, an edge Vietnam has over the US is the consistent message it has sent to the public about combating the virus, said Dr Todd Pollack, an infectious disease specialist with the Harvard Medical School Partnership for Health Advancement in Vietnam. The government's communications campaign includes posters in residential and office complexes, text messages, an app to help Vietnamese trace cases near them, regular updates on the Ministry of Health's web site and even a pop song encouraging hand-washing and social distancing.

COVID-19 News, 2020

According to the Johns Hopkins University and Medicine Coronavirus Resource Center, as of 19 June 2022 Vietnam registered 10,736,408 COVID-19 infections and 43,083 deaths. This is in a country with a population of almost 100 million people. Capitalist South Africa has a population of about 60 million people, yet according to the Johns Hopkins University and Medicine Coronavirus Resource Center as of 19 June 2022 South Africa registered 101,589 COVID-19 deaths. Capitalist South Africa has half the population of communist Vietnam – yet the number of South Africans that died from COVID-19 was more than twice that of communist Vietnam!

Bernie Sanders, the one-time socialist candidate for the US presidency, was berated for stating that Scandinavian countries followed "democratic social-ism". The countries that he specifically referred to were Sweden, Norway and Denmark. Sweden, Norway and Denmark are not socialist or communist countries like China, Cuba or Venezuela, but neither are they capitalist countries like the US, France nor the UK. However, insofar as they have strong welfare states, then is it safe to say that they are more socialist than capitalist in orientation? According to Martin (n.d.):

> Yet I find that the strong state-society relations found in the Nordic countries have persisted, that the social partners have jointly struggled to articulate non-zero-sum solutions (for example job-sharing to cope with unemployment) and that these efforts have helped to preserve greater social solidarity. The Scandinavian model enjoys a high level of coordination that resists a full embrace of neoliberalism and that sustains high levels of social investments (especially in skills for low-skilled workers), relative equality, and redistribution against post-industrial threats.

That Scandinavian countries have a relatively socialist outlook is captured by Macionis and Plummer (2012: 468):

> Sweden and the other Scandinavian countries are generally seen as a version of a more socialist approach – interventionist, corporatist and planned. But they are in the process of being pulled towards the German model, which is more inclined towards a social market.

At the beginning of COVID-19 Sweden seemed to have experienced some success with the herd immunity model. As time went on the number of infected and dying people in Sweden were becoming worrisome. Its neighbours, Norway and Denmark, who went into lockdown much earlier had far fewer numbers of citizens that were infected and dead. Commentators and analysts put it down to cultural factors – it was believed that the Swedes are a more trusting society. It appears that individualism in the UK is a tad bit different than the individualism of Sweden. COVID-19 demonstrated to the world that, seemingly, there are variations of individualisms as there are variations of capitalisms, communisms and socialisms:

> Sweden offers an appealing model to many people who are fatigued by the hardships of pandemic lockdown or who were never convinced it was entirely necessary. The Nordic country took some measures to control the

spread of the coronavirus. It banned groups larger than 50 people, called
for social distancing and put older students on video learning. But it did
not take a draconian approach. Schools for those under 16 remained
open, as did many bars, restaurants and gyms, with social distancing. That
raises the question of whether the example is worth emulating. Sweden
has reported 364.28 deaths per million people, compared with 94.4 for
Denmark, 53.7 for Finland and 42.8 for Norway. However, Sweden's death
rate remained lower than those of Britain, France, Italy and Spain, which
all imposed strict lockdowns. The virus ravaged Sweden's nursing homes,
which accounted for a large portion of the deaths; the government was
slow to restrict visits to them. What Sweden has demonstrated is the
advantage of a high degree of trust in government. People did not have to
be ordered to stay at home, wash their hands and flatten the curve; they
accepted the recommendations of the government and followed them.
In a public health emergency, this reflects common sense and good judg-
ment, a contrast to the noisy demands in the United States to break free
from government orders. The verdict is still out on Sweden. The near-
term costs of its approach seem to be high in death and illness, and not
inconsequential in economic pain, while the longer-term payoff could be
more resilience. The best outcome for all is a vaccine as soon as possible.

The Washington Post, 19 May 2020: 24

Still in the more Scandinavian socialist than capitalist countries:

Sweden's state epidemiologist, who led the country's controversial
approach to tackling the coronavirus pandemic, has admitted more
restrictions on movement and gatherings would have helped avoid a high
death toll.

KATE, 2020

But it seemed that all were not impressed with Sweden's response to COVID-19:

Norway and Denmark are to drop border controls between the two countries but have for the time being excluded their Scandinavian neighbour
Sweden, which has taken a lighter-touch approach to the COVID-19 pandemic and suffered a far higher death toll.

HENLEY and HARDING, 2020: 32

When compared to other Scandinavian countries – there was also the percep-
tion that Sweden had experimented with its citizens' lives:

Sweden, which has been criticised for its soft lockdown measures, has reported more than 3,200 deaths from the disease – several times higher than the number of deaths in neighbouring Scandinavian countries. The Swedish authorities have denied that their strategy was based on the overall goal of herd immunity.

LI, 2020

According to the Johns Hopkins University and Medicine Coronavirus Resource Center, as of 19 June 2022 Sweden registered 2,512,853 COVID-19 infections and 19,075 deaths. Norway registered 1,439,408 COVID-19 infections and 3,250 deaths. Denmark registered 3,197,228 COVID-19 infections and 6,470 deaths.

3   The Green Shoots of Socialism and Communism in Capitalist America?

Feelings relating to communism and socialism are strong in the US. It is as strong as feelings toward religion, gun ownership, and securing individual rights in the time of a global pandemic. A reader in a letter to the print media in capitalist US relates his experience about meeting a group of college students he had encountered enjoying themselves at a lake whilst they also took time out to express their disapproval of Donald Trump – and why Joe Biden would be their preferred choice for president of the US. The visitor took it upon himself to suggest that the students learn about socialism and communism. He then went on to share his research on the much-hated system – supposedly by many in the West – by apparently consulting the Webster's dictionary college edition:

Socialism is a system of social organisation which advocates the vesting of the ownership and control of the means of production, capital, land, etc. in the country as a whole. In Marxist theory, the stage following capitalism in the transition of a society to communism is characterised by the imperfect implementation of collectivist principles. Communism is a theory or system of social organisation based on the holding of all property in common, actual ownership being described to the community as a whole or to the state. Communism is a system or social organisation in which all economic and social activity is controlled by a totalitarian state dominated by a single and self-perpetuating political party. Totalitarianism means one political group maintains complete control under a dictator, such as Hitler.

ANDERSON, 2020

So that the students could have had an all-round education, the learned teacher of history and communism could have included the fact that Hitler and Nazism were defeated by communist Russia. The good Samaritan of political education then suggested to the students – who were really concerned about the exorbitant costs of college education in capitalist US – that they should learn about socialism and its workings in Russia, China and North Korea. Here too – so as to ensure the dispensation of an all-round education – he could have directed the students to his little socialist neighbour, Cuba, to study life under the US-backed Batista, compared to life under socialism.

In the US the disdain for any socialist green shoots' ideas and plans came thick and fast in the time of COVID-19:

> The violence perpetuated in our major city streets will cause the 'silent majority' to rise up in November and reject left-wing socialist anarchy and liberal, big government's absurd programs and ideas. People want good policing, calm racial improvements, less government and a free capitalist economy. In my almost 70 years, I have seen the Democratic Party drift further and further left to where I don't recognise it, and most of America is appalled that it now resembles countries like Cuba, Venezuela and other Marxist failures.
>
> SKELL, 2020

The only uprising that was of monumental importance in the US in the time of COVID-19 was of that by the rightwing anarchist movement on Capitol Hill. Joe Biden was declared president – only time will tell whether the Democratic Party will veer to the left. And had the US invested in a socialist health care system like Cuba, so many American lives would not have been lost – in the same way that if America had not involved its soldiers in the Vietnam and Iraq wars, American lives would not have been lost as well.

Whilst many around the world are fast becoming disillusioned with capitalism, it seems that American young adults in particular are beginning to see socialism as the saving grace for the US. It appears that the green shoots of socialism and communism are sprouting amidst the heavy ideological boots of capitalism in the US:

> Those feelings [that the capitalist system is rigged] have only accelerated this spring, particularly among the young. At the end of February, during the last week of the pre-COVID era, Forbes surveyed 1,000 American adults under age 30 about capitalism and socialism. Half approved of the former; 43% regarded the latter positively. Ten weeks, 80,000 deaths

and 20 million unemployment claims later, we repeated the exercise, and those already dismal results had flipped: 47% now approve of socialism, 46% of capitalism. You can see those changing sentiments playing out in public, as ideas such as universal basic income, rent amnesties and job guarantees move rapidly from the fringe to the mainstream.

LANE, 2020

To think that the country that went all out to destroy communist USSR and destroyed millions of lives and livelihoods in communist countries such as Vietnam would breed socialist ideas on its very own soil! This must surely make the most ardent of capitalist ideologues sit up, take note and then obviously go all out to smash any green shoots of socialism in the US. It appears that the seeds of socialism have indeed been sown in the US of A – and it's only a matter of time before its green shoots begin to appear:

Although it's very likely a Biden presidency would move the country in a more extreme-left direction, the more socialistic policies America's youth have come to believe are essential 'rights' wouldn't be put into place as quickly as they would under a Sanders presidency, a political reality many young leftists believe to be completely unacceptable.

HASKENS, 2020: 8

Who would dare believe that with capitalism being declared The End of History, that there would still exist a communist party in the 21st century in United States of America – the bastion of capitalism:

This year's election is an easy call for Bob Avakian, founder and leader of the Revolutionary Communist Party USA. The need to stop President Trump is so overwhelming that he has no qualms about backing Democrat Joseph R. Biden. Mr. Avakian says this is not the year for protest votes. Although he still considers Mr. Biden and the Democratic Party 'representatives and instruments of this exploitative, oppressive, and literally murderous system of capitalism imperialism,' Mr. Trump and the Republicans are even worse.

DINAN, 2020

If socialism failed in the USSR in the latter part of the 20th century, then apparently elements of socialism are working fine in some parts of the US – seemingly for the last 100 years! At least this is the view, albeit debatable, of a writer to the print media in the time of COVID-19:

Texas has had a much larger socialist base than Oklahoma for the last 100 years. Texas has funded its higher education system with money from state-owned oil and gas royalties while Oklahoma, having a much smaller state-owned royalty base, has funded its higher education budget from taxes. This also allows Texas to operate without an income tax. When businesses look to relocate, their leadership looks for places their overpaid executives can save the big tax bucks. The reason Austin was chosen is simply that Texas' public goodies are derived from socialist programs and Oklahoma's are much less so. Austin has always been able to afford to be more hip and accepting of change than Tulsa because it is funded from the public ownership of production, aka socialism. Harvard University's endowment is the largest at $36 billion, and the University of Texas system comes in third at $26 billion. It is amazing what 100 years of excessive socialism can buy. My solution: merge with Texas. They want our water, and we want their socialist free ride. And we have too many states anyway.

WITT, 2020

It therefore is prudent for broader and mainstream society to have regular, small and big debates on the meanings, views, interpretations, experiences, etc. on socialism and communism. In this way, it is hoped that global society will be better informed on the meanings and workings of socialism and communism – as opposed to the propaganda pushed out by the elite and powerful of the world.

4   Toward a Global, Mature and Sober Dialogue on Socialism and Communism

There had been talk about slavery and feudalism, but not as much as there had been about socialism and communism in the time of COVID-19. I guess slavery and feudalism are not of concern to 21st century society as socialism and communism are. With so much talk about socialism and communism in the time of COVID-19 – not by historians but by powerful people in powerful positions and places – it must surely be a sign that socialism and communism do not fall into the same category as slavery and feudalism. These are not systems of the past, but appear to be systems of the present, and maybe even of the future too. The capitalist class trembles at this thought – hence the flurry of views on these political systems in the time of COVID-19.

Francis Fukuyama was the declared prophet of the capitalist class when he delivered his The End of History doctrine. His disciples worship him and his brand of neoliberal ideology. But faith in The End of History ideology is day by day being violently shaken. With world events turning out in the way that they are, it is beginning to seem that Fukuyama's The End of History doctrine is not political or economic science but a dominant ideology parading as the iron law of historical and societal development. The End of History debate is not over, it seems. On the contrary it is only just beginning. Is capitalism The End of History? Is communism The End of History? Only our descendants in the distant future will know for sure. Or we might get lucky – or unlucky if you prefer capitalism – and wake up one morning to a whole new world called socialism or communism. But Eastern Europe has been to communism and back. In the meantime, it is best we stay awake and observe the social facts for ourselves.

Like Marx and Fukuyama, we can choose to take sides – and continue our guessing games about socialism's and communism's place in history. It is a challenge to say what capitalism is or is not – especially after the Great Crisis of 2008. One way to grasp what socialism or communism is, is to first say what I think socialism or communism is not – at least within my ideological framework. Socialism or communism is not the exploitation of nature. It is not the exploitation of man by man nor the exploitation of women by men, nor the exploitation of women by women nor the exploitation of man by machine. It is not each man for himself and an apparent god for all. Socialism or communism is not tyranny, authoritarianism and the anti-democratic culture in the workplace. It is not a system that works the worker to the ground – and leaves him or her physically and mentally exhausted at the end of the day, at the end of the week, at the end of the month and at the end of his or her life. Socialism or communism is not acquiring money for money's sake. It is not leaving an invisible enemy – such as COVID-19 – to be defeated by individuals with little or no power in society. It is not accumulation for accumulation's sake. It is not dropping bombs on a people based on lies, deceit and made-up evidence.

Socialism or communism is not dropping bombs on a people under the good intentions of exporting democracy, freedom and human rights to their lands. It is not sending millions of people from the lower social classes to their deaths in wars under the ideological banner of patriotism – whilst embarking on empire building and natural resource theft. It is not ruthless competition based on the law of the jungle viz. that only the fittest survives – as in the herd immunity practiced in the West in the time of a global pandemic. It is not leaving the tens of thousands of migrants to drown in the seas – whilst having meetings in suits and ties in glass buildings. Socialism or communism is not reducing man's lifetime activity to that of work – whilst looking forward to enjoying his life just before expiring from this world. It is not shouting out god's name – whilst mowing down innocent children, women and men. It is not using religious texts to claim that the land of Israel belongs to only the Jews – in the same way that some in the Bharatiya Janata Party (BJP) may believe that India belongs only to the Hindus, or a few in South Africa may believe that South Africa belongs only to Africans.

Socialism or communism is not having the democratic right to vote once in 4 or 5 years – but not having the right to democracy in the workplace, in the army, in the home, over a country's energy systems, etc. Socialism is not propagating the ideology that the "invisible hand" will ensure that all people will one day benefit from the selfish interests of a few. Socialism or communism is not leaving the huge challenge of climate change to the apparent hand of the capitalist market. It is not using taxpayers' monies to bail out the big banks and the rich – and enforcing austerity measures and neoliberal capitalist market ideologies on working and unemployed citizens. In other words, socialism is not socialism for the rich and capitalism for the poor – as was the case during the 2008 Financial Crisis. Socialism or communism is not pushing guns into the hands of the American people under an outdated and fatalistic constitutional amendment. Socialism and communism are not social systems whereby a handful of humans own planet earth – whilst the rest work very hard just to get by. Socialism or communism is not defeating an evil system like apartheid, securing a black-majority state, making a sprinkling of blacks filthy rich – but still ruling over the most unequal country in the world. It is not forcing people off of their lands – so that a few rich people can continue to acquire more riches. Socialism or communism is not burning and clearing the Amazon rainforests – under the narrow banner of economic growth, development and progress.

Socialism or communism is not leaving your life to be safeguarded by an apparent higher power during a global pandemic – or during any other natural or man-made calamity for that matter – such as hunger or homelessness. Socialism or communism is not waiting for more of nature to be destroyed, more warming of the earth, more of worker exploitation, more wars and so-called collateral damage – whilst striving for some imagined apex of economic growth and development. Socialism or communism is not men having social, cultural, political or economic power over women or other men.

It is one thing idealising what isn't socialism or communism. It is quite another saying what these systems actually are or entails. For this one has to turn to the experts. For example, Eagleton (2018: 57) provides a definition and description of communism in relation to capitalism:

Capitalist society generates enormous wealth, but in a way that cannot help putting it beyond the reach of most of its citizens. Even so, that wealth can always be brought within reach. It can be disentangled from the acquisitive, individualist forms which bred it, invested in the community as a whole, and used to restrict disagreeable work to the minimum. It can thus release men and women from the chains of economic necessity into a life where they are free to realise their creative potential. This is Marx's vision of communism.

Schumpeter (1950: 446) defines socialism as:

That organization of society in which the means of production are controlled, and the decisions on how and what to produce and on who is to get what, are made by public authority instead of by privately-owned and privately-managed firms.

According to Roemer (1994: 454):

I believe socialists want (1) equality of opportunity for self-realization and welfare, (2) equality of opportunity for political influence, and (3) equality of social status. By self-realization, I mean the development and application of one's talents in a direction that gives meaning to one's life. This is a specifically Marxian conception of human flourishing.

The following definition of socialism is provided in Lange and Taylor (1964: 32):

A socialist economy would eliminate the privilege that arises from wealth, since it stands for an equal distribution of income. Democracy's aim is to govern in the interests of the whole community; therefore democracy stands, in principle, for the satisfaction of necessities before luxuries. A socialist economy stands for this same principle, for equality in the distribution of income means that needs will be satisfied in proportion ~ their urgency.

Marxists are worse than Margaret Thatcher and Ronald Reagan. Whereas Reaganites and Thatcherites want limited state involvement in the economy – Marxists pine for a society where there is no state:

> Although, there needs to be a state in socialism, the state will not exist in communism.
>
> CAM ET AL., 2015: 389

Marx believed that socialism will precede communism. In the similar manner that the end-goal of ending apartheid was to do away with race discrimination, the end goal of communism is to do away with class discrimination. In other words, class exploitation will cease to exist. This will obviously not take place overnight but will be a process. For Marx, human potential and creativity can only be fully and meaningfully realised in a classless society viz. communist society. Humans will cease to be merely instruments for capital accumulation.

In some ways Marxists are like romantics and idealistic dreamers – singing along to John Lennon's song – *Imagine*. But for many of us who fought the evil apartheid system – we always imagined and dreamt of a better future – then the future that was planned and made for us – by the colonial and apartheid thinkers and planners of the past.

CHAPTER 6

Capitalism

Free to Choose – Even When Others Die

> Freedom in capitalist society always remains about the same as it
> was in ancient Greek republics: Freedom for slave owners.
> VLADIMIR LENIN

•••

> Your liberty to swing your fist ends just where my nose begins.
> JUSTICE OLIVER WENDELL HOLMES JR.

•
• •

1   Toward an Understanding of Freedom under Capitalism

The trade of anything – wildlife like bats included – will make any neoliberal,
capitalist or capitalist marketeer excited to the core – since this is what individual freedom is all about – do as you please – because this has been the
reigning ideology of capitalism for decades. The revered economic scientist of
modern capitalism is Adam Smith, the author of *The Wealth of Nations*. He has
this to say:

> By pursuing his own interest he frequently promotes that of the society
> more effectually than when he really intends to promote it.
> SMITH, 1776: 594.

The *Wealth of Nations* was written in 1776, the same year that England's subjects in the US decided to wage war against the mother country – and cut off its
colonial umbilical cord. Such was the urge for freedom and liberty by the stealers of the land of the First Americans in the US, which England tried hard to
resist with all of its military might – not the stealing of indigenous land, but the
yearning for independence, liberty and freedom by its subjects. The Chinese
also paid a heavy price whilst a colony of England – as a result of England's

growing appetite for greed. Thanks to England's greed for more since the building of its Empire, many of us are now capitalists in one form or another. But when the workhouse's Oliver Twist wanted more – the poor lad was severely reprimanded! The "more" philosophy is meant for the capitalist class – not for the poor masses like Oliver Twist. Again thanks to capitalism, the more philosophy is still with us today – more wealth, more poverty, more inequality, more unemployment, more guns, more violence, more crime, more wars, more cars, more environmental destruction, more loneliness, more mental health disorders, more suicides, more profit, more people on the planet and growing evermore, and there is much more of such mores under the much loved capitalist system of more is good. We need more – not less capitalism, they say! Even communist China bought into the more philosophy and embraced more production, more consumerism and more growth.

That the Chinese state would intervene and close down a free enterprise in Wuhan – the free market where wildlife is a sought-after delicacy by customers who demand such – is a fundamental violation of capitalism and free market ideology; the state must not intervene in the free market – even if it is a wild market! Apparently, the free market in Wuhan city traded in the following prized delicacies:

> Freshly slaughtered reptiles along with wolf cubs, donkeys, badgers, hedgehogs, porcupines, camels and even koalas.
> NAISH, 2020

By closing down the free market in Wuhan, the Chinese state revealed the evils of communist ideology – interference in the supply and demand by free individuals who should be at liberty to freely choose what they should eat – bats and wildlife included. Surely the same Western rules and values should apply to the Chinese: "Give me liberty or give me death!" So China finds itself in a double-bind – damned if you do, damned if you don't. If it involves itself in the free market – it is the evil communist state that the Western world shouts down. If it does not close down its free markets selling wildlife – it is putting the world at risk! No wonder China is schizophrenic in shape and form – it does not know whether it is communist or capitalist!

All sets of views of understanding the world we live in have their chosen and anointed leaders, who assume the highest position in human affairs, aspirations, ideals, values, ideas and ideologies. The world – according to their followers – should be shaped and formed in accordance with the thoughts, ideas, teachings and deeds of such thought-giants and great men of history. Christianity has Jesus Christ, Islam has the Prophet Muhammad (PBUH),

Buddhism, Buddha, Hinduism, Krishna amongst many other deities, etc. These were all enlightened men representing the very best of humankind's potential and aspirations. Such is their standing amongst humankind – that they have become gods or god-like in the eyes, brains and cultural practices of man. In the age of gender parity, it should be noted that Hinduism has female gods as well.

Whilst on the topic of earthly matters, whereas Karl Marx is known as the father of communism, capitalism has Adam Smith as its father, Milton Friedman as the son – and the capitalist market as the holy spirit or the invisible hand. Again, in the era of gender parity, it should be noted that neoliberalism's thought and practicing world has favourite daughters as well – key among them being Ayn Rand and Margaret Thatcher. Freedom itself has become synonymous with capitalism. This was made famous by Milton Friedman in his best-selling books – *Capitalism and Freedom* (1962) and *Free to Choose* (1980). Hence, capitalist societies are said to be free societies. Such freedoms were even demanded in the time of a global pandemic – especially in the US – the Land of the Free. With Donald Trump as president – the rebel, the outsider, the anti-establishment president – the US was becoming ever more nationalist in shape and form with his America First policy. This is in keeping with the self-interest thesis of Adam Smith.

But before Trump's rise to the White House, countries in Europe were already turning inward in selected matters. Donald Trump happened to lend his loud voice to this phenomenon in the age of globalisation. After the bombings of the Middle East by the countries of the developed world, citizens of war-torn countries embarked on the quest for a better life – and started the long and treacherous migration to the developed world. The Great Crisis of 2008 had impoverished much of Southern Europe, and this saw the breaking up of the European Union social spectrum into left and right politics – with the latter achieving more prominence. Populism was on the rise. Keep the borders closed and keep the migrants out became the call and order of the day. It seemed that the world was on the path to deglobalisation. Brexit was proof that there was a huge struggle between Europeanism and nationalism, the EU being accused of subverting democracy on a few occasions: during The Great Crisis of 2008 when Greece was most affected – and during the long-drawn out struggles of Brexit when the majority of UK's citizens voted to leave the European Union (EU). In both situations Western democracy was on trial. But this is the same West that preaches on the virtues of democracy to countries like China, Venezuela, Cuba, etc. COVID-19 was to place further strain on this tussle – and test it to its limits. It seemed that Brexit was not about the people's protest against globalisation per se, but against its uneven costs and benefits.

The working and lower middle classes seemed to have been the big losers of globalisation in its highly capitalistic form. Cheap migrant labour – and the competition for jobs and survival in a capitalist economy – saw migrants being targeted for much of Europe's woes. As the capitalist economy was taking strain, migrants were also viewed to be a burden on the social and health systems of the developed world. Ruthless competition under capitalism wormed its way into the social, cultural and political fabric of Europeanism. Capitalism thrives on unrestrained and ruthless competition – when such competition leads to profiteering for the system. Some refer to it as a dog-eat-dog world!

There were inklings of the unevenness of globalisation during the early stages of COVID-19. In parts of the world like South Africa, it became known as the traveler's disease – meaning that those who could afford to travel contracted the virus and passed it on to people in other parts of the world. They were not entirely wrong. Some referred to it as a white man's disease – black skins were supposedly immune from COVID-19. They were entirely wrong! Many blacks died from COVID-19. Science is an undeveloped social force for good – especially in the developing world.

Before COVID-19, globalisation seemed an abstract concept for many but the well informed. Within a few weeks of having been detected in Wuhan, China, COVID-19 had found its way to all parts of the world. The inextricable interconnectedness of all countries was laid bare. This interconnectedness would later on be glaringly demonstrated – most times worryingly – when supply chains of the global world order were disrupted. China was the epicenter for commodities production required by the world – in their quest to stave off and keep COVID-19 at bay. In its initial stages, much of the world was of the belief that COVID-19 was a phenomenon only applicable to China. Much of the world were in for a rude shock! Many countries embarked on naming and shaming China. Countries in the West also took the opportunity to do business with China – and sold-off much of their PPEs to the communist or capitalist monster during the early stages of COVID-19, a business exchange that would come to haunt them in the months ahead – as their own frontline workers experienced the shortage of PPEs. "Never let a good crisis go to waste" – especially if one is going to profit from such a crisis!

All capitalist countries consider themselves free societies – the freedom of choice being one of the pillars of its democratic foundation. Coupled with the laissez faire ideology – that the individual is best placed in society to decide his or her fate in life – would result in the best interest of the entire society – was allowed to play itself out in the Western world in the main – during a global pandemic! This long-held neoliberal ideology would soon turn on its head. For the Western world, saving the capitalist economy was their first priority. Saving lives seemed non-essential or secondary to the capitalist way of life – and left to the relatively powerless individual in the main to resolve. Capitalist countries were in a double bind – let the people work and shop and kill-off some of the people and save capitalism – or save the people and kill capitalism. Thrown into the mix was the political hot potato of the Western framework of rights and freedoms. But COVID-19 was to put the meanings of the Western framework of freedom, democracy, liberty and individual choice under the world's spotlight. These are deeply cherished and entrenched ideas and values – that have always been emphasised to be intrinsic and unique to Western civilisation. The West believes that these are values to be exported to all parts of the world – even if it has to be done by boots, bullets, bombs and brainwashing. Strangely, saving precious lives does not seem to fall within the framework of human rights supposedly held up by the West!

In the time of COVID-19, the real workings of freedom, democracy, liberty and individual choice under the capitalist order would put on a grand show for the world to witness – and try to make sense of as well. The ideological fault lines on which Western civilisation sits – spewed out contradictions and conflicts of all sorts. Whilst the citizens of Wuhan were subjected to more unfreedoms under communism, the citizens of the free world were all practicing their god-given freedoms: the freedom to work, the freedom to be unemployed in their millions – 40 million in the US around May 2020, the freedom to be homeless, the freedom to be in debt, the freedom to shop, the freedom to own guns meant for the battle field – and sometimes the freedom to kill with easily acquired firearms and ammunition. Whilst COVID-19 was ripping through most of the developed world, leaders of the free world exulted their freedoms and shouted it to the world – but first ensuring that the big media houses were free to be present. Such is the sacredness of freedom, democracy, liberty, and choice in the capitalist world – that even viruses were to have freedom of movement to devastate and destroy – especially those that were considered to be of little or no exchange-value to capitalist society – like the elderly in care homes.

In capitalist society, the raison d'être of freedom is the freedom to maximise profit. And when there was a realisation that the freedom to profit was being threatened by the freedom of COVID-19 to move about freely in society – those charged with being the custodians of freedom in capitalist societies – practiced their freedom to mobilise the state's resources to place a lockdown on society's many freedoms. But even during the lockdown – there were some in the Western world who were hell-bent on being free to go against the freedom of the state's declaration of lockdowns. So, the fanatics of free choice went about their free ways: barbecuing and sunbathing on the beach, walking up the mountains, etc. Then there were those that were free to infect others in society – most probably leading to the deaths of some – who most probably would have wanted to be free from infection and death themselves. The fortunate-living in the meantime practiced their freedom by snitching on the truly free – by freely taking pics of them enjoying their hard-won freedoms:

> These are people who time their neighbours on a morning run, or monitor how many family members leave the house at any one time, and then report their findings to the authorities.
> VINE, 2020: 17

With the KGB in mind, the writer titled the article "lockdown stasi are coming for you". Those with the visual evidence then freely handed such pics over to the authorities – who on previous occasions pronounced to the people that they were free to be on lockdown in their free societies. The authorities then freely handed out warnings and fines to the free-willed amongst them. Science was invoked in the time of COVID-19 to test the freedom to snitch on freedom-loving citizens:

> Plenty of people are confined to homes next to neighbours who are anti-social or disobeying lockdown guidance. A recent poll by Ipsos Mori and King's College London found that almost one in 10 had reported someone for breaking the rules.
> ADDLEY, 2020

All of this was happening in the Western free world and not in Russia or North Korea or China! There were also freebees from the business sector to front-line workers; long after volunteers and sections of civil society freely gave of their time and effort to lend a helping hand to the health workers, soldiers who freely sacrificed themselves on the frontline of an invisible enemy that went about freely infecting the human race and killing them off in the millions. As the capitalist economy sank deeper into trouble, the workers were freely compelled to wear masks and instructed to "go back to work"! This authoritarian command was freely given by the commander in the White House and by capitalist ideologues through mainstream and social media. Forced labour is alive and well in the free West, it seems!

In the most powerful and most resourced country of the world – the USA – health workers were free of any Personal Protective Equipment (PPE). Some practiced their free democratic choice – and felt at liberty to wear garbage bags as part of their Personal Protective Equipment (PPE). I believe such garbage bags were made freely available – but this cannot be for certain as there is "no such thing as a free lunch" in the USA. Milton Friedman must have been turning in his grave – for all the freebees that were handed out under the capitalist epoch – garbage bags included for use as PPEs.

Those who were in charge of sections of society – like sailors – were free to write a letter and complain about being cocooned on a navy ship and sailors dying of COVID-19. His line manager practiced the freedom to fire him. All this in the land of freedom, democracy, liberty and opportunity – the United States of America – The Land of the Free! Some in the Western world executed the total freedom to leave out the deaths of the elderly in the COVID-19 fatality statistics. According to the British Broadcasting Corporation (BBC), the elders who had died from COVID-19 were airbrushed out of the death figures. There were those in powerful positions in the state – who freely gave instructions on the need to be free of certain freedoms and then went on their merry little ways quite freely – one enjoying the comfort of her holiday home – not once but twice during lockdown measures! Double down on your freedom as much as you can during a global pandemic!

In capitalist India millions of migrant workers were free to walk many hundreds of kilometers to their homes in villages – after the leader of the world's biggest democracy insisted on his freedom as head of state – to give the people of India less than 4 hours' notice of a lockdown. He then went on to encourage the people to practice their freedom of religion – by asking them to light candles to stave off COVID-19. The masses freely acceded to this freely given BJP ideology. In many parts of the world, religious fanatics practiced their freedom to pray together in the time of a global pandemic – and at the same time the freedom to infect each other at their religious gatherings. The ideology of freedom of religion during a pandemic created the perfect conditions for the coronavirus to jump from one unscientific believer to the next. Big governments were free to use trillions of dollars of taxpayers or socialised monies to bail out the private capitalist class – the class that already own most of planet earth and the means of production in all four corners of the globe. And going against their sacred free market decree – the business sector freely demanded colossal bailouts from the state.

So smitten were some with their freedom to choose during a global pandemic – that they went out when COVID-19 was still a clear and present danger – and freely held up placards that read: "Stop the Tyranny", "Don't Use Fear to Steal our Freedom", "Don't Tread on my Rights", "Pro Common Sense", "America – The Land of the Free", "Let my People Go", "Those who would give up essential Liberty to purchase a little temporary Safety, deserve neither Liberty nor Safety", "Fauci Lied, The Economy Died", "Work Matters" (BBC).

In the lands where freedom to choose, transparency and accountability are said to be sacred cows – leaders of the free world freely told half-truths to their citizens, freely omitted information that was sought and freely took the liberty to deceive the populace with information such as COVID-19 was "merely a cold". Without freely providing any scientific evidence, some member countries of the free world clubbed together and pronounced that COVID-19 was the deliberate creation by China. In the UK – about 100 health workers died but the government freely lied through its teeth and said it was 20 (UK Nursing website). The *Daily Mail* had the following headline:

> 4,000 feared dead in our care homes – shocking virus death toll hugely under-reported warns experts (Wednesday 15 April 2020).

And when the leaders of the free world instructed people in a freely authoritarian and dictatorial manner to "go back to work!" – sycophants and cheerleaders of capitalist freedom gladly and freely cheered them on. So enamored were the free men and women in the Land of the Free – that they latched onto their freedom to drive on freeways and then marched to freely order businesses to open up, and for the workers to free themselves of the lockdown and make themselves free to once again be exploited in the free labour market. Again, the free protesters held up posters and banners claiming that "All Work is Essential"! Many free protesters also freely brandished huge guns and ammunition. Had they not held up American flags – one could have easily been fooled into believing that these were terrorists in the Middle East, hell-bent on protecting themselves from freedom, democracy, liberty and Western civilisation!

Then there were those who were free to spread fake news – and there were those who invoked their freedom to choose to remove perceived fake news from social media. Such freedom-loving persons were the owners and managers of the giant social media corporations of the world. Conspiracy theories were also freely distributed – to all and sundry – to even those who did not feel free to receive them. In a free society, we must all have the freedom to be confused as to what freedom really means! And whilst the Western world – in the main – fiddled with their many freedoms – Rome burned. Western civilisation, with its capitalist, neoliberal ideological brand of freedom and democracy, was freely on trial!

2   An Overview of Capitalist Countries' Response to COVID-19

New Zealand, with a population of about 5 million, is an island country in the southwest of the Pacific Ocean. Having been colonised by the British in 1841 – it gained its independence in 1947 (Wikipedia, 2021). Yet, New Zealand is still 'ruled' by a king. It seems that colonial influences do not make their exit with independence. New Zealand was one of the few Western countries to take COVID-19 seriously:

> The coronavirus outbreak started in December 2019 in Wuhan City, China, where cases of mysterious illness including pneumonia of unknown origin were noted. On 3 January 2020, New Zealand's government placed entry restrictions on those transiting through or travelling from mainland China requiring a 14-day period of self-isolation upon return to the country. On 28 February 2020, New Zealand reported its first case of COVID-19 in an adult male travelling from Iran. Beginning at 11:59 pm on 25 March, the alert level was moved to level 4, putting the country into one of the world's most stringent nationwide lockdowns until 11:59 on 27 April 2020
>
> BANDYOPADHYAY ET AL., 2020: 219

The leader of New Zealand, Prime Minister Jacinda Ardern, felt that it made sense to have a 72-hour lockdown rather than 72 hours of a community outbreak (Prebble, 2021). With its common-sense approach to a global pandemic, New Zealand was able to have effective control over COVID-19. After about a year, the rest of the world watched with envy as:

> New Zealanders went back to work and began attending concerts and sporting events, without the need to wear masks.
>
> HARTE, 2021

New Zealand had "become the poster child for fans of tough lockdown" (Creighton, 2020). According to the Johns Hopkins University and Medicine Coronavirus Resource Center as of 20 June 2022 New Zealand registered 1,283,295 COVID-19 infections and 1,338 deaths. Whereas major capitalist countries chose the economy over lives, New Zealand – like China – was able to save both lives and the economy:

> If anyone still needed proof New Zealand's pandemic response had been the right one for the economy, yesterday's S&P Global Ratings upgrade should suffice.
>
> DANN, 2021

Australia lies about 2000 km west of New Zealand. It has a population of about 26 million people. Indigenous people inhabited the continent for about 65,000 years. With British colonialism, the indigenous population was diminished through diseases and conflicts (Wikipedia, 2020).

Australia's COVID-19 situation gained world attention with the entry of the Ruby Princess into the country:

> The ship [The Ruby Princess] left Port Kembla just before 5pm on Thursday, after a month in Sydney in which it has been linked to more than 600 cases of coronavirus and 21 deaths among passengers who took its final cruise to New Zealand in March. That cruise, and the decision to allow 2,700 passengers to disembark in Sydney on 19 March, is now the subject of a criminal investigation and a special commission of inquiry.
>
> ZHOU, 2020

In the time of COVID-19 "Lifeboat Australia" was used as the metaphor to steer the country out of COVID-19. For some:

> Setting aside the economic questions, it seems as though the real question for Lifeboat Australia may not be what direction it heads in, but how long we're willing to float before we start to kick people out and leave them at sea. What brings the moral and ethical nature of the choices before our leaders isn't the question of where we go, but the brutal, indigestible fact that not everyone is getting out of this alive.
>
> BEARD, 2020

The Lifeboat Australia metaphor brought back memories of the Mignonette yacht that was shipwrecked off the coast of Australia in July 1884:

> Indeed, Lifeboat Australia isn't the first ship to have to consider these questions. In 1884 there was another yacht – the Mignonette – making its way to our shores. It shipwrecked with a crew of four. More than a week passed and rations ran out. It was becoming clear that not all of the crew were going to make it out alive. They discussed drawing lots to see who would be sacrificed so the others might live.
>
> BEARD, 2020

Whilst on the lifeboat, Richard Parker, the cabin boy, was killed and eaten by the other 3 men. Like the decisions taken on the wrecked yacht in 1884, Beard (2020) interrogates the decisions made by those in power in Australia in the time of COVID-19. It seems that on "Lifeboat Australia" all lives are not of equal value – even though they add tremendous value to Australian society:

> Those who are in Australia temporarily – to study, to work, to pick fruit, to be protected from persecution – have had their second-class status brutally exposed by the extremis of COVID-19. As the government has rolled out massive and unprecedented rescue packages for jobs and businesses – $214bn and counting – for those in Australia on temporary visas there is no safety net at all. Many work in jobs and industries severely affected by shutdowns. They have lost jobs in their tens of thousands. But they are excluded from all government support measures, including the center piece job keeper wage subsidy and jobseeker welfare payments.
>
> DOHERTY, 2020

When sections of Australian society chose life over risk of infections and deaths, the prime minister chose coercion and public pressure instead. Forced or coerced labour is alive and well in Western Australia, as it is in China and the rest of the capitalist world.

> The Prime Minister took a swipe at teachers' unions, saying workers – from bus drivers to supermarket staff – were showing up each day at work despite the risk of contracting COVID-19.
>
> JOHNSTONE ET AL., 2020

Australia had outdone many countries in the developed world in the war against COVID-19 – even though these countries have: "sophisticated, developed economies with good health systems" (Kelly, 2020). According to the former prime minister of Australia, Mr. Tony Abbott, Australia was one of the first countries to impose travel bans from China in early February. On 13 March the number of known COVID-19 cases were 198 with three deaths. Social, economic and cultural life were strictly curtailed so as to manage the pandemic. This included stringent quarantine rules especially for travelers to Australia (Abbott, 2020). Other factors that helped Australia in its response to and management of COVID-19 are its remoteness from other land masses, its low-density settlement and warm seasons (The Weekend Australian, 2020). According to the Johns Hopkins University and Medicine Coronavirus Resource Center, as of 20 June 2022 Australia registered 7,825,659 COVID-19 infections and 9,387 deaths.

Japan is in Asia on the northwest of the Pacific Ocean. It has a population of about 126 million. After its adventurism in war and tragically having two atom bombs dropped on its cities and people, Japan renounced its right to declare war (Wikipedia, 2020). Its war on COVID-19 was weak – especially being a highly developed country. For the Japanese it seemed life went on as normal. However, as infection rates started to increase, the Japanese state decided to impose some restrictions. Japan only declared a state of emergency on the 6 April 2020 – about three months after the world came to know about COVID-19! It seemed Japanese patience was one of a long slumber. Before that the Japanese government had been quite lax with those on board the cruise-ship the Princess Diamond that had landed in Japan. According to the director of Japan's Hygiene Research Institute:

> The first outbreak that originated from the cruise-ship Diamond Princess was contained around February. But Japan failed to stop imported cases from Europe and the US starting March, which caused the second wave.
>
> CAIYU ET AL., 2020

The following newspaper article reflects the sorry response of a G7 country to COVID-19:

> Hospitals in Japan are increasingly turning away sick people, as the country struggles with surging coronavirus infections and its emergency medical system collapses. In one recent case, an ambulance carrying a man with a fever and difficulty breathing was rejected by 80 hospitals and forced to search for hours for a hospital in downtown Tokyo that would treat him. Another feverish man finally reached a hospital after paramedics unsuccessfully contacted 40 clinics. Apart from a general unwillingness to embrace physical distancing, experts fault government incompetence and a widespread shortage of the protective gear and equipment medical workers need to do their jobs.
>
> AP, 2020

When common sense and science dictated that socio-cultural activities like sporting events are super spreaders of COVID-9, the Japanese elite and the Olympics Organising Committee insisted on going ahead with the Olympics in the midst of a global pandemic – against popular opinion. This was G7 ideology at its worst. According to the Johns Hopkins University and Medicine Coronavirus Resource Center, as of 20 June 2022 Japan registered 9,137,595 Japan COVID-19 infections and 31,029 deaths.

Capitalist South Korea, with a population of about 52 million, is the neighbour to communist North Korea (Wikipedia, 2020). Even though South Korea is in the east, it is considered ideologically Western with South Korean characteristics. South Korea is the first and only country to have conducted its full-scale elections during the pandemic. It was hailed as both a defeat against COVID-19 and the shining light of Western democracy. Much of the world also looked to South Korea as a model with which to deal with COVID-19. According to Dudden and Marks (2020: 1):

> The country acted fast when the virus began to spread. Strict quarantine measures and testing have helped to curb it. Most importantly, South Korea immediately began testing hundreds of thousands of asymptomatic people, including at drive-through centers. The country employed a central tracking app, Corona 100m, that publicly informs citizens of known cases within 100 metres of where they are. Surprisingly, a culture that has often rebelliously rejected authoritarianism has embraced intrusive measures. From 16 March, South Korea started to screen all people arriving at airports, Koreans included. South Koreans have universal health care, double the number of hospital beds compared to Organisation for Economic Cooperation and Development (OECD) norms (and triple that of the UK), and are accustomed to paying half what Americans pay for similar medical procedures.

South Korean pragmatism prevailed in the time of COVID-19. If ideology gave way to pragmatism and common sense in the West, then surely many lives would have been saved. Mainstream media highlighted South Korea as a shining example to the world of its handling of COVID-19. South Korea experienced renewed outbreaks of COVID-19. Lockdown measures were once again implemented. These included shutting down schools. The areas that were hardest hit with renewed outbreaks were Seoul, Bucheon and Gumi (Henley and Harding, 2020: 32). But just like China and Vietnam, South Korea's model included a massive surveillance system as well:

> South Korea is combing through mobile phone data and credit card records in an all-out effort to reach people potentially exposed to the coronavirus in a new cluster outbreak linked to clubs in Seoul's nightlife district Itaewon, as the number of infections rose to 102. The total number of cases stands at 10,936, with 258 deaths.
>
> CHOON, 2020

According to the Johns Hopkins University and Medicine Coronavirus Resource Center, as of 20 June 2022 South Korea registered 18,280,090 COVID-19 infections and 24,451 deaths.

South Africa is on the African continent but it is more Western than African. It has a population of about 59 million (Wikipedia, 2020). South Africa, termed "the miracle nation" – never mind that it is the most unequal country in the world and with an unemployment rate of more than 30% – went quite early into lockdown – when one person was identified as having contracted COVID-19 on his arrival from Italy.

As of 6 June 2020, South Africa recorded about 40,792 cases of COVID-19 and 848 deaths. One was of a prominent professor who was at the forefront of the fight against another virus – that of HIV-AIDS. Since then, many professors and doctors had lost their lives to COVID-19. Whilst the majority of South Africans obeyed the lockdown laws, a minority of citizens had to be slapped with harsher punishments so as not to endanger the lives of others – in the event that some of them could have been infected.

For many workers in South Africa, the cities are places of work whilst their homes are in villages in far-away rural areas, as well as in other provinces and neighbouring countries. Not anticipated by the state – hordes of people started to migrate out of the cities and suburbs just before the lockdown went into action. The South African state was not as qualified to deal with a public health crisis, in the way that the Vietnamese state, for example, was.

For most of its history, the majority of South Africa's people have been under some form of lockdown of one sort or another – but under an authoritarian and draconian state: the apartheid regime. With COVID-19 demonstrating very little room to manoeuvre South Africa's complex challenges, ideologues, and lobbyists of capitalism sanctioned the lockdown. South Africa's constitution – said to be one of the best in the world – was also tested. Apparently a COVID-19 patient refused to be quarantined, citing freedom of movement as a constitutional right. In the early part of the lockdown 53 people were jailed for attending a wedding during the lockdown period. There was one recorded death at the hands of soldiers. When weighed against South Africa's relatively new constitution – the soldiers acted with impunity, unconstitutionally and inhumanely. When weighed up against the history of police and military brutality in South Africa – it seemed quite insignificant. Considering South Africa's violent history and make-up, it is indeed pleasing to know that more people were not killed by the South African Defense Force. As recent as 2012, the world witnessed the brutal killing of 36 miners in South Africa by a trigger-happy police force. The miners were fighting for higher wages in a highly unequal and brutal capitalist country.

Police brutality in South Africa is merely the face of the brutality of capitalism. South Africa is a violent country – it has been that way since the days of colonialism and apartheid. It's why books with titles such as *Cry, The Beloved Country* have been written about this beautiful but troubled land. The violence continues under a democratic state in capitalist South Africa. Forced labour is prevalent in South Africa – as it is in the rest of the world. Contrary to capitalist ideology, there is no freedom to choose whether to go to work or not. When a single person chooses not to go to work, then the ideology of choice is granted. But when many choose not to go to work but are forced to, then we see through the ideology of free choice under capitalism. Mining is the backbone of South Africa's economy. In the time of COVID-19 an Impala Platinum Mine senior executive was apparently arrested for forcing people to go back to work in the time of a global pandemic.

Just before South Africa went into lockdown, there were 42,700 alcohol-related trauma admissions to hospitals. It dropped to 15,000 during the lockdown. With the unbanning of alcohol during level 3 lockdown, South Africa's: "booze binge set SA back in its fight against COVID-19" (Hosken and Nair, 2020: 5). Left toothless by the pressures of human rights organisations and big businesses in SA, all that the president could say was: "we are calling on all South Africans to behave in a manner that will take into account the rights of other people to health care". Without mentioning the words "herd immunity", after a considerable length in lock-down, it seems that the South African state followed their former colonial master – the UK – and went into "herd mentality" mode. We were reminded that infection and death numbers would rise in winter. We were also reminded that "this is hardly what was planned for" (Jonas, 2020:19).

There were free choices as well in South Africa in the time of COVID-19. The rich could choose to stay at home and enjoy the luxuries of a skewed and unjust economic system. The poor also had a choice to stay at home – but probably starve to death. Such is the character of freedom of choice in capitalist South Africa! One week into the lockdown, the minister of communications broke the lockdown law and chose to visit friends. In the age of social media, pics of the gathering were passed on – as a symbol of social status. The minister was apparently summoned by the darling president of a harsh capitalist society – Mr. Cyril Ramaphosa – to explain her freedom to choose in the time of the nationwide lockdown.

In June of 2021, the country experienced its third wave! With subsequent ineffectiveness by a state leaning towards capitalist interests, surviving COVID-19 was like weaving between speeding cars on a busy street – and hoping to come out the other side unscathed and alive. By 7 July 2021, South Africa was on the red list of many countries regarding international travel. According to the Johns Hopkins University and Medicine Coronavirus Resource Center by 20 June 2022 South Africa registered 3,986,601 COVID-19 infections and 101,604 deaths – the highest on the African continent even though it is the most developed country on the continent.

On 25 January 2020 France declared its first case of COVID-19. Around this time global cases rose past 900 with cases detected in Japan, South Korea, Singapore, Thailand, the US, Vietnam and Nepal; (Spencer et al., 2020). President Emmanuel Macron of France was one of the first Western leaders to invoke the language of war in the fight against COVID-19. This was to prepare the citizens of France to forgo some of their individual liberties and freedoms in order to do battle with COVID-19. This was not new to France in recent years – since France had imposed restrictions on its citizens because the country was subjected to a series of terrorist attacks.

Drone technology was used to monitor people and their movements. Big brother was there to both protect people as well as to impose punitive measures on those disobeying rules and regulations to contain COVID-19. By 2 April 2020 French police and authorities had handed out 359 000 fines for those violating lockdown rules. According to the Johns Hopkins University and Medicine Coronavirus Resource Center by 20 June 2022 France registered 30,279,240 COVID-19 infections and 150,078 deaths.

Italy was the first European country to have been terribly impacted by COVID-19. Daily reporting of the tragic situation in Italy had to melt even the coldest of hearts. As experts throughout the world tried to analyse and understand the increasing infection and death rate in Italy, some put it down to "it won't happen to me" mindset – as people continued to disobey the lockdown. Around mid-March 2020, about 70 000 Italians were fined for breaking the lockdown laws. With the increasing number of infections, deaths and fines, the enforcement of the lockdown laws also got more severe. In the case of Italy, it seemed to boil down to freedom to live – or freedom to die – as well as the freedom to enable the deaths of people within the societal tribe.

By end May 2020, Italy employed 60 000 volunteers to police social distancing rules. Italy probably took a page out of China's public health policy book when it came to taking care of its citizens – when tragic developments forced the state to do so. According to the Johns Hopkins University and Medicine Coronavirus Resource Center, by 20 June 2022 Italy registered 17,879,160 COVID-19 infections and 167,721 deaths.

In Spain doctors were apparently told to prioritise younger patients to that of 80-year-olds. The country also allowed a women's day gathering to go ahead on 8 March 2020 when warnings were already in place of the high risks of going ahead with such super-spreader events. Like so many rights, it seemed that woman's rights trumped the right to life during a global pandemic. By 16 March 2020, Spain became the second major European country to enter lockdown (Capurro, 2020). There was also talk of health care workers fleeing elderly care homes. According to the Johns Hopkins University and Medicine Coronavirus Resource Center, by 20 June 2022 Spain registered 12,563,399 COVID-19 infections and 107,482 deaths.

The UK, or Great Britain, is the once proud empire and exporter of colonialism and capitalism to all corners of the globe. With a current population of about 67 million people (Wikipedia, 2022) the UK could have had more people – had it not exported so many of its citizens to strange and forbidden lands during its heydays of Empire. In the time of COVID-19 it lost more of its citizens due to its Malthusian policy on COVID-19. It seems Great Britain has a history of messing around with its population numbers. When COVID-19 was decimating communities in other parts of the world, the UK appeared to have been humming "eeny, meeny, miny moe, let's play herd immunity with a deadly foe, if it attacks that's too bad, COVID-19 is a passing fad".

Whilst British stubbornness dug in its inaction heels:

> England's Chief Medical Officer, Professor Chris Whitty, has said there is a 'fair chance' coronavirus will reach the UK. He warned: 'what we don't know is how far it's going to spread – we need to plan for all eventualities'.
> GROVES ET AL., 2020

Unlike precision bombings in the Middle East, there was not much evidence of precision planning to do battle with COVID-19 – in about the most looked-up-to country in the world! In one of the most scientific lands of the world – and the country that gave the world The Enlightenment:

> Epidemiologists are still unclear about when the virus arrived in the UK, although modelling from Oxford University has suggested it could have arrived in mid-January and have been spreading undetected since then.
> NUKI and NEWEY, 2020

When containment at the geographical source of the pandemic was the best preventative measure against COVID-19, the Foreign and Commonwealth Office (FCO) instead:

> Advised any Britons to leave if possible, seemingly contradicting travel restrictions in China.
> LEDWITH, 2020

The man at the helm in the time of COVID-19 was Boris Johnson – a prime minister par excellence. Which other prime minister or president can be a jester and serious at the same time! He even got Brexit done – against the wishes and pushback from the Western world and the anti-democratic movements in the UK and the EU. Such is the skills-set of the man who must be the envy of all men and women longing to exude the same level of confidence with such a hairdo to match. He once called Muslim women wearing burkas – "letter boxes"! He was forced to later apologise. He even said that "anti-vaxxers are nuts"! He had a point.

You have to hand it to Bojo for his unique leadership qualities, and ability to weave in and out of London traffic on his bicycle – no African leader would be caught pedaling on his 2-wheeler in any of the African cities. African leaders need a convoy of BMWs, Range Rovers and blue light brigades to make themselves feel important and elevated above the toiling and impoverished masses. African leaders are good at preaching on the evils of colonialism – but also very good at accumulating wealth and power for themselves, their families and politically connected – whilst leaving masses of their citizens in poverty and destitution. In any event, such is the aura of Bojo that he even boasted visiting a hospital and shaking hands with COVID-19 patients. The man was clearly nuts! He was lucky to escape the death-trap of COVID-19. Millions of others around the world and hundreds of thousands in his United Kingdom were not.

Apart from the many lessons that COVID-19 has taught us, we also learnt new and strange concepts like "herd immunity":

> The concept of herd immunity, where the virus spreads in the population, eventually building up resistance in the population, was initially key to the British government's decision-making when battling COVID-19, reported British newspaper, *The Guardian*.
>
> LI, 2020

The question remains: did Bojo use himself as a guinea pig in order to justify Britain's "herd immunity" ideology? It seems that the UK wanted to prove the superiority of the British way of life. Communist China could not be seen to be superior in the eyes of the world – in the highly successful manner with which it went to battle with COVID-19:

> At the beginning, Boris Johnson stood behind 'the science' to justify a UK-only policy of 'delay' of the COVID-19 virus. This involved minimal intervention in what Johnson took to reminding us are the 'freedom-loving'

proclivities of the 'British people'. Too late, what looked like a cunning plan to exemplify the virtues of the British way collapsed utterly.

EDGERTON, 2020

It seemed the British state needed the Queen of England to ask: why didn't anyone see this coming:

> Several government advisers have said the lockdown, in late March, came too late. Prof John Edmunds, who is on the Scientific Advisory Group for Emergencies (Sage), said in June that the decision cost a lot of lives.
>
> WALKER, 2020

It was clear that decisions made at the level of the UK state determined whether citizens lived or died. It reminds one of the time that Great Britain was a great Empire – and the masses of colonised people that perished during British colonialism. The capitalist economy was never going to be allowed to perish by the state – but UK citizens were. And in the UK people died in large numbers:

> The government reports that over 26,000 people have died of coronavirus so far; the real number is estimated to be over 45,000. Despite our small population, the UK has the fifth-highest number of deaths in the world: of every 10 lives the virus claims around the world, one is British.
>
> OSAMA, 2020

Great Britain has a historical tendency to sacrifice its citizens to epoch-making phenomena – it seemed COVID-19 would be no different. Having been conceptualised and initiated in the UK, the herd immunity model has a singular unwritten and unspoken underlying code: allow the virus to circulate amongst the human race and let the strong live and the weak die. This Darwinian law of the jungle was applied to civilised society by the elite in British society:

> Outside Europe, criticism has been strongest in Australia and New Zealand, both of which imposed strict, early lockdowns and have contained their outbreaks. Scott Morrison, the Australian prime minister, said no country that had pursued herd immunity had achieved it, describing the strategy as a 'death sentence'.
>
> HENLEY ET AL., 2020

The weak did die in extraordinary numbers in the UK – especially the elderly in care homes. They had no or very limited power as individuals, to fight off an invisible but known enemy. The resourceful state and wealthy private sector did not go fully armed to the people's aid. Pragmatism in dealing with a deadly pandemic was missing in abundance in civilised UK. Instead, ideology reigned supreme. After many unwarranted deaths mainly of the weak, the UK state meekly changed course when the "herd immunity" model was proving to be a catastrophic failure – and an embarrassment to the state. This is the country that gave the world capitalism, the socio-economic infrastructure of progress, apparent civilisation and the good life! One would have expected that after centuries of selling capitalism to all and sundry, the goodness of the capitalist way of life would have done wonders for the citizens of the motherland. The world would be in for a rude shock!

COVID-19 swept aside years of built-up capitalist ideologies in the UK and exposed the real workings of the motherland of capitalism. Like priorities during the time of the Industrial Revolution, capitalism in the time of COVID-19 was about the profit economy – not about saving lives! The COVID-19 situation demanded pragmatism – but neoliberal and Western ideologies masquerading as Western values were blockades to the value and preciousness of life. The UK state was gradually exposed to be an ineffective and inefficient institution in British society when it came to the life and death matters of the British people. The state was more inclined to oversee the deaths of the British people:

> Prof Neil Ferguson of Imperial College London, one of the architects of that lockdown, said that had the Government acted a week earlier the national death toll may have been halved. Such are the stakes when dealing with a disease that spreads exponentially.
>
> CAPURRO, 2020

Citizens attempted to fill in the gaps for the inefficient and ideological UK state in the time of a global pandemic:

> A woman who shared a final photo of her dying mother in hospital has said she did so to warn the public about the dangerous realities of COVID-19.
>
> QUINN and PARVEEN, 2020

Emotional pleas were continuously made in order to uphold the notion of a free and thinking people in the Western world – after health workers lost their lives – with a message of "stay at home for them". Clapping on a weekly basis was meant to keep the spirits of the health workers on the frontline high. An adequate supply of PPEs in one of the world's wealthiest countries would have been a more noteworthy life-saving contribution.

The country that guarantees a constant supply of guns and ammunition to the authoritarian state of Saudi Arabia and to the apartheid state of Israel was not able to secure basic life-saving apparel for its health workers. Instead, the state sought to rubbish any talk of shortages of PPEs. However, evidence confronted conservative state ideology in the UK:

> The BBC has stood by its defence of a Panorama investigation exposing shortages of personal protective equipment (PPE) among healthcare workers, after a formal complaint from the culture secretary.
>
> QUINN, 2020

The UK state's response to COVID-19 was steeped in the Western ideology that the individual – and not the state – is best placed to make responsible decisions regarding citizens' well-being and health. The idea that the herd knows best gave way to the individual knows best – and finally gave way to the state knows best. With time, UK society went from a request society to an advised society, to a guided society – and finally to an ordered society. The response to COVID-19 was continuously metamorphosing: the UK did not know whether to be the United Kingdom – or to be China! Instructions changed from "Stay Home" to "Stay Alert"! As Western states and China-haters accused China of not being transparent and truthful with COVID-19 fatality statistics, back in the UK:

> About 5,300 care home residents have died from coronavirus – but the true toll could be even higher as doctors are told they do not have to declare COVID-19 on death certificates, it has been claimed.
>
> DILWORTH, 2020: 10

Out of apparent genuine respect for doctor's independence of judgement and their rare skill and expertise, they were informed that:

> COVID-19 may be mentioned in another area of the form relating to indirect causes of death 'should the doctor wish'.
>
> DILWORTH, 2020: 10

For the many already dying from a slow, painful, and very lonely death with loved ones not being able to be present, to have them not recorded as having succumbed to COVID-19 is indeed "the final insult really" (Dilworth, 2020). As the virus was allowed unrestricted freedom to infiltrate and saturate British society, the important subject of freedom came under the spotlight:

> Then there's the tech mogul who has been breaking lockdown from the start, using his gardener's car to escape to London where, his friends believe, he either visits his mistress or his plastic surgeon.
>
> TAYLOR, 2020

"Do as I say and not as I do" seemed to have been the messaging sent out to the commoners in the UK. "Only go out when necessary" was the constant message to the UK people. However, chief medical officer for Scotland Catherine Calderwood believed that going to her holiday home – twice – was a necessary outing. She was paid a visit by the no freedom of movement police in the time of COVID-19 and given a formal warning:

> If only Catherine Calderwood had followed her own advice. Instead, in an act of mind-blowing hypocrisy, Dr Calderwood chose to – two weekends in a row – travel to her second home in direct contravention of the public health rules she had carefully and repeatedly set out.
>
> STEWART, 2020

Dr Calderwood has since apologised to the public and the frontline workers for her bad behaviour – on two separate occasions!

There were many in British society who in one way or another expressed their dissatisfaction with the notions about freedoms without responsibilities and consequences:

> Police are being bombarded with calls from the public snitching on their neighbours and others flouting lockdown. Forces have received almost 200,000 reports of gatherings and anti-social behavior. Across the UK, forces have been inundated with 194,314 calls or emails about so-called 'covidiots' gathering in groups of more than two for parties or picnics.
>
> CAMBER, 2020

Labels such as "police state" were branded about. Caught between the holiness of individual freedoms and ring-fencing the populace from an invisible but known enemy, the police were accused of being "heavy-handed". They were instructed by their bosses to "engage and not enforce". In the meantime, COVID-19 was enforcing its devastation on the masses of British society. Not expressing grave concern about the free movement of COVID-19, human rights organisations pronounced on matters of civil liberty through ideological lenses and not pragmatism and common sense in the time of a global pandemic:

> Civil liberties campaigners are concerned that people may be 'coerced' into sharing data about their movements through a coronavirus contact-tracing app being developed by the government. The health secretary, Matt Hancock, says the app, which will be available within weeks, is 'crucial for holding down the rate and the level of transmission of COVID-19'.
>
> WEAVER, 2020

As the pandemic took hold in and of British society, the contradictions of freedom of choice in capitalist society grew sharper:

> Two weeks ago I was handed a letter, along with other residents in my care home in Wiltshire, and asked to sign it. It stated that if I fell ill, I agreed that I did not want to be taken to hospital.
>
> DIACON, 2020

Incisive observers pointed to the hypocritical UK in relation to transparency and truth-telling. The writer clearly felt let-down by the UK state and its shenanigans:

> China's in the spotlight again, having added nearly 1,300 people to its COVID-19 death toll while at the same time denying any suggestion of a cover-up. But it's a bit rich strafing China when our own official coronavirus stats are about as reliable as the 100m times put up by Ben Johnson when the Canadian sprinter was fuelled by pharmaceuticals. What should make us very, very angry in this country is that the UK, in theory, accounts for roughly 10 per cent of those deaths despite having less than 1 per cent of the world's population and the experience of other countries, where things got nastier earlier, to inform its approach. But even that 10 per cent figure is open to debate. It might very well be higher because the commonly quoted stat in Britain, the one I'm using to make the calculation, refers only to deaths in hospitals. It doesn't include deaths in care homes or of people who succumb in their own homes before they get as far as calling 111.
>
> MOORE, 2020

As if children live on their own in society without sick and elderly family members – the man who was happy to see-off British soldiers to an illegal war, his organisation was now more than happy it seems, to see-off children to face an invisible but still present enemy:

> A comprehensive international study by Tony Blair's Institute for Global Change argues that full lockdowns are unsustainable. It says that once new virus cases are falling in Britain, schools should reopen first. 'Children are at very low risk, and economic and education costs of school closure are high,' the report says.
>
> JOHNSTONE ET AL., 2020

Being Boris means being optimistic – even if you have to lie through your dishevelled blonde hair:

> Boris Johnson claims 'there will be many people looking now at our apparent success'. Of all the lies foisted on the British public, all the empty slogans, all the promises on the side of buses, this could yet prove the greatest.
>
> OSAMA, 2020

From Italy to Australia, critics have accused a complacent British state of "massively underestimating" the gravity of the coronavirus crisis after the UK reported the highest death toll in Europe (Henley, et al., 2020). According to the Johns Hopkins University and Medicine Coronavirus Resource Center, by 21 June 2022 the UK registered 22,664,435 COVID-19 infections and 180,204 deaths. These are the deaths of people that belonged to 180,204 families. These were people who were once part of British society – even though neoliberal conservative ideology would have us believe that "there is no such thing as society"! Whilst the citizens of the UK were being infected and dying, conservative politicians partied at 10 Downing Street during lockdown. The many parties held at 10 Downing Street depicted the disdain of the ruling class for the commoners in the UK. It seems that in a country that believed devotedly in the herd immunity model, it was not difficult for the rulers to also believe the *Animal Farm* ideology of "four legs good two legs better!" Capitalism divides society into royalty and commoners. The UK clearly portrayed this state of affairs under capitalism in the time of COVID-19.

Brazil is home to 211 million people (Wikipedia, 2020). It is also home to the world's largest green lungs – the Amazon rainforest. The president in the time of COVID-19 in Brazil was Jair Bolsonaro. Apparently, his role model is Donald

Trump. Like his counterparts in the Western world – Bolsonaro downplayed the severity of the virus and was slow to respond. More than a year later as countries in other parts of the world had COVID-19 more or less under control, Brazil was still experiencing increasing infection and death rates. Right-wing states and anti-science stances seem to go together in the modern world. In Latin America you can't get more right-wing than Bolsonaro. Like the US – and similar to the UK – Brazil lacked a coherent and scientific response to COVID-19.

Like South Africa – Brazil is a highly unequal country. These two combinations would prove fatal for many Brazilians. Bolsonaro, "the Trump of the Tropics decried the 'hysteria' of the press for spreading fear, dismissing the virus as a 'little flu'" (Marshall, 2020) and opposed any form of lockdown. Some cities in Brazil called him out for his deceit and lies – and not daring to put their citizens' lives at risk – decided to impose lockdowns of their own. But with the most powerful man in the country not lending support to saving lives during a global pandemic – the inevitable was occurring:

> Brazil is the current leader in the race for the world's most inept response to the COVID-19 crisis. In the words of Celso Rocha de Barros — a leading columnist for Folha de São Paulo, Brazil's largest newspaper, Bolsonaro is the president who ordered Brazilians to die. This is a president who, with his unruly brood of politician sons unleashed a barrage of fake news urging Brazilians to break with the quarantine.
>
> FOGEL, 2020: 1

Instead of motivating people to live, the maverick president of Brazil seemed to have motivated people to look forward to dying:

> When criticised for his actions, Bolsonaro reassured those listening that 'we are all going to die one day'. He has also claimed that Brazilians possess a special type of natural immunity that will protect them from the virus.
>
> FOGEL, 2020: 1

To add insult to injury, the president did the unthinkable and fired the health minister. The second health minister resigned under pressure. This is the same right-wing president who allowed the Amazon rainforest – the green lungs of the world – to burn in the name of unrestrained capitalist development and progress. Right-wing censorship went into full-gear and the Brazilian state then decided to censor the statistics on COVID-19. Some in the justice sphere pushed back. Bolsonaro was democratically elected to rule Brazil. But this tin-pot ruler had little interest in saving the lives of the Brazilian people:

> The move was widely criticised, with Brazilian doctors, medical associations and state governors attacking what they called an attempt to control information. Federal prosecutors announced an investigation on Saturday – using the Brazilian constitution and freedom of information law as justification – and gave the interim health minister 72 hours to explain the move. 'The manipulation of statistics is a manoeuvre of totalitarian regimes,' tweeted Supreme Court Judge Gilmar Mendes. The trick will not exempt responsibility for the eventual genocide. The data was 'adapted' because it did not 'portray' the moment the country is in', tweeted Bolsonaro – who has flouted isolation measures, dismissed the virus as a 'little flu' and shrugged-off the rising death toll because death was 'everybody's destiny'.
>
> PHILLIPS, 2020

The highest court of the land overturned neoliberal ideology and ruled that concealing COVID-19 statistics from the people was unlawful. As early as 7 July 2021, Brazil was on the red list of countries regarding international travel. According to the Johns Hopkins University and Medicine Coronavirus Resource Center, by 21 June 2022 Brazil registered 31,611,769 COVID-19 infections and 668,693 deaths.

The United States of America (USA), commonly known as the United States (U.S. or US) or America, has a population of 328 million people. It is the third most populous country in the world (Wikipedia, 2020). The US is the land of denial, death and so-called democracy. It is a capitalist country with the highest form of neoliberalism. Before that it was Native American country – until violence, murder and theft turned it into the Land of the Free and the Home of the Brave. It is probably the only country in the world whose national anthem has the words "rockets" and "bombs" in it. Anyway, it also symbolises the US's preoccupation with war in the modern world.

The US had its first case of COVID-19 about the same time as South Korea. Donald Trump was the 45th president when COVID-19 entered its borders. A US advisor had advised Trump of the developing COVID-19 situation in January 2020. Dr Ryan of the World Health Organisation (WHO) stated that the WHO informed the world on 5 January 2020 that COVID-19 was a developing situation. America's borders are manned and heavily resourced to keep out Muslims and Mexicans. COVID-19 was given a free pass through one of the most secure borders of the world. The US was effective and efficient to lock down the borders to keep immigrants out. The same political will and abundant resources were not present – and not evident – when it came to the invisible but known enemy entering its borders – and given many months to kill more than a million Americans. Whereas China took the liberty and freedom to defeat the invisible enemy – in America the invisible enemy was given the liberty and freedom to defeat and kill-off the American people.

Former United States Secretary of State – Madeleine Albright once said:

> If we have to use force, it is because we are America. We are the indispensable nation. We stand tall. We see further into the future.
>
> *The Today Show*, 1998

Insofar as the US using untold force on parts of the world, she was 100% on the mark. Insofar as America standing tall and seeing further into the future, there was no evidence of this – when it came to COVID-19 and saving American lives. White House ideology was being ripped apart by the devastation caused by COVID-19.

The US is a country comprising 50 states. Red states are predominantly Republican states – and blue states are predominantly Democratic states (Wikipedia, 2020). Whereas effective countries had a national response to COVID-19, in the US the response was fragmented and not even half-baked. The US's response to COVID-19 was disastrous. 2020 was also an election year in the US – and what was a national response in successful countries turned out to be a red and blue response in the US. Donald Trump is the "Xi Jinping" – the supreme leader – of the red party in the US. What was a public health response to COVID-19 in successful countries, became a political and ideological response in the US. Whereas the reds did a splendid job in China, Vietnam, Cuba, etc. the reds in the US failed abysmally in preventing COVID-19 from infecting and killing Americans in droves. The blue states preferred restrictions and lockdown of sorts – whereas the red states wanted a freed-up neoliberal capitalist economy. In order for money-making to resume, neoliberal Western notions of liberty and freedom were demanded in the time of a global pandemic. In Michigan:

> Hundreds of protesters, many not wearing protective face masks and some armed legally with 'long guns', gathered inside the statehouse in Lansing on Thursday as lawmakers debated the Democratic governor's request to extend her emergency powers to combat the coronavirus pandemic.
>
> GRAHAM, 2020

Western ideology flows from the head. Supreme leader Trump:

> Has rooted for states to lift many of the tightest restrictions on movement and commerce and allowed a national stay-at-home recommendation to expire Thursday night. Hundreds of people, including a militia group armed with military-style rifles, rushed the state Capitol in Lansing on Thursday, with some forcing their way into the building and facing off with law enforcement. An angry mob screamed 'Lock Her Up' and insults about Whitmer.
>
> GEARAN ET AL., 2020

We demand our freedoms, but we'll take away your freedom by locking you up! This was the madness of US right-wing ideology in the time of COVID-19! The US is always prepared for war against other countries and people – even if it has to do so under make-believe intelligence. Even though the Spanish Flu began in the US – spread to all parts of the world – and killed more than 50 million people worldwide – the US chose not to learn the lessons from this historic and devastating pandemic:

> The United States has not faced a pandemic of such devastating proportions since the 1918 Spanish Flu. Despite being the richest and the most scientifically advanced country in the world, it has been the worst affected with the number of cases due to shortly cross the two-million mark. More than 100,000 Americans died due to the virus by the end of May.
>
> CHERIAN, 2020

This was in May 2020! The number of dead Americans rose drastically as the months dragged on in the time of COVID-19. But ideology trumps science in the mighty US of A. Trump blamed federal governments for not stocking up on medical supplies. US responsibility for the deaths of its own citizens was missing in abundance:

> The world is now suffering as a result of the malfeasance of the Chinese government, Trump said. Countless lives have been taken, and profound economic hardship has been inflicted all around the globe.
>
> CHERIAN, 2020

Being the world's richest nation and the best resourced to wage a global war against COVID-19, the President of the US instead walked away from that war.

Where and when global solidarity was necessary to wage war against COVID-19, the US betrayed global institutions and left them vulnerable and weakened in the time of a global pandemic:

> Despite there being no takers for the U.S. President's allegations against the WHO, he has gone ahead and done the unthinkable. He will now have the dubious reputation of being the only head of state to turn his back on the WHO and its dedicated team of scientists and doctors in the midst of a raging pandemic. The United Nations and the WHO issued an SOS in the last week of May calling for 'global solidarity' in the fight against the pandemic. It was at this critical juncture that the Trump administration chose to formally walk out of the WHO. President Donald Trump sent a letter to WHO Director-general Tedros Adhanom Ghebreyesus in the last week of May announcing the decision. The Trump administration also announced that it was cutting-off all funding to the organisation.
>
> CHERIAN, 2020

The US response to COVID-19 was American exceptionalism at its very best! In a leaked recording, Barack Obama, the former president of the US, frustratingly described the US response to COVID-19: "leaders aren't even pretending to lead and called Trump's handling of the crisis an absolute chaotic disaster" (Pilkington, 2020: 21). Sometimes leaked reports are meant to be strategically leaked. In a country that proudly houses the magnificent Statue of Liberty, the workers did not have the freedom to choose between life and death. Forced labour is a covert reality in the Land of the Free. COVID-19 merely exposed this reality so long hidden under the heavy weight of neoliberal ideologies:

> Iowa, Oklahoma and other states reopening soon amid the coronavirus outbreak are issuing early warnings to their worried workers: Return to your jobs or risk losing unemployment benefits. The threats have been loudest among Republican leaders in recent days, reflecting their anxious attempts to jump-start local economic recovery roughly two months after most businesses shut their doors.
>
> ROMM, 2020

In a world of Facebook, Instagram, Tinder, TikTok, YouPorn, Pornhub, etc. saturated with private data in the capitalist market sphere, private individuals in the US protested against their private data being used in the time of a global pandemic – even if such data would help save precious lives:

An exception to federal medical privacy law allows health departments to warn police and firefighters responding to a home where someone has tested positive for COVID-19. But that's not happening in the county that is home to Chicago, one of a handful of jurisdictions where patients' rights are trumping first responders' need to know. 'We run into dangerous situations on a constant basis, but COVID-19 is different,' said Joseph Lukaszek, police chief in Hillside, Illinois. 'I could possibly die from this or bring this home and my wife and children could die. I have a responsibility to my family, and it doesn't make any sense that we can't get information that can save our lives'.

MORDOCK, 2020

Unlike the capitalist market that breaks through all privacy boundaries by requesting all sorts of private information and most times secures it, the frontline workers had no intention to make money from the use of private data. Capitalist society is highly hypocritical in the important affairs of privacy – we are all aware of how our private data is a free-for-all for companies and corporations of the capitalist market. COVID-19 was a practical challenge that required a practical response – but in most parts of the Western world the response was mostly ideological:

'We are not asking for gender, age or any personal information, and we are not asking to keep this information indefinitely,' said Tom Weitzel, police chief in Riverside, Illinois. 'I don't understand the resistance. We are not asking it to be public'.

MORDOCK, 2020

So strong is neoliberal ideology regarding Western forms of individual freedom in the US that a guard was shot dead by a customer in a store – for attempting to enforce the using of masks. If doctors were silenced and journalists kicked out in China, Mr. Trump's White House made it its duty to also kick out reporters, and silenced U.S. state medical professionals who disagreed with it. A country that demands transparency and accountability from other countries proved to be strong on preaching – and extremely weak on practising transparency and accountability itself:

COVID-19 numbers are likely an undercount, because the CDC report says not all states with coronavirus cases in such facilities contributed data. The prevalence of testing also probably played a role, the CDC found, with more infections reported in places with more testing.

GEARAN ET AL., 2020

Whilst the hawks in the White House and mainstream media in the US were pushing the narrative that COVID-19 was manufactured in a lab in Wuhan, China, the United States intelligence professionals were of a different view, that the virus made the jump to humans in a non-lab setting in southern China – and have said so publicly (Fadden and Jones, 2020). All the while sections of the American populace – covered from head to toe with neoliberal ideologies – went into the streets and branded big guns on the one hand and placards on the other – some of which read: "Stop the Epidemic of Tyranny!" "Shutdown the Shutdown!"

In order to distract the world from the chaos and confusion that depicted the US in the time of COVID-19, the billionaire and South African born Elon Musk – with supreme leader Donald Trump by his side – sent a rocket to the International Space Station. Whilst Rocket Man was sending rockets across South Korea and Japan in the East, Rocket Men in the West were sending rockets into space in the time of a global pandemic! Symbolic ideology under arch capitalists failed to unite a broken and dying nation. On another vanity project in the time of a global pandemic – on 10 December 2020 – one of Musk's rockets exploded upon landing back on planet earth. The rocket's explosion symbolised the overall disaster that plagued the US under Donald Trump's presidency.

American society had never been this polarised in a long time. It became glaringly evident in the time of COVID-19, that the capitalist state is not a human-centred state:

> Many states have also failed to put in place public-health infrastructure to contain the virus. In the Miami area, local mayors say, the state has hired so few contact tracers that only 17 per cent of people who test positive for COVID-19 are contacted by the program. 'Eighty per cent of the people that are told they're positive are not given instructions, their contacts are not reached out to, they are not told to be quarantined,' Miami Beach Mayor Dan Gelber said outside Miami City Hall.
>
> MORROW, 2020

The country that is world-renowned for spying on all and sundry fell far short of spying on the spread of COVID-19. Contrary to ideological talk of American values – that the world has become used to, COVID-19 helped shine the light on aspects that the American elite value in reality:

Cramped slaughterhouses and crowded prisons have helped drive outbreaks, while Florida and other states declared churches 'essential' and
allowed thousands to keep attending services in person.

MORROW, 2020

Capitalist America was the epitome of anarchy in the time of a global pandemic:

In the United States, where the death toll on Tuesday approached 100,000,
crowds flooded newly reopened beaches and other public spaces over
Memorial Day weekend, even as the virus claimed more than 2,000 additional lives. At a club in Houston, dozens splashed around the pool and
sipped on drinks on the patio. In North Carolina, thousands packed the
stands shoulder to shoulder at a speedway on opening night, where face
masks were the exception. In Daytona Beach, Florida, even after an event
called 'Orlando Invades Daytona' was cancelled, hundreds of people still
danced in the street and on top of cars near the boardwalk.

DENNIS ET AL., 2020

They stuck to ideology in the White House like glue stuck to paper. The consequence of White House ideology in the time of a global pandemic was the loss
of precious American lives:

The death toll would have probably been much lower had the Trump
administration acted more quickly, Bright told the hearing. He said his
efforts to obtain early viral samples from China was met with 'frustration
and dismissal' from the Department of Health and Human Services.

MILMAN, 2020

Protestors on beaches also did not let go of Western ideologies in the time of a
global pandemic:

Beukers, 48, said afterward that he was willing to get arrested and that
the discussion had less to do with the beach than the constitutionality of
the closure. 'Where do we go from here?' he recalled asking the officers.
'What side of history do you want to be on? Someone has to stand their
ground. We're on a slippery slope, and we might end up where we might
not want to be'.

CURWEN, 2020

I am certain many Americans did not want to end up with ventilators in hospitals and most certainly not in coffins! Whilst ideologues were holding onto Western notions of freedom in the White House and on the streets and beaches – Americans were left to perish. By the end of April 2020, the "virus had killed nearly 65,000 people in the United States" (Gearan, et al., 2020). If China delayed when it came to know about COVID-19, then why did Western countries delay, dither and dawdle when they first came to know about COVID-19? The West had the opportunity to "teach China a lesson" on the "just in time" response – but they decided to procrastinate instead:

> Trump made no mention of the early warning the WHO had issued to the international community. And, of course, there was no question of owning responsibility for his administration's colossal failure that allowed the virus to spread like wildfire in the country and beyond its borders. Instead, Trump insisted that the world needs answers from China.
> CHERIAN, 2020

Another writer states:

> That the US now has the largest numbers of COVID-19 infections and deaths goes beyond expectations. China locked down Wuhan – the Chinese city hit the hardest by the epidemic – on January 23, sending early warnings of the novel coronavirus outbreak. The US, with sufficient time to prepare, the most advanced medical system and technology, as well as rich experience in dealing with public health crises, should have performed well, or at least not so poorly amid the epidemic.
> NING, 2020

From the very beginning when the pandemic was declared – Western ideology and not pragmatism informed the US response to COVID-19:

> As the first American evacuees from Wuhan, China, touched down at a California military base a year ago, fleeing the epicentre of the coronavirus outbreak, they were met by U.S. health officials with no virus prevention plan or infection-control training – and who had not even been told to wear masks, according to a federal investigation. Later, those officials were told to remove protective gear when meeting with the evacuees to avoid 'bad optics,' and days after those initial encounters, departed California aboard commercial airline flights to other destinations.
> DIAMOND, 2021

In the land that prides itself on life, liberty and the pursuit of happiness – the US response to COVID-19 was the antithesis and contrary to life, liberty and the pursuit of happiness. According to the Johns Hopkins University and Medicine Coronavirus Resource Center, by 22 June 2022 the US registered 86,452,232 COVID-19 infections and 1,013,974 deaths – the highest in the world! The US is quite exceptional in this regard. After decades of ideological brainwashing about the wonders of American capitalism – the unthinkable questions were being asked: "with no end in sight to the COVID-19 carnage, we need to ask ourselves how it is possible for a country with unlimited financial, medical and communications clout to screw up its response so badly"? (Picard, 2020). Western and capitalist ideologies kill and it killed many in the time of COVID-19!

Capitalist India is the neighbour of communist China. India is the world's largest democracy – and also the country with the greatest number of gods. India sits uncomfortably next to China. It is highly capitalist in shape and form – and is usually measured up against China – as a model for the world to look up to. It is a country of about 1.5 billion people (Wikipedia, 2020). India seeks to model itself in the image of the West – but with Indian characteristics. If one puts aside India's Bollywood movies and GDP figures, one sees India for what it really is – a country of hundreds of millions of Indians living and working under wretched conditions.

India is a country in chaos and of chaos. Had it not been for critical and social media, the true picture of India would remain hidden from the world at large. Omitting the real picture of conditions in capitalist countries has thus far been a deliberate and effective strategy of capitalist ideologies. This is made possible through ideologically embedded mainstream media within the capitalist system. COVID-19 gave us a glimpse into the real India – in the same way that it gave us glimpses into the true workings of other countries – in the important affairs of life, livelihoods and death under the capitalist epoch.

Images of millions of Indians , mostly migrant workers leaving for their villages – were plastered on television sets and printed media throughout the world. Social media via YouTube, Facebook, WhatsApp and Instagram, for example, brought more of real India into the global collective consciousness. If there is one aspect of capitalism that has been truly globalised in the 21st century – it is that of capitalist ideologies – a fabrication and socially engineered construction of reality by the ruling class and its many mental or intellectual workers – the busy bees of ideological construction. COVID-19 turned this ideological world upside down – and inside out. The Indian state gave the hundreds of millions of migrant workers just under four hours' notice of the lockdown. Capitalist piety came to the fore when Narendra Modi – the prime minister of India – requested India's citizens to switch off all their lights and light candles in order to boost the country's morale. He also suggested that they practice yoga and drink herbal tea. At that time, it seemed a much better suggestion than that of his good friend Donald Trump in the West – who suggested that people drink disinfectant and clean out their insides to kill off COVID-19!

Capitalist authoritarianism and ideology reared its ugly head when the Indian government applied to the Supreme Court – in order to have all reporting on COVID-19 go through its ideological censorship machine. The Supreme Court over-ruled the application – and the brutal character traits of capitalism were exposed – as chaos and confusion signified India – the world's largest democracy with the greatest number of holy men. Religion is really "the opium of the masses" in capitalist India. Gender parity seems a challenge in the affairs of overt holiness in India. In the country that prides on calling itself the world's largest democracy, the Solicitor General of India – referred to the media as "vultures" and as "prophets of doom spreading negativity".

In the time of COVID-19, India witnessed the biggest exodus since 1947 when colonial Britain drew a line on the map of India – thereby artificially creating the country we now know as Pakistan. When COVID-19 struck, the usually invisible class in capitalist India was made shockingly visible. In order to distract the world from the mess that is India, the ruling class invoked Indian nationalist ideology to drum up the country to wage war on communist China. Twenty Indian soldiers were needlessly killed and sacrificed in border skirmishes with China due to the loss of Indian pride in the time of COVID-19.

One commentator on the BBC stated that the true COVID-19 statistics in India may never be known – because the untouchables are an invisible class in India and their deaths are not counted. If the untouchables in India are invisible in life – they seemed to be invisible in death as well. In India: "the lockdown – one of the harshest in the world – was due to end Sunday, and the government is still struggling to contain the growing outbreak" (Gearan, et al., 2020). According to the Johns Hopkins University and Medicine Coronavirus Resource Center, by 22 June 2022 India registered 43,319,396 COVID-19 infections and 524,890 deaths. The view is that India had massively underreported its COVID-19 infections and deaths. Capitalist India was no match for communist China – in the life and death matters of the respective country's citizens. In India's ideological war with China – the common people of India were the innocent casualties of this war. As India attempted to project the illusion of normalcy, with mass gatherings at holy festivals, cricket matches and elections – the death toll climbed. Burning bodies on pavements in many parts of India was a grim reminder of the pain and lowest level of civilisation that

capitalism can take humanity to. India epitomised this grimness and pain in
the time of COVID-19!

3   An Inconvenient Truth in the Age of Comparative Statistics and
     Measurement

We live in an age of comparisons. The US and UK are freer societies – when
compared to China. Men overwhelmingly occupy powerful and key positions
in society, when compared to women. Black men outnumber white men in
prisons in the US. Kate and William are much more adored by the British
Media than Meghan and Harry. Even though by a small margin – Americans
felt that, when compared to Donald Trump, Joe Biden would make a better
president. The Pfizer vaccine is said to have a higher efficacy, when compared
to the AstraZeneca vaccine. With regards to countries responses and COVID-19,
the elephant or dragon in the room is China. Whatever the amount of Western
ideological spin, there is no running away from the fact that China responded
efficiently and effectively to COVID-19.
     However Western powers wish to demonise and defame China – the Johns
Hopkins University and Medicine Coronavirus Resource Center data will forever demonstrate that China outsmarted COVID-19, and COVID-19 outsmarted
the Western world. However Western powers attempt to name and shame
China on its Human Rights abuses, they must at the same time pronounce
on China's admirable ability to secure "the right to life" of the Chinese people – whilst Western powers failed to secure or abandoned "the right to life" of
its citizens. China's success in dealing with COVID-19 has become a blind-spot
in the global narrative on COVID-19. Western and capitalist countries made
certain to keep this inconvenient truth buried deep within the heaviness of
Western ideologies.
     However Western powers and ideologues propagate that responses by
different countries to COVID-19 cannot and should not be compared, there
is no getting away from the fact that the COVID-19 Dashboard by the Center
for Systems Science and Engineering (CSSE) at Johns Hopkins University has
painstakingly made the comparisons – in number form – between countries
on their handling of COVID-19. No amount of Western ideological attacks can
alter the numbers relating to the infected and dead in respective countries. Ask
a man or a woman whether they prefer being locked up for life and losing all
of their freedoms – compared to the death penalty. My guess would be that 10
out of 10 will prefer losing their freedoms for life – than being condemned to
death – as was the case in the Western world in the time of COVID-19.

The West administered the death penalty to its citizens in the time of COVID-19. Neoliberal ideologies masked the reality of the preciousness of life – during a global pandemic, and made freedom and liberty to be paramount over life and living. Life is precious. If we need reminding that life is precious, then ask the many millions in the world who lost loved ones to COVID-19: moms and dads, grandparents, husbands and wives, children, friends, partners, colleagues, babies, journalists, doctors, workers, academics, nurses, policemen and women, etc. Nature makes life possible – and pronounces death as an eventual necessity. But what are we to make of a particular type of society – that makes death so easily possible? What are we to make of Nazi Germany – that made the deaths of millions of Jews so easily possible? What are we to make of colonial society – that made it so easy to kill off indigenous peoples and steal their lands and natural resources? What are we to make of Western and capitalist countries – that made it so easy for its citizens to die in such large numbers – in the time of COVID-19? By 22 June 2022 more than 1,013,975 Americans had been reported to have died of COVID-19. What if 1,013,975 Chinese, Vietnamese or Cubans had died from COVID-19? Would the Western world have called for genocide charges against these communist leaders and states?

France called the retraining of Uighurs in China a genocide. Would France call the death of 1,013,975 Americans a genocide? Would it call the death of 669,161 Brazilians a genocide? According to the Johns Hopkins University and Medicine Coronavirus Resource Centre, by 22 June 2022 the number of people in capitalist US that died from COVID-19 was 1,013,975 – the highest in the world! The number of people in capitalist UK that died from COVID-19 was 180,271. The number of people in communist Cuba that died from COVID-19 was 8,529. The number of people that died from COVID-19 in communist Vietnam was 43,083. The number of people that died from COVID-19 in communist China was 14,622.

How did the richest and most powerful country in the world – allow more than 1000 000 of its citizens to die – whilst China allowed only 14,622 of its citizens to die? Why was the death rate 70 times more in capitalist US – than that in communist China? In an age of statistics, measurement and comparisons, this is the inconvenient truth that the Western world will have to live with – in the years, decades and centuries to come. In a world where "all men are created equal" – why were Chinese lives more important than American lives? Why were Vietnamese lives more important than British lives? Why were Cuban lives more important than South African lives? Why was the value of the grandparent that died in the US lower than the value of the grandparent that was saved in China? Why was the value of the healthcare worker that died in the UK lower than the value of the healthcare worker that was saved in China? Capitalism has a case to answer for. The Western world has a case to answer for. If China was not an important enough country to take lessons from – then Italy and Spain were. By negating pragmatism and clinging to neo-liberal and Western ideologies, countries like the US, Japan, the UK, India, etc. demonstrated to the world's audience how dogmatic and dug in their heels they were – in the important affairs of saving lives and keeping its citizens healthy. The leaders of these countries failed their citizens. Capitalist and neo-liberal ideologies in the Western world failed its citizens. Capitalist states were in the main failed states – when it came to protecting its citizens.

COVID-19 revealed how imprisoned and chained Western states were – under capitalist ideologies – in not being enabling agents – to formidably defeat a global pandemic. If Big Brother or the nanny state did not step in – albeit very late in capitalist economies – and save more people from sicknesses and deaths, then capitalism would have proceeded on its "merry way" – with more swathes of sick, dying and dead people – under the umbrella of unintended consequences. To use the language of Western ideology when waging war on Middle Eastern countries and killing innocent civilians – as a result of "collateral damage".

COVID-19 has taught us that an intelligent species – Homo sapiens – foregoes some freedoms if and when the need arises. Most people understood this – except the capitalist class and its representative – the capitalist state. The neoliberal state was ill-prepared to respond to a global pandemic. Only when it transformed its neoliberal make-up and shed some of its Western ideologies were countries able to respond effectively to a global pandemic. COVID-19 indicated to us the diverse nature of states – for example, good communist states and bad capitalist states – when it came to saving lives during a global pandemic.

Many centuries of capitalism has not given the entire of humanity the same chances at survival in the time of a global pandemic. Instead, we sat glued to our television screens – and witnessed the chaos of the neoliberal capitalist system. We witnessed people die needlessly. We witnessed people being given undignified funerals. We witnessed chaos and confusion in the developed world. We witnessed bodies being taken out in body bags and coffins. We witnessed the lonely journey of dead bodies – in military vehicles on their way to crematoriums and cemeteries. We witnessed bodies being stored in refrigerator trucks. We witnessed bodies left on the roadside. We witnessed bodies being cremated on pavements. These were bodies of the human race – a natural species with tens of thousands of years of culture. This surely must be one of the lowest points of human civilisation in general – and of Western civilisation in particular. And most of this was taking place in the developed world – that part of the world that all other countries are expected to emulate in terms of Western civilisation and progress. Western ideology about the falsity of meaningful individual power and agency for the majority in capitalist society had already set the stage for the needless deaths of citizens. COVID-19 merely exposed this fault line:

> It goes without saying that today we are all neoliberals, increasingly under pressure to make key life decisions, publicly and privately, collectively as well as individually, according to market logic. It remains the case that in today's neoliberal society, people are expected to become entrepreneurs of the self who can take full responsibility for their personal choices. In this way, we enact what has come to be called neoliberal governmentality.
> SCHRAM ET AL., 2018: xix

Many in the Western world – with resources that the developing world can only dream of – were not able to put together and implement an effective, efficient and just-in-time plan and strategy to deal with COVID-19. The just-in-time model was conceptualised and implemented first in Japan – and then exported to many parts of the world – to increase the pace and speed of profit. Unfortunately, the just-in-time model was not put to effective and efficient use in the Western world when it came to saving the lives of its citizens. Because the governments of the developed world faffed, fidgeted, fiddled, and farted whilst COVID-19 wasted no time in infecting millions – the citizens of the developed world fell like flies.

The evidence thus far has shown that under capitalism – freedom also means freedom to exploit workers, freedom to exploit nature, freedom to fire workers, freedom to throw people out of their homes if they cannot afford rentals, freedom to drive communities away and take their land in the name of progress and development, freedom to pollute the land, air, rivers and seas, freedom to cause global warming and climate change, freedom to cause species extinction, freedom to mass produce guns that leave people maimed and dead, freedom to extend the working pensionable age of workers – who have given their entire lives to the capitalist system, freedom to apply sanctions on the poor and destitute of a country, the freedom to tell outright lies that a country has weapons of mass destruction, the freedom to then bomb the living daylights of the country and then the freedom to live life as if nothing has happened, the freedom to place profit over people and planet, the freedom to report on certain news events and not on others, the freedom to continue with coal production – even though the evidence is overwhelming that coal is bad for the environment, the freedom to adopt socialist principles to bail out the banks and the rich by strong states and leave the middle and working classes exposed to the vagaries of the capitalist market – that collapsed the banks in the first place, the freedom to kowtow to authoritarian states like Saudi Arabia – whilst at the same time practising the freedom to name and shame countries like China and Cuba for human rights abuses, the freedom to profit from health care, the freedom to profit from education, the freedom to profit from old-age, the freedom to profit from mass murder as in war, the freedom to collect citizen's data through mass surveillance, the freedom to burn the Amazon rainforest and to profit from this burning, the freedom to hoard vaccines in the time of a global pandemic, the freedom to peddle ideologies in the name of freedom, etc.

The double-standards of the values of freedom are alive and well in the Western world! The UK and US did not support the freedom and liberty of South Africa's black majority during the dark days of apartheid. We do not see the powerful and free world fighting for the freedom and liberty of the Palestinian people. We do not see the free world standing up for the freedom and liberty of ordinary citizens in Saudi Arabia. When one considers the chaos and confusion manifesting itself as freedom in the West – one is forced to turn away from the ideology of Milton Friedman to consider Lenin's thought on freedom in capitalist society: "freedom in capitalist society always remains about the same as it was in ancient Greek republics: freedom for slave owners".

COVID-19 demonstrated that freedom from want is the most fundamental freedom for the human species. Maslow's hierachy of needs shows this to be the case. But decades before – Karl Marx warned:

> The simple fact, hitherto concealed by an overgrowth of ideology, that humankind must first of all eat, drink, have shelter and clothing, before it can pursue politics, science, art, religion, etc. (1883).

And before humankind can do all of these things, it must first be given a chance to stay alive. Whilst pragmatism in China saved millions, the "overgrowth of ideology" in the Western world in general – and in the capitalist world in particular – enabled and allowed its citizens to be killed in their millions!

CHAPTER 7

Workers under Capitalism

Creators of Value – Even during a Pandemic

A working-class hero is something to be.
JOHN LENNON

• • •

Workers of all lands unite; you have nothing to lose but your chains.
KARL MARX

• •
•

1   Health Workers: Soldiers on the Frontline in the Time of COVID-19

Our heroes in capitalist society are usually celebrities, sport stars, pop stars, rock stars, Winston Churchill, Christopher Columbus, Spiderman, Harry Potter and Mr. Bean in *Johnny English*. Now and again society remembers the war heroes – the soldiers who perished in the two World Wars – fighting for their respective countries. Even rarer is to consider a worker a hero, as John Lennon had done through his song *Working Class Hero*. COVID-19 has reconfigured paradigms and changed perspectives!

Nelson Mandela spent 27 long and hard years in prison and is rightly a celebrated hero in South Africa and abroad. Chris Hani who was assassinated just before South Africa's democratic transition – because of his communist vision for a post-apartheid South Africa – has not yet assumed the scale of hero adulation. But history has the tendency to make and remake heroes – for some there seems to be a historical time for worship and a historical time for vilification. Who would have thought that statues of heroes in the West would be vilified and brought down – in the way that they were – in the time of COVID-19! Even the statue of Winston Churchill was eyed to fall – but thanks to the strong presence and intervention of the nanny state, Churchill was cladded up and prevented from falling from grace. Good thing that the absolute freedom and liberty of citizens of the UK were disabled by the state. It seems that freedoms and liberties, after-all, have their limitations in the Western world. Winston Churchill still stands! The statues of other heroes did not have such state protection. For many in the developing world, Churchill is a colonial villain. But in the West – he is a hero. Ideological perspectives weigh heavily on humankind.

Like any war, COVID-19 included, countries require soldiers and heroes to do battle with the enemy. As to whether the human race can befriend itself in a post-COVID-19 world – instead of being in perpetual enmity with itself under capitalism – currently seems unimaginable. In any event, in the time of COVID-19, twenty-first century society discovered new heroes – heroes on the frontline of COVID-19. In my extended family, health workers had to confront the invisible enemy on a daily basis. One family member had to undergo at least three tests and be quarantined – after being exposed to COVID-19 positive patients. She was pregnant – which meant that it was not only her, but her unborn baby too – that was on the frontline in the war with COVID-19. These were trying times. Health workers in all parts of the world were the frontline soldiers fighting in a deadly war – a war that was allowed to drag on for about 18–20 months in the Western world in the main.

In South Africa, which is primarily Western in its ideological make-up, when and where alcohol is freely available and plentifully consumed – hospital admissions are increased. This meant added stress on an already deficient public health system and on health care workers in capitalist South Africa. The dominance and persistence of capitalist market ideologies meant that casualties and deaths were increased manifold in the time of COVID-19. Accident and murder rates go up in South Africa when the capitalist market is allowed total liberty and freedom. Come to think of it, we do have a chain of alcohol stores in South Africa called Liberty Liquors! If accident and murder rates went up when alcohol was freely available, so did the stresses and strains on the health care workers in the time of COVID-19.

In many parts of the world, health care workers were at breaking point. It was not just the health care workers that were under huge and continued pressures; their families were also consumed by the spill-offs of such pressures in their daily worries and support for their loved ones. In all parts of the world, health care workers were at the coalface in the war against COVID-19. Like soldiers on the battle field, they fought the enemy with both braveness and fear. Like soldiers on the battlefield they witnessed their fellow-workers killed by the invisible enemy. Like soldiers on the battlefield, they had to push family life to the back or out of their minds when fighting the deadly enemy. But unlike soldiers on the battlefield, their respective countries commanded them to do battle without the necessary defensive equipment. In the Western world in the main, health care workers were sitting ducks for COVID-19. All they got was "clapping Thursday" and "bin bags" as protective gowns (Gerard, 2020).

The Western world in the main pronounced that they were going to war – a war against an invisible enemy. But in a short space of time, the commanders and generals of the war economy abdicated their responsibilities to their foot soldiers in the time of a global war on COVID-19. According to Dr Michael Ryan of the WHO:

> Health workers are the canaries in a cage when it comes to pandemics. It is sadly the death of a care worker on the frontline that triggers a response.

The standard and quality of the response by capitalist nations to the COVID-19 war is in the death statistics of their citizens. Frontline heroes died in their numbers, as the capitalist system was not geared for the one war that needed sterling planning, preparation and execution:

> By May 2020 the UK had already lost many health care workers to COVID-19. A spokesperson for the Doctors' Association UK said: 'it is a tragedy that nearly 200 healthcare workers in the UK have died due to COVID-19. We had a pandemic stockpile of PPE lacking essential items like full gowns and eye protection; other equipment was out of date. There has been recurrent and systemic failure of the PPE supply chain, leaving staff in some instances with makeshift or no PPE'.
> SIDDIQUE, 2020

Another COVID-19 war correspondent stated:

> The deaths of more than 50 hospital and care home workers have been reported to Britain's health and safety regulator, which is considering launching criminal investigations, the Guardian has learned. Nazir Afzal, former chief crown prosecutor for north-west England, said: 'sending someone into a high-risk situation against one of the most infectious diseases we've come across in 100 years without proper protection needs investigation and may meet the threshold for criminal sanction'.
> DODD ET AL., 2020

It seems that the UK state committed war crimes against its own frontline soldiers:

Doctors are taking legal action to force the UK government to launch an independent inquiry into its failure to provide adequate personal protective equipment for NHS staff and other frontline care workers.

SIDDIQUE, 2020

As in war, the frontline workers were herded onto the COVID-19 battlefield. As in war, many lives were cut short in the time of COVID-19:

A nurse who died with COVID-19 shortly after surgeons delivered her baby had felt 'pressured' to return to work despite having concerns for her safety, an inquest into her death has heard.

DA SILVA, 2020

The country that was once the factory of the world did not – or could not – manufacture PPEs for its frontline soldiers:

Britain is facing a shortage of the gowns required to protect medical staff against coronavirus, with NHS hospitals resorting to flying in their own stocks from China.

MALNICK and DONNELY, 2020

In one of the nuclear powers of the world – India – doctors were asked to wear raincoats and sunglasses in order to do battle with COVID-19. This is the country that invited the entire world to come and "Make in India"! In Italy a nurse killed herself. She became the symbol of the stress and strain that health care workers had to deal with – in the time of COVID-19. In the US, health care workers had had enough – and protested at the lack of war apparel against the deadly virus. Some held up placards that read: "Hey CDC – we don't have PPE". Health workers needed masks in America – but the "greatest country on earth" could not produce masks for their frontline soldiers. Lawrence Summers asked: "why can't the greatest nation on earth produce face masks"?

One health care worker wrote a will. She tweeted to her children that if she had to die, then she died trying to save lives. Nurses in New York could not get tested. One was afraid of speaking out publicly – for fear of being fired from the hospital she worked in. The hospital in question had told her that it does not test staff for COVID-19. The result was that she wore the same mask and the same gown for 5 days – and went about treating patients. By the end of the 5 days – and when she finally did have a test – she was found to be positive.

Health care workers fought the virus with all of their might. Their battle against COVID-19 would have been that much more effective had they received the type of support that healthcare workers in countries that were successful against COVID-19 had received. But in the capitalist West, people are expendable – profit is not!

2   Workers: The Exploited, Unsung, Expendable, Sacked and Unknown Soldiers in the Time of COVID-19 in the Capitalist Era

We knew the names of the leaders and the many celebrities in the time of COVID-19. We also got to know the names of the important scientists and the important issues such as climate change and Black Lives Matter – and rightly so. We hear and see a lot about entrepreneurs, politicians, celebrities etc. but very little about the working men and women in capitalist society. If there were soldiers on the frontline, then there were also the unknown soldiers – the workers that are invisible in capitalist society. Media workers – "key workers" (Gerard, 2020) were also on the frontline bringing the world the news on COVID-19. Thanks to good journalism the world got to know about the existence of workers – the unknown soldiers – and the conditions under which they exist in the capitalist world. In all parts of the world, COVID-19 showed up the layers of society that are least protected and least secure under capitalism:

> It didn't take long for the pandemic to exacerbate existing inequalities; while the army of 'knowledge workers' can safely work from home, majority of the precariat are either continuing to go to work in unsafe conditions, or have already lost their jobs as a result of rapidly applied social-distancing measures.
>
> AL-BASAM, 2020

Workers are the bedrock of the capitalist economy – yet they are the ones that carry the most burdens in society. COVID-19 made transparent the hierarchical and exploitative structure of capitalist society:

> Incompetent and heartless governments put the hammer down on society without any planning or concern for those with few resources. It is one thing for the elite or the middle class to stay at home, work using the Internet, and muddle through teaching their children from home; it is another for the billions of migrant labourers and day labourers, people who live hand to mouth, and people who have no homes. Lockdowns, quarantines, social distancing – these words mean nothing for the billions of people who work hard each day to socially reproduce the world

and to produce the millions of commodities; they have not benefited from their work.

PRASHAD, 2020

Nowhere was the plight of workers more noticeable than in holy India. If India has a population of about 1.5 billion people, then the world got to see first-hand a part of the population of India in the time of COVID-19. If workers are hidden in the private property workspaces of capitalist society, then COVID-19 made them shockingly visible – thanks to sterling journalism and social media on the ineptitude and infantile ideology of the Indian state.

COVID-19 demonstrated that work under capitalism is just that – work for the purposes of survival and not as a life-long activity meant to be enjoyed by Homo sapiens. When there was no work, all that the Indian workers yearned for was to go back home to their families – much like the rest of us – during a day's work under capitalism. Work is drudgery under capitalism. The creators of Indian value – and contributors to global value – were left to walk hundreds, and in many cases, more than a thousand kilometres back to their villages. Whereas communist China had the backs of their workers, the workers in capitalist India were "thrown to the wolves". The Indian state's lockdown plan was a joke and a tragedy. Instead of containing COVID-19, the consequence of the Indian state's half-baked planning and implementation meant that COVID-19 had an easier and accelerated route into much of the Indian populace. The Indian migrant workers were forced to rub up against each other, as they moved about in a frenzy through and out of the big cities of India. Mother India was a complete mess in the time of COVID-19! The absorbers of Indian mess were the hundreds of millions of state-abandoned Indian migrant workers.

COVID-19 brought out into the open the human infrastructure that makes Indian capitalism possible. Workers make India but India breaks workers. This is the non-negotiable formula for the success of Indian-style capitalism. There were no omnipresent and omniscient gods, deities and holy men to protect the many millions of migrant workers – as they were compelled to walk the Indian battlefield – in the time of COVID-19. Many were taken before their time as they were mowed down by speeding vehicles on India's chaotic roads. If they were running away from COVID-19 and greedy Indian landlords in the big cities of India, then starvation, exhaustion and dangerous Indian driving saw to it that they meet death earlier than expected. They wanted to go home – that place of refuge and sanctuary under the harshness and brutality of Indian capitalism. But, instead, they got to experience the law of the jungle that informs capitalist India. Many did not make it back to their villages and homes because of the Indian state's ideological disdain for workers – demonstrated by the lack of proper state planning when it came to migrant workers.

Together with the Indian state, greedy Indian landlords shored-up a key partnership side to Indian capitalism:

> Earlier, even in the worst of times, migrants found their way home on a bus, train or truck. But today, they have been made to beg and suffer for no fault of theirs. It is clear that, even after so much outcry, migrant workers continue to be treated as irritants.
>
> KRISHNA, 2020

Ever since the time that capitalism forced itself upon England – and England forced capitalism upon the world – the workers have borne the brunt of capitalism's modus operandi. As far back as 1845, Friedrich Engels, a practising capitalist, an aspiring communist, friend and financial supporter of Karl Marx wrote:

> This class [manufacturing class], feeling itself the mighty representative class of the nation, is ashamed to lay the sore spot of England bare before the eyes of the world; will not confess, even to itself, that the workers are in distress, because it, the property-holding, manufacturing class, must bear the moral responsibility for this distress.
>
> ENGELS, 1845: 17

These sentiments ring true for the India of today. The Indian state and the capitalist class it represents "must bear the moral responsibility for the distress" of the workers of India – both in the time of COVID-19 and under the capitalist epoch. The entire world got to see the chaos that was India – the world's biggest democracy – a country with a thousand gods and a billion Bollywood movies – maybe more of each. One Indian migrant worker said on international television:

> They told us to wear masks, wash hands, maintain social distancing but what is government's responsibility? If we do not die of Coronavirus then we'll die of starvation. Another Indian migrant worker stated that everyone takes advantage during troubled times.
>
> AL JAZEERA, 2020

In about the same time that England colonised India, it had also generously exported capitalism to South Africa – even though the then South Africa's peoples did not ask for it. There was no referendum to decide whether colonialism or capitalism was good for the country or not. Instead, violence and wholesale looting of the country was the language spoken by the British Empire. As in England, workers have built South Africa – as cheap slave-like-labour under colonialism and apartheid – and as free workers under non-racial capitalism. They have done so under the command and control of effective and efficient states – working in tandem with the capitalist class. When and where workers demand more, they are not given a rebuking as *Oliver Twist* was; they are at times met with the full might of the South African state – sometimes violently. Marikana – 2012 is a graphic reminder of what happens when the tenuous balancing act between workers and capitalism becomes disrupted. Violence ensues. Capitalism wins!

Capitalism has a love-hate relationship with labour; a love relationship when labour is cheap – a hate relationship when labour is expensive. When and where labour is cheap, capitalism employs human energy in its millions. When labour raises its value, capitalism discards human energy and looks to other forms of energy – coal, nuclear and gas being the primary forms that capitalism depends on in all parts of the globe. In fact, this is the modus operandi of capitalism: it requires a constant and cheap supply of energy in general – and human energy in particular. The dirt-cheap human-energy of men, women and children is what fed the Industrial Revolution in England in the 18th and 19th century. The cheap human-energy of men, women and children is what feeds the capitalist enterprise on a daily basis in the 21st century – in countries where labour laws are weak. In South Africa, human-energy remains unemployed at levels of 34.4%. The unemployment of youth human-energy is as high as 70%!

COVID-19 took the wind out of capitalism's sails; the unemployment of human-energy in all parts of the world has risen, thereby depriving capitalism of its only source of value – human energy. Capitalism hates interruptions to its historical profit-making project. It therefore has to play catch-up. If workers stand still – then capitalism stands still. If workers move – then capitalism moves. Hence when the profit-economy was forced to open whilst COVID-19 was still very much part of global society, capitalism had little appetite to instil health and occupational annoyances to its functioning:

> As the economy slowly reopens amid the coronavirus pandemic, many workers have been forced to balance their health and safety with their ability to eke out a living. The trade union federation contended that 'thousands of employers are not complying with the new occupational health and safety protocols and conditions set out to reopen the economy'.
> SMIT, 2020

History matters in South Africa – as it does in all parts of the world. South African workers – whose ancestors once owned land in a country where land and the bounty of nature is plentiful – were compelled to sell their human-energy on the labour market in the time of COVID-19. Surely this state of affairs cannot be the hallmark of The End of History ideology!

First World countries depend on labour that is immersed in Third World conditions. At a slaughterhouse in Alberta, Canada:

> 935 employees at the facility that accounts for 36 per cent of the coun-try's beef production had tested positive. One employee has died, Bui Thi Hiep. A Globe and Mail investigation into the Cargill outbreak revealed an environment in which employees, who are largely immigrants and temporary foreign workers, said they felt pressured to work even as the COVID-19 cases continued to rise. A number of employees said the com-pany's medical staff cleared them to continue working despite symp-toms, positive COVID-19 test results, incomplete isolation periods and recent travel abroad. Ms. Hiep, the Cargill employee who died, was in her 60s and worked at the Alberta meat-packing plant for more than two decades. Her death, two weeks ago, has left her husband, Nguyen Nga, uncertain of his future. 'In this country, if you work they'll think of you. When you no longer work, I'm not sure you'll be remembered'. She's been known as 'the worker who died', Marichu Antonio, executive director of Action Dignity, said. 'We want to put the face to it and emphasise that these people are human beings'.
>
> TAIT ET AL., 2020: 1

In Ontario, Canada: "More than 950 migrant farm workers in Ontario have tested positive for COVID-19, according to a Globe and Mail tally of local public-health units" (Stone et al., 2020). If the premier of Ontario chose not to compare Canada's response to the pandemic with that of China's – he chose to make a questionable comparison between Canada and the Third World:

> 'We're Canada, we aren't in some Third World nation that you have to run from the authorities. We're here to help you, not to hurt you,' Mr. Ford said at the time.
>
> STONE ET AL., 2020

Still in Canada:

> Bonifacio Romero, 31, died of COVID 19 on May 30, and Rogelio Muñoz
> Santo died on June 4. Both were migrant agricultural workers from
> Mexico and previously healthy. 'That we don't know anything about
> Bonifacio and Rogelio is the point,' says Hennebry. 'We think of them as
> workers rather than people with families and interests who have sacri-
> ficed a lot to be here. That's one of the problems with the system; they're
> seen as interchangeable'.
>
> GERBER, 2020

The working class is the most important component of the capitalist infrastructure and scaffolding in First World countries. In Europe migrant workers are:

> Needed to pick strawberries, oranges, melons, tomatoes and asparagus.
> Germany has in recent weeks received 30,000 seasonal workers from
> Eastern Europe and expects another 30,000 by the end of May, most for
> asparagus and strawberry harvests. In theory strict guidelines govern
> their journeys and living and working conditions. But reality is proving
> messy.
>
> CARROLL ET AL., 2020

The West is known to preach idealism to the rest of the world whilst accepting, downplaying or denying the messiness of reality back home. In a part of
Europe that is treated as somewhat of an outcast:

> The stakes are particularly high in Italy where crops risk rotting in the
> fields and a political battle is escalating. The sector relies on hundreds of
> thousands of migrants, most sub-Saharan Africans without proper work
> permits. Many live in squalid shacks cobbled from wood and plastic that
> bake in summer and freeze in winter. Tonino Russo of the CGIL labour
> union in Sicily said that 'without these people, agriculture in Italy is on
> its knees'.
>
> CARROLL ET AL., 2020

It seems that Britain has not lost its appetite for slavery. In the UK:

> Labour has called on the government to ensure proper legal action
> is being taken against UK companies found to be doing business with

overseas PPE suppliers accused of abhorrent modern slavery practices. The Independent which showed the government has repeatedly sourced PPE from companies in Malaysia facing modern slavery allegations, despite promises to crack down on suppliers accused of labour abuses.

LOVETT, 2021

A stint as a COVID-19 patient made the UK prime minister conscious of the relevance of workers in British society. Boris Johnson stated after his discharge from intensive care that "cleaners, cooks, etc. at the NHS kept coming to work". On the other hand – free choice is a double-edged sword when it comes to work in capitalist society.

In the US, where one has a chance of becoming president – and most of becoming economically and socially insecure and irrelevant:

> Governor Gavin Newsom explained that there are many reasons Latino workers, including farmworkers who make up 93% of the state's agricultural labourers, are bearing the brunt of California's cases. Farmworkers in particular often live in crowded housing, sharing space with other families. Many are transported to job sites in packed vans, and they have little access to healthcare, including testing, and personal protective equipment. When they fall ill, the realities of lost wages may drive them to work anyway, exposing others. But according to advocates for agricultural employees, the coronavirus is also ravaging Latino farmworkers because they have long been treated as disposable labour in California, risking their lives in heat waves and pesticide-laden fields to help put food on people's tables.
>
> CHABRIA, 2020

Capitalist ideology and myth about the virtues of a country's economic growth, success and security were exposed in the time of COVID-19. Capitalism – it seems – means success and security for the few, hardship and insecurity for the many:

> COVID-19 has brought into sharp relief the contrast between the experiences of the higher-income Americans who receive deliveries and the lower-income Americans who fulfil them, between those who can work safely from home and those who must expose themselves to risk, often with inadequate protection, between those who have the power to safeguard their health and their living standards and those who do not.
>
> SUMMERS ET AL., 2020

Next to the greatest nation on earth – and in the corridor of labour reserves feeding the capitalist monster:

> The Mexican government released a plan to gradually reopen the economy, beginning on 18 May, although many factories never stopped. All along the 2,000-mile border, maquila workers have died of COVID-19. In Ciudad Juárez, 18 workers at a textile factory owned by the American Lear Corp have reportedly died of coronavirus. The re-openings came after weeks of pressure from US officials.
>
> WATTENBARGER, 2020

In Texan prisons – prisoners were apparently forced to make soaps and sanitisers which they themselves were not able to use. This is not in North Korea or in China. This is in the United States of America – where forced labour is apparently frowned upon. Investigative journalism exposed the dark, dull and dreary spaces of capitalism in the time of COVID-19:

> The Centre for Disease Control and Prevention said coronavirus cases were confirmed among thousands of workers in meat and poultry processing facilities across the country in April, affecting more than 100 plants in upward of a dozen states. The CDC said it examined data from 115 meat or poultry facilities in 19 states. These plants employed more than 130,000 workers, more than 4,900 of whom had confirmed cases. At least 20 coronavirus deaths were reported.
>
> GEARAN ET AL., 2020

Like slaves under slave society – and peasants in feudal society – workers are not considered to be fully human in capitalist society:

> 'There's been a lot of talk about essential workers', said Rob Baril, president of Service Employees International Union, which represents nursing home workers in Connecticut and Rhode Island. 'They're treated like they're expendable workers'.
>
> MULCAHY ET AL., 2020

Some workers saw through capitalist ideologies and demanded pragmatic solutions to their plight:

> Just two weeks ago, President Trump had personally extended his gratitude to truckers, welcoming representatives of the industry to the White

House and calling truckers 'the foot soldiers' in the war against the novel coronavirus. But now, 'the American truck driver needs help, and we need it now,' said Santiago, a 21-year veteran of the industry from New Jersey. 'This is our distress call to our commander-in-chief to address the problems we are facing. He has called us heroes – his heroes need his help now'. The economic pain truckers say they are facing comes on top of difficult conditions on the road, with long waits to pick up and drop off goods and only limited options for health care suitable for someone driving a large truck.

DUNCAN, 2020: 20

If capitalists own the means of production, then it means that their lives and livelihoods are secured under capitalism. Since workers do not own the means of production, the insensitive and ruthless character of capitalism was shored-up in the time of COVID-19. In Australia:

US-owned laundry giant Alsco has sacked 155 low-paid workers across Australia after telling them to use up their annual leave during the COVID-19 crisis, in conduct their union called an 'industrial massacre'. Workers, some of whom have been with the company for more than 30 years, said they were given a couple of hours' notice and ordered to clean out their lockers and leave the premises. If Alsco has the money to buy their major competitor, then they can afford to keep on their loyal and hardworking staff. It's yet another example of a company kicking workers while they're down. It's a case of a corporation securing its own short-term profits at the expense of the public good.

HANNAN, 2020

The profit-economy is comfortable with people being casualties – but never with profit becoming a casualty. This is the reigning ideology of capitalism. In Thailand – the country that served as a US military base for the unpopular capitalist war on communist Vietnam and its people – migrant workers also experienced extreme hardship in the time of COVID-19:

Four months pregnant, unemployed and relying on money borrowed from friends, War War Hywe, a 29-year-old migrant worker from Myanmar's city of Mandalay, wishes she could go home. 'If I wasn't pregnant, it would be fine if I skipped a meal. But now that I'm four months pregnant, I'm very worried about the baby's health,' she said, stroking her bulging belly.

All she can do now is keep telling her baby to be strong while waiting for
her husband to come back soon.

CHAROENSUTHIPAN, 2020

Most workers were battling to survive in the time of COVID-19, but one Al
Jazeera correspondent put it aptly: Capitalist society was "kicking someone
when they are already down".

Sex is a free gift of nature between consenting adults – but it is a paid-for
and expensive commodity under capitalism. There are almost 300 000 sex
workers in capitalist Japan. Many of them put their lives at risk by visiting cli-
ents at their homes. It's always the stark choice between COVID-19 and starving
to death with their children. People the world over have witnessed the ruthless
DNA of capitalism; Boeing asked workers to volunteer for retrenchment. The
company did not want to accept government subsidies to keep workers on.
The working class has always had it bad under capitalism. Friedrich Engels
captured the wretched lives of the working class under early capitalism well
in his 1845 *The Conditions of the Working Class in England*. Even in the dying
days of feudalism, the workers were the worse-off in society when pandemics
occurred:

> The succession of pandemics in the fourteenth and early fifteenth centu-
> ries decimated the working classes, with their poorer diet and sanitation,
> even more than the better to do.
>
> FRIEDMAN, 2003: 43–44

It was no different in the time of COVID-19 under the system called capitalism.

3   Workers: Creators of Value – Even during a Pandemic

People needed masks and hand sanitisers in order to reduce the risk of contracting COVID-19. Masks and hand sanitisers are made by workers in different
parts of the world. Health care workers needed gowns, visors, swabs, etc. in
order to do battle with COVID-19. Gowns, visors, swabs etc. are made by workers
in different parts of the world. People needed ventilators and other life-saving
equipment in order for them to have a chance at life after having contracted
COVID-19. Ventilators and other life-saving equipment are made by workers in
different parts of the world. People needed body bags and coffins in the time
of COVID-19. Body bags and coffins are made by workers in different parts of
the world. Capitalists, politicians, celebrities and the privileged working from

home needed groceries, fruit, vegetables, meat, fish, toilet rolls, home exercise and training apparel, indoor games, etc. in order to stay alive and stay sane in the time of COVID-19. Such commodities are produced by workers in different parts of the world.

If millions died but billions survived – it is because workers in all parts of the world kept the livelihoods economy going – as they always do under capitalism. They picked the fruit and the vegetables and sorted them. They drove the trucks that transported the fruit and vegetables. They kept the treadmill of the livelihood's economy moving in the time of COVID-19, most times at risk to their own and their family's lives. The workers are the central cogs in the capitalist production and distribution machine. COVID-19 provided the empirical evidence and data for this fact of life under capitalism. Workers had to keep moving – whilst the rest of the world had to stop moving – in order for the world to have a chance of winning the war against COVID-19. The workers left their homes in the early hours of the morning – and arrived back late at night. They delivered food to homes in cars, on bikes and on foot. They made the coffins, transported the dead, dug the graves and laid the dead in the ground. Workers picked the fruit and milked the cows so that humankind could have fruit and milk and the better off in capitalist society could have strawberries and cream. As is usual when capitalism is deprived of its oxygen to stay alive, those with symbolic and ideological capital help to mobilise the armies of labour that lie scattered about in capitalist society:

> You know you have worries when the future king is warning about food security. Prince Charles this week implored workers furloughed by the pandemic to get out into the fields and 'pick for Britain. If we are to harvest British fruit and vegetables this year, we need an army of people to help' he said.
>
> BOOTH ET AL., 2020

COVID-19 made clear how the capitalist economy rests uneasily on the backs and shoulders of the working class. These were the essential workers – soldiers securing lives, livelihoods and dignity in death – in the time of a global pandemic.

That labour is what provides humankind with life and livelihoods was recognised by Adam Smith in his *The Wealth of Nations* (1776) – about 250 years ago:

> The annual labour of every nation is the fund which originally supplies it with all the necessaries and conveniences of life which it annually

consumes, and which consist always either in the immediate produce of
that labour, or in what is purchased with that produce from other nations.
SMITH, 1776: 12

Workers of the world cooperated in order to produce commodities such as
masks, gloves, gowns, etc. This is owing to the specialisation of labour – the
primary pillar for capitalism's functioning. Humans have to work with nature
in order to survive. Let us take rubber gloves, for example, that are an integral
part of the PPEs for health care workers. Large tracts of land are cleared in
order to make way for rubber trees. Workers are central to the land clearing
process. The equipment required for clearing the land are themselves made by
workers in many parts of the world. Workers are required for planting the rubber trees when they are mere seedlings. Workers are required for watering the
rubber trees, tending to them and ensuring that they grow into mature trees.

Once the rubber trees are mature, the worker must make a nick into the rubber tree. The instrument she uses to make the incision is also made by workers
in many parts of the world. The worker then harvests the rubber in the form
of latex. This is known as tapping. The latex rubber is collected in small non-
metal containers that are suspended onto the rubber trees. The containers
themselves are made by workers in many parts of the world. Once the containers are full with latex rubber, the rubber is emptied into larger containers and
transported to rubber factories. Here too the forms of transport used are made
by workers in different parts of the world. A variety of labour is necessary and
employed in making the production of PPEs – such as rubber gloves – possible.
Once in the rubber factories, workers are responsible for converting the liquid
rubber produced by nature into sheets of rubber. The machines used to assist
the process are themselves made by workers in different parts of the world.
The sheets of rubber are then transported to glove-making factories where
they are made into rubber gloves which are then transported to countries in all
parts of the world for use by health care workers.

Like all commodities – whether these are mobile phones, coffee, indoor and
outdoor bikes, board games, etc. – rubber gloves are made by armies of workers in all parts of the world. Adam Smith in his *The Wealth of Nations* outlined
the cooperative nature of workers under capitalism in so far as the production
of commodities are concerned: "without the assistance and co-operation of
many thousands, the very meanest person in a civilised country could not be
provided" (Smith, 1776: 27). Cooperation amongst producers – instead of competition – is therefore a fundamental requirement for the making of rubber
gloves – which health workers so desperately needed in the time of COVID-19.
It is the same for all other commodities required by humankind. It is the same

for vaccines and the infrastructure that supports vaccine manufacture and distribution. Capitalism is highly productive because man as a worker has the
potential to be highly productive – more so when he cooperates with his fellow
man – instead of when he competes with him!

But the capitalist economy expects the worker to produce not only use-value
but exchange-value as well. We thus see the two-fold nature of the economy in
capitalist society. Hence in the time of COVID-19; society was torn between
producing use-value commodities and exchange-value or profit. We witnessed
this contradiction of the capitalist economy with regards to vaccines. The free-
marketeers and their state supporters wanted exchange-value or profit. The
rest of society wanted use-value or useful commodities such as masks, sanitisers, food, PPEs, vaccines, etc.

The workers create both use-value and exchange-value in the capitalist
economy. They produced useful commodities of all sorts for COVID-19 society's
consumption – as well as exchange-value or profit for the capitalist class. With
their human energy and time – the working class continued to create value in
the time of COVID-19. If the wealth of Jeff Bezos, Elon Musk and other mega
capitalists increased many-fold in the time of COVID-19, then the workers in
many parts of the world – with their human energy and time – generated value
and the biggest chunks of the value created were channelled to the kings of
the big corporations under the ideology of profit being a necessity for business owners. Such a phenomenon has been going on for a long time: "since
the 1970s, our number of working poor has increased sharply. Nearly all of
our much-vaunted newly created wealth has gone to the richest" (Friedman,
2003:1).

Where surplus-value is created in a society premised on equal exchange,
then the surplus-value generated is the equivalent to the quantity of the
human energy and time of the workers of that society. If the capitalist contrib-
utes his human energy and time, then he too acts as a worker – adding value
to the already vast reservoirs of value in capitalist society – most of it stored in
banks and private property. As to why the capitalist extracts most of the value
created – and the worker is given very little of the value created – this is a question for a post-COVID-19 society to ponder upon. Even in the time of COVID-19,
value created by the working class was ingeniously extracted from them by
capitalist ideologies backed by the state and its laws:

> Even in the best of times, gig work offered few protections. But the pan-
> demic has increased the stakes of operating without a safety net. Most
> on-demand companies offset thin profit margins by offloading the risk
> onto workers, who are classified as independent contractors and have to

provide their own vehicle and gas. There is a lack of basic employee protections. Take-home pay is volatile, and there is no minimum wage or overtime pay.

TIKU, 2020

If the workers gave their all or most in the time of COVID-19, then capitalism made sure that they get least in return:

As workers have become less able to share in the profits generated by their firms, income has been redistributed from employees to the owners of capital. That has contributed to higher income inequality along class and race lines.

SUMMERS ET AL., 2020

But it was observed much earlier on in the life of capitalism that the productive worker receives far less – whilst the less productive capitalist receives far more of the productive fruits of the capitalist economy. Friedrich Engels – as far back as 1845 – about one hundred and seventy-five years ago, observed:

What is to become of those destitute millions, who consume today what they earned yesterday; who have created the greatness of England by their inventions and their toil; who become with every passing day more conscious of their might, and demand, with daily increasing urgency, their share of the advantages of society?

ENGELS, 1845: 16

As to why contemporary society comprises a few million capitalists – but billions of workers amongst the human race – is another question for a post-COVID-19 society to ponder upon. We can however take a cue from the economic scientist and scholar, Karl Marx, who made it known that:

One thing, however, is clear – Nature does not produce on the one side owners of money or commodities, and on the other men possessing nothing but their own labour power. This relation has no natural basis, neither is its social basis one that is common to all historical periods. It is clearly the result of a past historical development, the product of many economic revolutions, of the extinction of a whole series of older forms of social production.

MARX, 1867: 121

And because the workers are not part owners of the means of production, and were forced to sell the only property they own on the labour market viz. their human energy – they died in their numbers, whilst the capitalist class were mostly insulated from COVID-19. In the main, those who owned the means of production lived – whilst many who owned nothing but their human-energy as their only commodity by which to eke out a living – perished:

> If the economic burden of the lockdown has been destructive for capital, it has been devastating for labour. Most workers own little means of subsistence and are precariously dependent on the market for their labour power. They retain in the form of wages part of the wealth they create and realise for capital. But any disruption in the operation of capital is immediately detrimental to its very existence. Labour under capitalism is not awarded the same liberty as capital in separating its personhood from its economic entity. While the latter can lawfully bankrupt itself without a sliver of threat to personal well-being, any downturn in economic conditions precipitates into a crisis of social reproduction for labour. So, while for capital the lockdown is a crisis of preserving and furthering wealth, for labour it is a matter of sustaining life.
>
> DEEPAK, 2020

Like the underclass on the *Titanic* that went under – the workers of capitalist society were destined to be the sacrificial lambs in the time of COVID-19. Whilst many countries in the Western world were likely contenders, no other country better demonstrated this fact than capitalist India – the neighbour of communist China. Workers of the world carried the world on their shoulders and backs in the time of COVID-19 – as they usually do under capitalism. They paid the heaviest price in the time of COVID-19 – as they usually do under capitalism. When one accepts this as fact, then it is not difficult to understand why Karl Marx has the following maxim engraved on his tombstone in Highgate cemetery in London: *"Workers of all lands unite – you have nothing to lose but your chains"!*

CHAPTER 8

The Ideology of the Invisible Hand or Capitalist Market under Capitalism

There are no limits to what free men, free women, and free markets can accomplish.

JACK KEMP

• • •

This country has socialism for the rich, and rugged individualism for the poor.

MARTIN LUTHER KING JR.

•   •
•

1   The Invisible Hand and Capitalist Market in the Time of COVID-19

COVID-19 not only gave us a glimpse into the poor state of public health in so many parts of the world – and exposed the West's chaotic understanding of freedom and liberty and the tenuous conditions of the working class under capitalism – it also heaped onto society the science of the economy – at least the science of the economy as put forward mainly by the defenders and supporters of the capitalist economy. Like so many economic terms – both familiar and unfamiliar – that made an entry into the global discourse in the time of COVID-19, a much-cherished economic science concept that came to the surface of capitalist society was that of the "invisible hand":

> At this stage of the pandemic, the main problem afflicting the economy is the heavy hand of government. It is because the government is unwilling to allow the supply and demand sides to freely transact with each other. Curfews are not justified by the pandemic. The COVID-19 virus does not travel any more swiftly by night than by day. Using the night time for work (as well as play) allows more physical distancing in the daytime.

The invisible hand promotes cooperation without coercion, at no financial expense.

MANGAHAS, 2020

We all know about the continued bombardment of advertisements and the
coercive impact such advertisements have on people – to part with their hard-
earned monies. We are also aware of how workers were coerced to go back to
work in the time of a global pandemic. The writer goes on to proudly announce
the names of the economic scientists and scholars that he is a staunch disciple
of – and how it came to be that he is able to practice his ideological craft of
distorting economic reality with economic myths and economic fake news –
which tend to have staying-power in capitalist society:

> Adam Smith, one of the founders of economics, observed centuries ago
> (The Theory of Moral Sentiment, 1759; The Wealth of Nations, 1776) that
> there is 'an invisible hand' that keeps an economy in order, and benefits
> society as a whole, even as individual people freely pursue their personal
> self-interest. It was my good fortune to study at the University of Chicago,
> and learn first-hand from the great economic freedom fighter Milton
> Friedman (Capitalism and Freedom, 1962: Free to Choose, 1980). For
> Friedman, freedom is the end, and capitalism is a means. I am a founding
> member of the Foundation for Economic Freedom (fef.org.ph), where
> the prevailing general sentiment, I believe, is that the people's economic
> well-being has already suffered too long from the government's overly
> restrictive policies.
>
> MANGAHAS, 2020

We in South Africa also have economic freedom fighters – in the form of a
political party known as Economic Freedom Fighters. Like Milton Friedman –
they are ardent economic freedom fighters. Unlike Milton Friedman – they
wish to see the back of capitalism in South Africa asap! Who can blame them
when one witnesses the devastation caused by the development of capitalism
in the country!

The writer is so wrapped up in the smothering ideological garb of Adam
Smith and Milton Friedman that even his thinking has become restricted from
moving – from its fairy-tale position on the workings of the capitalist economy to a common sense understanding of the failures of the capitalist market
– and the invisible hand – in shaping and contributing to a liveable and well-
being society for all. The invisible hand is a metaphysical expression for the
capitalist market. Just like the many gods that occupy the minds of much of

humankind – the invisible hand has been secured a divine presence amongst the countless deities created by man's astounding imagination. When it suits the disciples of capitalist market theology, they argue for the capitalist market to be rescued by an effective state. Once the capitalist market is on its feet again, they argue aggressively for it to be allowed free reign to continue on its disparaging ways:

> Pandemics, wars and national catastrophes pose a particular challenge to free-marketeers. It is not just that they require an enormous dose of centralised, government intervention, policies that are anathema to small statists in ordinary times. An even greater problem is that central planning and huge expansions in welfare are extraordinarily addictive.
> HEATH, 2020

I wonder if capitalist marketeers would object to welfare and state support being handed out to the private sector on a continual basis? How about supporting free market monies like Bitcoin? We don't hear the loud voices of free marketeers on the Libra money that Facebook intended to put out in society?

In the US – antagonists and critics of the state – even when they are an integral part of that state – championed the capitalist market. Then again, we are all too aware that capitalist marketeers will not chop-off the branch that they are sitting on. The state is the tree trunk from which the capitalist class spreads out its supportive branches. But under capitalism, the fruits and soothing shade of the capitalist economic tree are meant for a select few – not for the many:

> US energy secretary Dan Brouillette told a global summit that democracies should choose the free market over tax and regulation. 'My country is abandoning none of our fuels, and not one iota of economic opportunity, in the quest for a clean energy world'.
> *The Guardian Weekly*, 2020

Those in the West who believe religiously in capitalist market functioning – and waste no time in freely dishing out their gospel – pushed for their citizens to not support the free market comprising commodities produced in China. Capitalist market nationalism or capitalist market apartheid is one of the ideological pillars of capitalism. Here we learn first-hand how the invisible hand works in tandem with visible lobbying and state-bashing, mainly by ideologues in the West:

Meanwhile, the authoritarian Chinese Communist Party recently approved a national security law that curtails free speech and pro-democracy protests in Hong Kong. As a society, we can peacefully protest by refusing to buy Chinese goods. Contact companies such as Walmart, Amazon and big-box stores and tell them to stop importing Chinese products. Importing from other nations, or better yet, having products manufactured in our country to help our workers and citizens, will hit China in its pocketbook.

Santa Fe New Mexican, 2020

What the writer actually conceded was the fact that the capitalist market in the US has not resulted in the workers and citizens becoming better-off.

Making an argument for the gambling industry to not have any state regulation in the Philippines, another writer in the time of COVID-19 states:

The great Adam Smith, known as 'The Father of Economics,' wrote about the invisible hand in his book, 'The Wealth of Nations' in 1776. It is an economic concept carried on for centuries, studied to this very day, yet misinterpreted by few, including Supreme Court justices. Smith hypothesised that society benefits from the individuals' self-interested actions, free from any form of regulation. The invisible hand has become an argument against government regulation, suggesting that self-centric activities can redound for the greater good i.e., pursuit of my business for profit has unintended benefits such as jobs creation and fiscal revenue for the government. Money aside, one cannot discount the truth that Pogos provide jobs to the Filipino people and is an economic stimulant, much needed now in the time of COVID-19.

GUTIERREZ, 2020

To think that people would be speaking and writing about economic scientists in the midst of a global pandemic! The extent of ideological learnings and leanings towards the capitalist system came thick and fast in the time of COVID-19:

Adam Smith, the economist commonly known as the Father of Capitalism, famously wrote of an 'invisible hand' that regulated capitalism. His theory, considered to be one of the cornerstones of our modern economy, was that in a free market consumers and sellers pursuing their own self-interest would lead to everyone ending up better off. The constant back and forth between buyers and sellers looking out only for themselves would, thanks to the invisible hand of the market, lead to lower prices, quality goods, and fair profits.

SCHOTTENFELD, 2020

These defunct ideologues wish for us all to believe that the entire world became better off when some countries in the developed world were looking out for themselves and pursuing their own interests – by buying and hording vaccines! Countries in many parts of the world were waiting for the "greater good" to come to their shores under the gospel of self-interest – but it seems that the Second Coming was more probable than receiving meaningful supplies of vaccines from self-interested countries! Self-interest rewards the self – no greater good comes out of self-interest! The developed world was already selfishly giving 3rd vaccine doses and booster shots to its citizens – whilst only about 5% of the population of Africa was vaccinated!

As if visible and known capitalists like Jeff Bezos and Elon Musk were not trying to make huge profits in the time of COVID-19, ideological fanatics of the capitalist market continued to wrap the capitalist market in a mystical shroud – absent of conscious and planning capitalists:

Amid the chaos and the disorienting paradigm shifts, though, something profound is also happening – the invisible hand is operating on itself with dispatch. Even without government intervention, the invisible hand is doing its own work.

LANE, 2020

In capitalist South Africa, adorable thoughts on the capitalist market is never in short supply:

The market will be watching closely to see whether the government stays on the path of fiscal consolidation it outlined last year to contain SA's spiralling public debt level, which Mboweni warned could see SA face a sovereign debt crisis within a few years if action was not taken.

JOFFE, 2021

What the writer may have actually meant when she says "the market will be watching closely" is that the capitalist class will be watching the South African state very closely. Her capitalist market ideology conceals the fact that the capitalist class is a key player in the capitalist economy – and the one monitoring the state, rewarding the economy when it proves profitable and punishing the economy when it proves unprofitable for the capitalist class:

And though market players are expected to be supportive of higher spending on a vaccine rollout, they will be looking at whether the government sticks to its attempt to cut the public sector wage bill as a bellwether signal of its commitment to cut its debt in coming years.

JOFFE, 2021

With threats like these – who needs bank robbers!

2   Producing and Reproducing Lives and Livelihoods through the Capitalist Market

We once hunted and gathered our food before we became bartering and free market animals. For our cultural and leisure lives, we did not buy our paints and rocks from Walmart – we made our own paints and painted on the rocks of the Drakensberg Mountains in South Africa, the Maros-Pangkep caves in Indonesia, the Dordogne region of France, in the Kakadu National Park in Australia, in the Cantabria region of Spain, the Magura Cave in Bulgaria, and elsewhere on planet earth. Our bows, arrows and spears were made by us – after mixing our labour with nature – and not ordered through Amazon.

Our clothing and jewelry were not bought from Harrods but made by us – with nature as the substratum. There was no invisible hand bringing commodities to our valleys, mountains and plains – the act of producing and reproducing one's life and livelihood was concrete and material in shape and form. Using our very visible hands, we had to mix our human energy and time with nature – in order to make a life and a livelihood. If there was no free market – at least nature was free for the taking. But we took little from nature as hunter-gatherers. We take without limits from nature under capitalism. The word for this under capitalism has come to be known as greed.

If we wanted water – the rivers and lakes were abundant in nature for Homo sapiens – free of modern affluents, pollution and nuclear reactive waste – like the one that countries like Japan wish to empty into the oceans. If we wanted fruit and vegetables – nature provided. If we wanted medicine – nature provided. When we wanted energy feedstock – we took the wood from nature and used it to warm our caves and ourselves in winter. As hunter-gatherers the price we paid to take the free gifts of nature was our human energy and time. We did this for hundreds of thousands of years. With experience, mistakes and best practices, we learnt to exchange two deer for one beaver. It's probably because twice the amount of human energy and time were spent hunting beaver than deer. If exchange is predicated on equality – then how one gains more of the deer or beaver – viz. a profit – must be a mystery to any 21st century economics scientist! I guess the Queen of England has a thought or two on the calibre of mainstream economic scientists of our time.

In any event, we still hunted and gathered – but we found a way to exchange our surplus commodities. We introduced barter or exchange into our economic and social lives. In the act of exchanging one beaver for two deer – we may have created the first exchange market. There was no state telling us what to exchange on the market. Then again there was no state printing money and pouring it like liquid into the market – thereby forming what is known as a liquidity market. Our wives may have instructed us as to what to take from our caves and exchange in the market. Otherwise the markets were free then.

Nature determined what could and could not be exchanged. Only those countries with gold could use it as a medium of exchange. Some used shells. If we wish to have a totally free market now, then the state must be removed from the equation of printing and controlling money. It seems it's what the innovators had in mind when they invented Bitcoin. Bitcoin – like climate change and Jerusalema – has made a name for itself in recent times. It's what Facebook had in mind when it wished to come up with the currency it called Libra. This project was soon quashed – by the capitalist market itself it seems – in tandem with the capitalist state! I wonder if capitalist marketeers would push for states to not have control over money in a post-COVID-19 economy? If he who pays the piper calls the tune – then he who prints the money that pays the piper creates the tune.

When it comes to creating the conditions for the unrestrained functioning of the capitalist market – no power does it better than the state! The invisible hand is no match for the state in securing the capitalist economy! In any event, ever since the exchanging of deer and beaver – humans have been making stuff and exchanging them in markets:

> Although an actual economy is a complex entity with many facets, mainstream economics focuses in large part on what is called 'the market'. Markets, as places of exchange and trade, have existed since antiquity. However, they were less important in the distant past, because most production of necessities took place in households. It was only in the sixteenth century that markets became a primary way to satisfy daily needs and a place where prices were formed. Adam Smith elevated the study of markets in eighteenth century England to a position of prominence in an era characterised by agriculture and small-scale manufacturing. Here farmers would lay out the leftover vegetables and eggs that they did not use themselves and trade them for money to buy other things such as the

products of various smiths or artisans. In these environments purchasers could take their usually hard-earned money and carefully choose what was most needed or desired for their lives without too much in the way of manipulation or compelling authority. Contemporary mainstream economics believes that in an almost magical way 'the market' will generate the maximum possible human well-being by generating the largest possible number of most desirable goods and services for each member simply attempting to achieve his or her own self-interest. In the words of Adam Smith – 'it is not from the benevolence of the butcher, the brewer, or the baker that we expect our dinner, but from their regard to their own interest'. Thus, the basic concept of how economies are thought to work in a 'free market' situation is that consumers will purchase goods and services to suit their own conception of the psychological satisfaction each purchase will make and that suppliers will shift to make what people want, for that is where they make their own largest profit. As consumers purchase additional commodities, they will get less satisfaction from the extra one and shift to another commodity. Market is often imbued with nearly mystical power. Former President Ronald Reagan often spoke about the 'magic of the market'.

HALL and KLITGAARD, 2018: 6–7

For the past few centuries, we have been told that we have to get what we need through the capitalist market. So of late we have decided that we need an endless quantity of products and services. The preachers of the capitalist market have insisted – and continue to insist – that in order to get stuff from nature we have to go through the capitalist market. If we decide to hunt and gather under capitalism, then this would be regarded as poaching and a punishable crime.

Capitalist society has also foisted it upon us to be institutionally educated. Here too, we have to ensure that we get our education through the capitalist market. All other forms of education – not accessed through the capitalist market – are stigmatised as less than superior. So indigenous knowledge does not have the same standing as other forms of knowledge – especially the forms of knowledge that come from the West. Sickness is a prevalent feature of capitalist society. Mental health challenges, burnout, stress, etc. are epidemic in capitalist society. But having a chance at getting better in capitalist society means that one has to go through the capitalist market. Some dying with COVID-19 in private hospitals were more concerned with how they were going to pay their bills than losing their lives. This is the capitalist market that Milton Friedman elevated to god-like status and won a Nobel Prize in economics for!

Ideologies, myths and fake news in economics are well rewarded – materially – and in terms of social status! Good health will have a better chance of being secured when humankind finds a cure for capitalism itself. Even sex – a free gift of nature between consenting adults in civilised society – is now a pricey commodity – thanks to the capitalist market. Self-interest in matters of sex is bound to leave one alone and lonely – no greater good is bound to come out of sex predicated on self-interest and individualism. You need two to tango! Sex sells – thanks to the capitalist market. Books like "No Money, No Honey" and songs like "No Romance Without Finance" are reminders of the beauty and sexiness of free market capitalism!

Markets have become extremely complex beasts with the development of economic man. We may not readily be able to get beaver and deer through the capitalist market – but we certainly can get a million other stuffs like paint, bows, arrows, spears, body jewelry etc. that may suit our tastes. But markets themselves are informed and shaped by the availability of commodities made by workers in all parts of the world.

3   Toward Uncovering the Fake News about the Invisible Hand and Free Market under Capitalism

The world is drowning in a sea of commodities – thanks to the capitalist market and the invisible hand – except in China where the state has a steady hand in the capitalist market – as it had in its response to COVID-19. Everybody has the freedom to participate in the capitalist market. The capitalist market enables innovation, creativity, hard work, etc. The capitalist market allows for people in all parts of the world to cooperate in producing commodities that people need and don't need. The fundamental principle of the capitalist market is that of competition. It is important and necessary for vaccine manufacturers to compete with each other in order to produce the best vaccines, to produce these in record time, to produce these with the least cost, and to sell these at the lowest price to countries and people in all parts of the world. The capitalist market prides itself on competition; and so, by the beginning of 2021, after about a year since COVID-19 was known; wealthy countries started to roll out vaccines. It was a world record – thanks to competition amongst countries. History and ideology was part of the mix as well. Russia was first to develop the Sputnik V vaccine. China developed and rolled out the Sinovac vaccine. The US developed and rolled out the Pfizer and Johnson and Johnson vaccines. The UK developed and rolled out the Moderna and AstraZeneca vaccines.

But untrammelled competition, it seems, did not deliver the best for human-kind; AstraZeneca, after first being abandoned by South Africa – was refused by one country after another – after it was allegedly found to be deficient in quality. Instead of saving lives – the AstraZeneca was allegedly found to be putting some lives in danger. Then in April of 2021, the US state halted the use of Johnson and Johnson – also for allegedly putting lives in danger. South Africa followed suit. Capitalist market competition – instead of bringing out the best in innovation – was apparently proving to be a danger to life and limb. The Western world did a splendid job when – instead of competing with each other – it collaborated and cooperated in bombing Iraq in 2003. They also did a splendid job when – instead of competing with each other – they collaborated and cooperated in bombing Libya in 2011. Competition – it seems – would have been messy for the warmongers of the West!

If the US capitalist market could not supply PPEs to its health workers, it is because the magic of the US capitalist market turned out to be a nightmare in the time of COVID-19. If the many COVID-19 patients were not able to get ven-tilators, it is because the invisible hand directing ventilators to sick and dying patients was nowhere to be seen in the US. I guess to expect to see something as an invisible hand is to invite concern for one's mental state. The US presi-dent had to step in to make the capitalist market – with its huge resources – work for sick Americans: "last week Trump first invoked the emergency powers to compel auto giant General Motors to produce ventilators" (Brenner, 2020). The invisible hand had to be given a rap on the knuckles – in order to get its disappearing act together:

'As usual with this General Motors, things just never seem to work out,' Trump tweeted. 'They said they were going to give us 40,000 much needed Ventilators, very quickly. Now they are saying it will only be 6000, in late April, and they want top dollar'.

CAVAZUTI ET AL., 2020

Top dollar and self-interest is what motivates the capitalist market – not saving lives! The vaccine market was also severely constrained by vaccine national-ism and vaccine apartheid in the time of COVID-19. Here it was quite the vis-ible and heavy hands of Western states – fanatics of Adam Smith who turned against their fellow children, women and men in the time of COVID-19. Some in society felt that COVID-19 had upended the ideology of the invisible hand and capitalist market:

Market economies? Laissez-faire and the invisible hand? These are all antiquated terms that exist only in textbooks. Adam Smith may be rolling over in his grave as widespread nationalisation of financial markets has taken hold. So, how to trade these moves? Always bet on the wealthy. The rich will lobby governments to bail them out, so I doubt markets will collapse. Once in a while, however, investors will get jittery when they hear the worst isn't over and try to cash out. This will be followed by pro-recovery news from governments and the financial press they exist in a symbiotic relationship with – which will cause more rallies. Should markets be rallying? No. Are markets rallying? Yes. Ignore fundamentals, and don't bet against the Fed. Invest with a long-term time horizon, and you should do well even if real economies don't – that is, of course, if you can stomach the roller coaster ride it's going to be.

ARVAS, 2020

Thanks to the capitalist market and the invisible hand that make it possible for two people – the buyer and seller – who agree on the price or money that the one wishes to depart with and the other wishes to attain. In fact we do this everyday – apparently happily and harmoniously – and apparently without any coercion and influence such as constant advertisements from those with power in capitalist society. We depart with our monies for so much of stuff – most of which would most probably end up not being used and taking up healthy spaces in our homes. All praise, glory and worship must go to the capitalist market and the invisible hand for the many unused mobile phones, pc notebooks, clothing, kitchenware, toys, tools, shampoos, dildos, etc. that we collect and hoard – as part of our main mission in life under capitalism! As it is saturated with commodities, the capitalist world is awash with capitalist markets – the fish market, the wet market, the wildlife market as in Wuhan in China, the housing market, the car market, the financial market, the drugs market, the education market, the health market, the travel and tourism market, the food market, the sex market, the money market, the stock market, etc. The most recent and important market is the so-called vaccine market.

The antithesis to the capitalist market and the invisible hand is that of the state: "what we urgently need, for both economic stability and growth, is a reduction of government intervention not an increase" (Friedman, 2002: 38). Had China followed Adam Smith's self-interest ideology and left all and sundry to the capitalist market, it would not have lifted 850 million of its citizens out of poverty. A conscious state with a well thought-out plan is more likely to be successful at taking people out of poverty than the capitalist market, which has a history of pushing people into poverty. The beauty of the market is that people could also be stolen from Africa and sold on the market. The invisible hand and market saw to it that husbands could be separated from their wives, and children from their parents and each other – thanks to the slave market. It's the magic of the market! Let the invisible hand do its work!

Questioning the fallacy of no state support for renewable energy in the capitalist market – a writer to the print media in the time of COVID-19 states:

> If renewable energy is the cheapest option, why do we have to set Renewable Energy Targets and provide special subsidies and incentives to build renewable energy plants? If they are so cheap we should stop all subsidies and Renewable Energy Targets and let renewables compete on an open free enterprise market. Until this happens any claim that renewable energy will provide cheaper electricity is just rubbish.
>
> JOHNSTON, 2020

It seemed not to have occurred to Adam Smith and his self-interested ideologues that – in order for the butcher to serve his own interest – he has to ensure that his customer's interest in meat was worth seeing to; that the brewer's cutomer's interest in good beer may serve the brewer's interest to sustain a livelihood; and that the baker has to make fresh and affordable bread – in order to keep up the interests of customers wanting bread. It would serve economic scientists steeped in self-interest ideology well to know that interests are mutual and co-dependent. That in attempting to meet one's self-interest it is encumbent on one to meet the interest of the other. It is in the interest of all people in all countries to be vaccinated – not just a few. As we were continuosly reminded by the WHO – "no one is safe until everyone is safe". It is in the interest of a man to ensure that his partner's or wife's interests are taken care of – in order to decrease the likelihood of his interests not being taken care of. It is in the interest of the rich and well-off, if the poor are not left to suffer under conditions of unemployment, improper health-care, neglect and indignity. It is not only for the sake of their material interests – but for their moral interest as well. It is probably why Jeff Bezos has agreed to the rich paying more taxes when COVID-19 exposed the sorry state of affairs among much of humankind in the age of capitalism. It is in the interest of the state to ensure that citizens have a good and happy life. Then only might the poor not find it in their interest to engage in revolution.

The Western world, in the main, tried everything in their power to leave the capitalist market and the invisible hand to dominate in the time of COVID-19. But COVID-19 made visible the true and real workings of the ideology of the invisible hand – so worshipped in mainstream economic science upholding capitalism:

> Just look at the government's response to the coronavirus pandemic. Some money was spent on directly helping the American people, but the vast majority of aid was directed at propping up corporate America and a market that has become completely untethered from the real economy that most Americans experience. No rational person can look at a stock market reaching new highs while our economy is on life support and believe the market is reflective of the current state of our economy. Instead it is reflective of a system that is supporting those in society who need that support the least. While the current rhetoric from conservatives in Washington attacks progressive social programs designed to lift those at the bottom as socialism, the truth is that they're the ones giving away irresponsible handouts. Thanks to massive amounts of corporate welfare given out through Fed intervention, lax regulation, and billions of dollars in fiscal stimulus, our free market capitalist society has been replaced by a new era of corporate socialism.
>
> SCHOTTENFELD, 2020

The invisible hand working to enrich the wealthy at the expense of the rest of society was not only evident in the time of COVID-19, but during the Great Crisis of 2008 as well. In the midst of the Great Crisis of 2008 – in a letter to the print media – a reader had this to say:

> Having just been thrown under the bus by the invisible hand, I am grateful for having been missed by the wheels. I fear the invisible hand may stop the bus and back it up for another run at me. I may not be so lucky next time. I'm no socialist, but it seems like the invisible hand does not always deal out benevolence.
>
> KELLY, 2008

In the real capitalist world, the invisible hand and free market are modern economic myths. They are economic superstitions that mask the real workings of the capitalist system and the embedded nature of the state in securing and maintaining the status quo – in favour of the capitalist class and the profit-economy.

Nothing moves without energy. Our entire modern civilisation is premised on energy. Our entire lives revolve around energy. So when the price of oil goes up – then the price of every other aspect of economic life goes up: "so much of our energy system, and by extension the economy, is supported by the use of cheap, abundant fossil fuels" (Merritt, 2016: 1–2). Yet the price of oil is not under the auspices of the so-called free market. It is under the control of the Organization of Petroleum Exporting Countries (OPEC) formed in 1960. It is a cartel:

> By definition, being a cartel is defined in economic terms. Based on the economic definition, a cartel is able to control the price of a good or service by coordinating several top firms in the industry to cooperatively fix the price. To do this, the cartel must control the production rate of the goods or service.
>
> MERRITT, 2016: 10

The capitalist market and the invisible hand will continue to defraud society to complete poverty if the state allows it to do so. For example, the European Commission fined major banks for forex rigging:

> The Commission said the banks – Barclays, the Royal Bank of Scotland (RBS), Citigroup, JPMorgan, UBS and MUFG Bank – had colluded over 11 currencies, including sterling, the euro, the US dollar and the Japanese yen and imposed a fine of €811.2 million on Barclays, RBS, Citigroup and JP Morgan in relation to a case referred to as the 'Forex – Three Way Banana Split' cartel. The second decision related to the so-called 'Forex – Essex Express' cartel and resulted in a total fine of €257.7 million for Barclays, RBS and Bank of Tokyo-Mitsubishi [now MUFG Bank].
>
> DEUTSCHE WELLE, English edition, 26 Dec 2019

It seems that the so-called free market is also the freedom to form cartels. Thanks to states that do involve themselves in the market to break up cartels! Capitalist marketeers and capitalist ideologues have saturated society with the ideology that the capitalist market takes risks in the spheres of innovation, that it is involved in research and development – and therefore the capitalist market is best placed to lead humankind out of poverty and despair – and into prosperity and happiness. It is true that the private sector and private individuals are innovative. But the credit and value allocated to the private sector is overvalued – and most times, fallacious. For example in the area of medicine:

> Government scientists often develop these drugs, and in other cases the government finances the research that leads to the development or

clinical trial of new drugs. But instead of reigning in the drug monopolies, the U.S. government actually works to protect these companies' high prices.

ADLER, 2009: 85

We are all too aware of how the capitalist market tries every economic trick in the book in order to get us to part with our hard-earned monies. Watching a YouTube video only happens after you are forced to sit through advertisements continusouly dished out by the capitalist market. There's no freedom in this! Many have been conned out of their monies – in one way or another – by the capitalist market. There are many – especially in the developing world – who are subjected to high borrowing interest rates when the market is left free to decide on interest rates for borrowed money. Capitalist market theft – enabled by small and endless print on contracts and the reinterpreting of terms and conditions (ts & cs) is not an uncommon practice – even in the time of a global pandemic:

> Australia's consumer watchdog has warned the travel sector it must honour the refund policies that existed at the time of bookings, after widespread complaints that operators were creating new conditions and applying them retrospectively during the COVID-19 crisis.
>
> KNAUS, 2020

The US and much of the world were witnesses to the devastating impacts of the opioid crisis in the US – when the invisible hand and capitalist market were allowed unlimited power. By seeking our own individual interests, we seemed to have damaged or destroyed the interests of others and the interests of future generations. Adam Smith's invisible hand and self-interest ideologies have become fatal ideological weapons – working against humans and nature:

> But despite *laissez faire*'s mediocre track record and despite powerful arguments that it cannot possibly provide what it promises, the notion of the unqualified benefit of the free market has become deeply embedded in our mythology. Apologists have exulted in claims that glorify free market mythology at the expense of reality, and also at the expense of society. Free market principles, even though they have failed in economics, have been eagerly applied to sectors ranging from politics to education, where they have contributed to societal dysfunction.
>
> FRIEDMAN, 2003: 2

If we wish to have a totally free market – then let's all be pure free marketeers and completely get rid of the state! I wonder how many free marketeers would agree to this liberating free market call?

4 The Invisible Hand and Capitalist Market: Mid-wives of Profit and Accumulation for the Rich – and Insufficiency, Insecurity and Misery for the Poor

So, man – the hunter-gatherer who had the bounty of nature to take from – has to now go through the capitalist market in order to produce and reproduce his life and livelihood. But the dominant ideology of the capitalist market is to make a profit – producing and reproducing lives and livelihoods are incidental to the dominant ideology of profit-making. Profit is primary – producing and reproducing lives and livelihoods are secondary – if at all considered. Its why the food indutry turned to feeding cars and aeroplanes instead of people, when sugar cane, corn, etc. started to be converted into biofuels. The invisible hand and capitalist market are primarily premised on exchange value – not use-value:

> In the Third World, there's a two-tiered society – a sector of extreme wealth and privilege, and a sector of huge misery and despair among useless, superfluous people. That division is deepened by the policies dictated by the West. It imposes a neoliberal 'free market' system that directs resources to the wealthy and to foreign investors, with the idea that something will trickle down by magic, sometime after the Messiah comes. The free market is for the poor. We have a dual system – protection for the rich and market discipline for everyone else.
>
> CHOMSKY, 1992

The dominant ideology of the so-called free market in capitalist society has meant that:

> Over the past four decades, governments have sought to prune the welfare state and shift responsibility for services and care onto individuals. Increasingly, citizens are expected to 'live life like an enterprise', 'stand on their own two feet', and not look to the state for 'handouts' or forms of support that one could provide oneself. The demands of the competitive market are remorseless: privatise everything, relinquish the concept of the state as an institutionalised model based on social rights to

market-based model, reduce the range of protection and safety nets such as welfare provisions and labour rights, reduce the cost of labour and maintain a pool of unemployed to discipline those lucky enough to have a job.

AL-BASAM, 2020

The ideology of the so-called free market or capitalist market serves to extract value from the many and direct it to the few. And when the so-called free market is no longer capable of doing this – then the powerful who make the economic rules in capitalist society have no qualms about violating free market principles: "by bending the free market rules that have proven so pliable when elite interests are in peril" (Klein, 2014: 13).

Under capitalism we are no longer creatures of nature. We now belong to the labour market. The task of the labour market is to cheapen humans as much as possible. We no longer exchange beavers for deer – because only a few in capitalist society have become owners of nature – whilst the rest of us have become mere spectators of the wonders of the natural world. We may choose to exchange money for bows, arrows and spears. But nature does not make money, it makes gold, silver and copper – which we humans have ingeniously converted into money. So the only property that most of us have – with which to exchange – is our labour. We do this on the labour market on a regular basis. Every day we are free to sell our labour on the labour market. We compete vigorously with each other for jobs. The swathes of unemployed people under capitalism ensures that vigorous and ruthless competition is kept alive – hence ensuring that the price of labour is continuously driven downwards.

The majority of us are lucky to own labour-power or human-energy which we freely sell on the labour market in order to produce and reproduce our lives. But as to how we have come to be free to sell our labour on the labour market is still a question to be answered. To again invoke Marx:

One thing, however, is clear – nature does not produce on the one side owners of money or commodities, and on the other men possessing nothing but their own labour power. This relation has no natural basis, neither is its social basis one that is common to all historical periods. It is clearly the result of a past historical development, the product of many economic revolutions, of the extinction of a whole series of older forms of social production.

MARX, 1867: 121

It seems, thanks to capitalism, we are free workers – freely selling our labour until we no longer have the strength to do so. Thanks to the invisible hand, we have become freed of property – and therefore free to follow our self-interests which apparently will then contribute to the benefit of all. And, as free individuals in a free market economy, we must feel free to ask the following questions: Should the free market be allowed to decide the quality of vaccines? Should the free market be allowed to decide that an endless supply of cars should inhabit planet earth? Should the free market be allowed to decide whether opioid use is a consumer choice? Should the free market decide that coal and other fossil fuels are the ideal and cheap energy feedstocks for society and the climate? Should the free market decide that children should have the freedom to choose whether to work or not? Should the free market decide that owning guns is a matter of demand and supply?

If society demands free markets, shouldn't society demand free workplaces with free workers as well? Should the state allow the free market to continue in its present hegemonic form? In an age of scientific excellence, should we still hang on to the old and tired ideology and ingrained superstition of an invisible hand – apparently leading all of humankind to a future of prosperity, well-being, nirvana and eternal happiness?

CHAPTER 9

The Nanny State in the Age of Capitalism

The most terrifying words in the English language are: I'm from the government and I am here to help.

RONALD REAGAN

• • •

If Singapore is a Nanny State, then I am proud to have fostered one.

LEE KUAN YEW

• •
•

1   COVID-19 and the Nanny State

The concept of a "nanny state" also made its entrance into global discussions in the time of COVID-19. Some were livid that the state wanted to take control of the unfolding situation during a global pandemic. They wrote letters to the written media:

> We are losing our freedoms as the nanny state is dictating to us, and aren't people tired of having to stay in their 'huts'? After all, we really are social animals. Nanny state, please let us live in dignity and give us our freedoms back.
>
> STEIN, 2020

It is indeed interesting that the writer demanded individual freedom to be a social animal. In South Africa the following sentiment was expressed:

> Instead, like young children, they want mommy – as embodied by the state – to intercede, to banish the nasties and make it all better with a kiss. As a result, the currency of most of our leaders, in every sphere of modern life, is one of honeyed reassurances. Whether it's actual bodies from a foreign invasion or bruised feelings from hurtful words, the assumption from government and governed alike has been that the state

must and will intervene. So go wash those hands, keep your social dis-
tance, and look out for yourself instead of crying for nanny. Helen Keller,
who also wrote 'life is either a daring adventure or nothing', would have
been proud of you.

SAUNDERSON-MEYER, 2020

So as to make all South Africans who relied on the state to protect them from
COVID-19 feel as guilty as hell, the writer quoted president Ramaphosa and
reassured South Africans that they do not need the help of the nanny state:

It's going to get much worse before it gets better. He [Ramaphosa] was
also frank about the limitations to what the government and its agencies
could do: 'It's now in your hands'.

SAUNDERSON-MEYER, 2020

Still in troubled South Africa:

The president stated in parliament that it was difficult to determine when
the ban on the sale of tobacco would be lifted. Can he and his nanny-
comrades provide the following data: 1) the number of smokers who died
without using ventilators. 2) the number of smokers who died notwith-
standing using ventilators.

GILLITS, 2020

After rescinding the ban on alcohol during the pandemic, the nanny state
again imposed the alcohol ban a month later – after COVID-19 numbers sky-
rocketed and motor car accidents, grievous bodily harm and murder rates went
up – putting pressure on an already weakened public health infrastructure in
the most capitalistic country on the African continent.

In the UK, sentiments against the nanny state were just as strong: "the coronavirus pandemic has proved that the many are an ungrateful, nanny stated,
whingeing, criticising culture" (Farmer, 2020).

It is good that the UK has a 'criticising culture', which allows the writer to
criticise with such freedom and zest. In Scotland, liberal idealism and ideology
about freedom from the state in the time of a global pandemic was dished out
in the land of the brave hearts:

Adults should be trusted to be sensible – and, of course, face the consequences of bad decisions. But the nanny state has no place in the weeks

that lie ahead as we enjoy a restoration, in limited form, of cherished freedoms.

Scottish Daily Mail: 2020

Do the rich and powerful face the consequences when they make bad decisions that affect billions of people – as was the case that led to the 2008 financial crisis?

For a while, Australia claimed victory over COVID-19, but then the invisible enemy struck again, and Melbourne had to go back into lockdown. Some were not happy with the nanny-state telling them what to do:

> Now, after temporarily relocating to Melbourne and with the NSW Victorian border closed, I find myself trapped in the nanny state and considering that perhaps NSW Premier Gladys Berejiklian isn't so bad.
>
> NSENDULUKA: 2020

Still in the land down under, in a letter to the media, a citizen questioned the motive behind the nanny state ideology:

> Ms Webb said Tasmanians had saved more than $42 million in gambling losses since COVID-19 restrictions closed pokies venues on March 23. But Premier Peter Gutwein firmly rejected the idea, accusing Ms Webb of wanting a nanny state. Rather than the fear of creating a nanny state, perhaps Mr Gutwein is more concerned about the loss of revenue for his government should the opening of poker machines be further delayed.
>
> MARTAIN, 2020

In Ontario, Canada, the premier was ideologically against more government intervention in people's lives – but nonetheless argued for why emergency measures were necessary in order to help the people of Ontario:

> I'm dead against big government, I'm dead against the big brother nanny state telling you what to do. That's just not me. But we have to help the people of Ontario get through this. There's certain things we must do to move on, and we can't sit around and wait three or four weeks. We have to move in hours.
>
> JEFFORD, 2020

It seems the premier realised the necessity to set aside ideology and be pragmatic in a situation that required efficient and effective state action in response to a virus fast on the move.

In crazy, confused and chaotic India, the nanny state that nurses capitalism but showed many of its citizens the fastest way to their early deaths – apparently offered to take the infected to quarantine facilities and regularly check on their condition:

> Only one unpleasant incident marred my family and my recovery and – this was the persistent telephone calls from the interfering, ignorant nanny state, in this case the capital's municipality.
>
> FRESCO, 2020

The ideological and non-pragmatic reason for wearing a mask played itself out in parts of the Western world. In the US:

> Worse, the outright refusal to wear a mask has become a bizarre badge of honor among some who see conspiracy theories and nanny state tyrannies lurking behind sensible public health guidelines. Self-styled freedom fighters against masks risk infecting others, and being infected themselves, with an as-yet unstoppable pathogen. What sort of freedom is that?
>
> *The Philadelphia Inquirer*, 2020

The Fourth of July is a sacred day in the US – it is the day that the Queen of England's subjects decided to tear away from their colonial nanny state in 1776. One would have thought that it would have been an opportune moment in history – for a people that do not believe in the existence of a nanny state – to use the occasion to create a country of free individuals – without having to deal with a nanny state. Instead, the Founding Fathers went on to create what would in time become the most powerful nanny state in the world. So strong was their belief in the state – that they actually called the land violently stolen from the indigenous peoples – the United States of America. Ever since – the love-hate relationship with the state seems to be part of the American way of life. In New Hampshire, the chairperson of ReopenNH – under whose auspices the Fourth of July event was to be held during a global pandemic stated:

> By all means, if you want to wash your hands or wear a mask, be our guest, but keep your nanny-state snootiness to yourself. Happiness means

different things to different people, and in America, that is ok so long as
government stays out of the way.
Pawtucket Times: 2020

I think millions around the world – who lost loved ones – would certainly be
happy if the nanny state did more to save their loved ones from an invisible
enemy – as did nanny states in China, Vietnam, Cuba, New Zealand, etc.! Let
the record show that where the nanny states stood out of the way in the time
of a global pandemic – millions of people needlessly died. It seems all of the
critics of the nanny state were singing from the same hymn sheets of Ronald
Reagan, Margaret Thatcher, Ayn Rand, Milton Freedman, Friedrich Hayek, and
other pioneering capitalist marketeers. These were the champions of free market ideologies for no or little state involvement in society and the economy.

The concept of a "nanny state" has been used as an ideological weapon to
denounce state support, protection and looking out for the common man and
woman. It is and has been effectively used to drive a wedge between the state
and the citizens of a country. The economic concept used to indicate the ideology of the state to remove itself from the workings of the economy is known
as neoliberalism. As indicated in the previous chapter, all of humanity has to
now go through the capitalist market – in order to try and secure lives and
livelihoods in a harsh and uncaring economy. Neoliberalism is identified with
minimal state intervention and minimal public expenditure in services such as
health services, social services and education (al-Basam, 2020).

If countries like New Zealand, South Korea, Vietnam, China, etc. had taken
the ideologues seriously on the ideology of the state getting out of the way in
the time of a global pandemic, the number of dead in their respective countries would not have been amongst the lowest in the world. If countries like
the UK, US, Brazil, India, etc. had not taken the ideologues seriously on the
ideology of the state getting out of the way in the time of a global pandemic –
the number of dead in their respective countries would not have been as high
as they were. If people were saved from death in the time of COVID-19, it was
thanks – in the main – to the nanny state! If people have loved ones alive and
well – it is thanks – in the main – to the nanny state in the time of a global
pandemic!

2   The Nanny State and Saving Capitalism in the Time of COVID-19

Whilst nanny state ideology was spewed on relatively powerless citizens for
their reliance on the state to save lives and livelihoods, the powerful private

sector looked to the nanny state to maintain its bottom line. The term nanny state is also used to denounce socialism – a socio-economic and political system in which the state assumes the regulator, overseer and arguably the provider for society at large. But many in the capitalist world appealed to the nanny state to help save capitalism from the capitalist market's inability to generate profit in the time of COVID-19. People were afraid to go to work. People were afraid to shop. People were afraid to travel. People were afraid of being in close contact with other people. When and where businesses requested support and intervention from the state – there was no mention of the words nanny state. In Britain about 1,500 artists signed an open letter to the nanny state requesting that:

> Until these businesses can operate again, which is likely to be 2021 at the earliest, government support will be crucial to prevent mass insolvencies and the end of this world-leading industry.
>
> AFP, 2020: 2

Still in the UK:

> The scheme [Eat Out to Help Out], which will cost taxpayers about £500m, aims to help the devastated hospitality industry, which employs 1.8 million workers, get back on its feet. Anyone visiting a participating restaurant, cafe or pub on Mondays, Tuesdays and Wednesdays throughout August will receive the half-price discount of up to £10 per person.
>
> WEARDEN ET AL., 2020

Who would have thought that the nanny state is perfectly capable of ensuring food security for its country's citizens! Eat Out to Help Out! This is no self-interest ideology! This is a public-good project: help out the people whilst helping businesses at the same time. The world would be a much better place if such common-sense practices replace neoliberal capitalist market fundamentalism and fanaticism. If the common people depended on the nanny state to protect and keep them alive, the capitalist class depended on the nanny state to keep the taps of their profits flowing:

> What successes there have been are felt only by a select few. While small businesses die and millions line up for universal credit, Amazon adds billions to its sales and profits and Richard Branson begs for a bailout.
>
> OSAMA, 2020

If the nanny states in the Western world were reluctant to impose lockdowns at the onset, in order to break COVID-19 transmissions and save lives, they did not hesitate to move social monies to the already well-off private sector of capitalist society:

> Since March, the Fed, Bank of Japan and European Central Bank have bought over $5 trillion in securities. To put that into perspective, in the 15 years prior, including the Great Recession of 2008, these three central banks spent less than $10 trillion in total. Initially, the Fed only bought bonds indirectly through exchange-traded funds (ETFs) whereas now they are buying bonds on the secondary market. This doesn't help the corporations selling them; it helps the holders of these bonds that purchased them from the corporations that issued them. In other words, this is a massive bailout for the rich. The Bank of Japan now owns nearly 6% of publicly traded firms in Japan. The Europeans are all bailing out firms integral to their economies. The Fed is on a shopping spree.
> ARVAS, 2020

Nanny states were readily available to meet the financial hunger of big corporations: "PPP rollout—the first $350 billion tranche gobbled up within days by the bigger, better-connected companies that knew how to play the game" (Lane, 2020). If the capitalist class depended on the nanny state for huge amounts of public monies, it just as well relied on the nanny state to herd scared and fearful workers back to the autocratic work-space in the time of a global pandemic:

> Yet laid-off workers who fear returning to work in Iowa, for example, could be targeted by state officials who have gone so far as to post a public call to companies to get in touch if an employee refuses to return to work.
> ROMM, 2020

Forced labour thrives in the democratic, free-choice and civilised West – all praise must go to the nanny state – for aiding and abetting the so-called free market and its compulsion to have workers back at work during a global pandemic! Neoliberal and free market ideologues have for a long time been successful in creating the illusion of a minimalist state as the rationale for the progress and prosperity of society. COVID-19 has exposed this lie. Time and time again writers in the time of COVID-19 highlighted the reality and necessity of the nanny state to rescue and aid big businesses:

> So far, the government has budgeted to spend more than $200bn on peo-
> ple and businesses impacted by the virus. That's close to the world's big-
> gest fiscal package – hence the government's budget deficit is tipped to
> exceed $100bn, and federal government debt might reach $1 trillion.
>
> ABBOTT, 2020

All across the globe, nanny states were on full alert and on standby to prevent
the infrastructure and scaffolding of capitalism from collapsing:

> Some rescue policies also cover emissions-intensive firms, such as air-
> lines, that face bankruptcy or significantly reduced revenue as a result
> of COVID-19. Examples include Russian tax breaks for airlines through
> the Anti-crisis Fund (Ostapets et al., 2020), AU$715mn of unconditional
> Australian airline relief through the Coronavirus Economic Response
> Package (Commonwealth of Australia, 2020), and US$32bn of bail-
> outs including grants and loans for US airlines through the CARES Act
> (Courtney, 2020). Fossil fuel industries, facing extraordinarily low oil
> prices (Ngai et al., 2020), are likely to request future tax breaks or bailouts.
>
> HEPBURN ET AL., 2020: 7

Nanny states ensured that businesses contributing to man-made climate
change were also nurtured: "the US has given at least $3bn in pandemic bailout
cash to more than 5,600 fossil fuel companies" (*The Guardian Weekly*, 2020).
Saving failing capitalism in the time of COVID-19 was not the exception to the
rule; on the contrary the ideology of the nanny state in the capitalist era is precisely to ensure that capitalism is prevented from failing.

3   The Capitalist Market's Covert and Overt Dependency on the Nanny State in the Age of Capitalism

Free market ideologues are quick to shout nanny state when the poor and
unemployed are assisted by the state. They are noticeably silent when the
nanny state intervenes in the economy – to protect and insulate the wealthy
from the ravages of the capitalist market economy. The term nanny state is:

> Of British origin that conveys a view that a government or its policies are
> overprotective or interfering unduly with personal choice. The term 'nanny
> state' likens government to the role that a nanny has in child rearing.
>
> WIKIPEDIA, 2020

Nannies take care of children when their parents are unable to do so. Nannies feed children, play with them, take them to school, read to them, help them cross the road, comfort them in times of pain and sorrow and some are even known to breast-feed children – otherwise known as "wet nursing" or "cross-nursing" – where the mom is no longer able to do so for one reason or another – or when the mom is no more.

Presidents have nannies to take care of their children. Royalty have nannies to take care of their children. Working people who have no time under capitalism – and who can afford to do so – also have nannies to take care of their children. For the well-off, nannies are an integral and significant component of family structures in capitalist societies. If we care to look carefully, beyond the veil of ideology dressing capitalism – we find that capitalism too had and continues to have the nanny state – to protect capitalism, ensure its continued functioning, survival and flourishing. We witnessed this in the time of COVID-19.

Capitalism depends on the nanny state to do its dirty dealings for it. When in capitalist US, George Floyd tried to pay for a commodity with counterfeit money during a pandemic – not dissimilar from the counterfeit fiat money that circulates and saturates the world after 1971 – the business owner did not depend on his own individual capacity to find a solution to the disputed economic exchange that took place in his free market of commodities. He called on the nanny state – a collective of people and resources to intervene in his individual economic dispute. Upon arrival, the nanny state sided with the owner of commodities against George Floyd – and murdered him by crushing his neck with its knee for 9 minutes and 29 seconds! This – even after the people protested and pleaded with the state to let go – but the nanny state did not listen to the reason of the people present.

George Floyd's counterfeit money was not the same counterfeit money produced and sanctioned by the capitalist class. The response was capitalist violence in its most brutal form. The outcome was death. Being black in capitalist America means that violence is amplified and sustained against black people. Violence was amplified and sustained against black people under apartheid capitalism in South Africa. George Floyd happened to be black – his main crime was that he challenged the ideology of capitalist forms of money. Capitalism has a monopoly on counterfeit money. There is no longer any real money in capitalist society. Money is printed by the state and backed up by the ideology of god: "in god we trust". Floyd's money attempted to compete with the dominant form. The nanny state protects capitalism and its various ideological forms. In actual fact this is how capitalism came to be – historically – with the aid of nanny states meting out untold violence to indigenous peoples.

The nanny state protects the interests of the rich in the main. The nanny state in the age of capitalism protects the coal companies – and leaves the natural environment and the climate unprotected. In South Africa – with the transition to democracy in 1994 – the black nanny state made a handful of blacks extremely rich and left millions unemployed and still hoping for the elusive better life under the ANC-led government. Apartheid capitalism became deracialised capitalism in South Africa's transition to democracy in 1994. But the term white monopoly capital is still very much part of the South African lexicon – by those who wish to remind South Africans – about the mainly racialised-ownership of the capitalist economy. Black comrades – who had very limited or no business skills – are now part owners of the commanding heights of the capitalist economy in South Africa – thanks to the democratic nanny state. It was not the free market that made former ANC terrorists extremely wealthy – it was the political decisions taken by the nanny state since Nelson Mandela was president. Having gotten used to the taste and smell of money – made by the working class in South Africa – ANC comrades have been on a never-ending looting spree aided and abetted by the nanny state. The free market ended up capturing the nanny state.

In a world of free market fantasies, individuals are expected to settle their own disputes – and have no reliance on the state. In the real world masked by capitalist ideologies – big business – in this case Lonmin Mines called in the South African nanny state to act on its behalf. The world watched as 36 platinum miners were massacred in Nelson Mandela's Rainbow Nation. This was in August 2012 – just after capitalism experienced its most failing moment in 2008. Thanks to the nanny state, ever since 2008, failing capitalism has been given a helping hand – so it could get onto its feet again – to once more continue on its path of ruin and ravage.

The Great Crisis of 2008 demonstrated how utterly dependent capitalism is on the nanny state. It burst asunder the dominant capitalist ideology for decades – that capitalism's success is as a result only of the neoliberal free market – and no or limited state intervention in the economy. A mere handful of persons responsible for the 2008 financial crisis went to jail for their economic crime against the entire of humanity. For decades the entire world was under the ideological spell that capitalism functions independently of the state. Capitalism and the state are happily married when the state creates the conditions for profit-making and maximisation. Capitalism threatens the state with a painful divorce if the latter attempts to take care of her children – by threatening disinvestments out of a country, job losses, downgrading by economic rating agencies and so forth. The Great Crisis of 2008 showed how the nanny state took monies meant for her needy children, showered the rich kids with it and made the poor children suffer instead.

Greece experienced the harsh ideological pangs of capitalism first-hand. Prior to the 2008 global financial crisis, neoliberal forces continuously attacked the nanny state forcing it to deregulate markets – especially the labour market and to refrain from implementing state intervention type policies (Martin,n.d). When the Great Crisis of 2008 struck, the ideology that was scripted by the ideologues of the elite of the world – and hammered into the already dominant ideological global discourse – was that "the banks were too big to fail". Suddenly and without warning the priests of individualism and free market miracles and magic, converted themselves and the unsuspecting masses into a global collective – just so failing capitalism and the capitalist class could be rescued:

> We had all just watched as trillions of dollars were marshalled in a moment when our elites decided to declare a crisis. If the banks were allowed to fail, we were told, the rest of the economy would collapse. It was a matter of collective survival, so the money had to be found. In the process, some rather large fictions at the heart of our economic system were exposed.
>
> KLEIN, 2014: 12

What Klein also meant by "fictions" – I think – is capitalist ideologies. One would have thought that countries like Venezuela and Cuba – and not Goldman Sachs – are too big to fail. But this did not stop the West from setting such big countries on the path to economic failure – through state intervention in the economy by way of sanctions! One would have thought that states in the West are too big to fail – but the world witnessed how the big states failed their citizens in the time of COVID-19. The one area where the hand of the nanny state is quite visible and actively intervenes in the economy – mostly in the interest of the already well-off in capitalist society – is that of taxation:

> The drastic reduction of top tax rates was the signature issue of the 'conservative revolution' waged by the Republican Party under Ronald Reagan in the United States and the Conservative Party under Margaret Thatcher in Britain in the late 1970s and early 1980s. The ensuing political and ideological shift had a marked impact on taxes and inequality not only in the United States and United Kingdom but also around the world.
>
> PIKETTY, 2020: 31

Even the ideological god of capitalism, Adam Smith, acknowledged about 250 years ago, the intimate and integral role that the nanny state plays in the capitalist economy:

> [Workmen] are disposed to combine in order to raise, [masters] in order to lower, the wages of labour. The masters, upon these occasions [strikes and other labour actions] never cease to call aloud for the assistance of the civil magistrate, and the rigorous execution of those laws which have been enacted with so much severity against the combination [union] of servants, labourers, and journeymen.
>
> ADLER, 2009: 122

Ronald Reagan and Margaret Thatcher were the iconic capitalist symbols for the last 50 years for no state intervention in the economy. Margaret Thatcher was ironically known as the Iron Lady – one who used her nanny state iron-fist to ensure that profit flourished in both the United Kingdom and in its former colonies – at the expense of the working class and former-colonised peoples. She did not leave profit-making entirely to the free market and invisible hand. When she died – many in the UK chanted "Ding Dong the Witch is Dead" – in celebration of the demise of the Iron Lady of capitalism and individualist free market ideology. The angrier amongst those celebrating her welcomed death took the word 'witch' one step further and replaced 'w' with 'b'. Many were enraged at the harshness and brutality of capitalism – and for them Margaret Thatcher symbolised the harshness and brutality of the capitalist system. She was after all known as the Iron Lady. In actual fact, she was the Iron Lady to the working class but always the Lady-in-waiting to the capitalist class.

At the ideological level, neoliberalism implies that the state does not intervene in the economy. But when we look beneath the surface of capitalist and neoliberal ideologies, it means that the state must be a passive and sometimes an active force in defence of the capitalist class and the capitalist system – at the expense of the common people:

> Neoliberalism involves centrally re-orienting the state to use its coercive power to discipline people to be market compliant in furtherance of creating a more thorough, robust market-centered society, where market logic reigns supreme over all decision-making across all social spheres and at all levels, personal and political, individual and collective.
>
> SCHRAM ET AL., 2018: xxi

Laws and legislations are ideological extensions and tentacles of the capitalist nanny state – ensuring that profit-making by the capitalist class is insulated and protected from the unsuspecting ideologically drenched masses. To highlight the myth and fake news of free market functioning in a deadly part of the economy:

> In our own society, despite the damage done to both lives and the economy by tobacco, industry officials have been able to use part of their profits to purchase considerable clout in Congress, which time and again has enacted legislation favourable to the industry. Hilts notes that every item of health legislation since the 1960s has specified an exemption for cigarettes. Even after the perfidious tactics and strategies of the tobacco industry had been exposed, Congressional leaders introduced a $50 billion tax credit for the cigarette industry in the 1997 budget bill.
>
> FRIEDMAN, 2003: 31–32

In the fantasy world of contemporary economic science – markets are free. In the real economic world – the free market is intimately linked to the nanny state:

> Consider patent protection, which functions to support successful research and development (R&D). It assures those who develop new products of an interval in which they will be free from competition and will be entitled to exact monopolistic prices. Government will intervene to prevent others from copying those products. Such an institution violates the conditions of a free market. It creates an artificial monopoly and raises the prices of those goods. Abolishing patent protection would be an economic positive in the near term, resulting in lower prices and greater consumption.
>
> FRIEDMAN, 2003: 25

The nanny state and the free market are Siamese twins:

> Would Bill Gates and his fellow techno-billionaires have been able to build their businesses without the hundreds of billions of dollars of public money invested in basic research over many decades? Would the quasi-monopolies they have built by patenting public knowledge have reaped such enormous profits without the active support of legal and tax codes?
>
> PIKETTY, 2020: 28

Capitalist and neoliberal ideologies have in the main successfully muddied the waters – insofar as the functioning of real-world economies is concerned. Capitalism is clear in its goals and strategies – either weaken the state to max-imise profits – or strengthen the state to maximise profits. Maximum profit is the end goal. The state is the means to this end. The nanny state is alive and well in the life of capitalism – and protects the economy of the rich in the main – to the detriment of the poor and disenfranchised in capitalist society.

About 175 years ago Karl Marx warned us about the biasness of the state in favour of the ruling class:

> The bourgeoisie has at last, since the establishment of Modern Industry and of the world market, conquered for itself, in the modern representa-tive state, exclusive political sway. The executive of the modern state is but a committee for managing the common affairs of the whole bourgeoisie.
> MARX, 1848: 15

COVID-19 gave us the material evidence to support Marx's argument. The world witnessed how the modern state in capitalist societies favoured mainly the capitalist economy – at the expense of the people. The modern state is here to stay – regardless of the many Ronald Reagans and Margaret Thatchers that live among us – and would like us to believe otherwise. To believe in no govern-ment or no state involvement in the economy and in society – is ideological, idealistic and utopian in the extreme.

CHAPTER 10

The Life of Capitalism

The essential notion of a capitalist society is voluntary cooperation and voluntary exchange.

MILTON FRIEDMAN

• • •

Capitalism is a social system based on the recognition of individual rights, including property rights, in which all property is privately owned.

AYN RAND

•••

1   The Grandeur of Capitalism!

With the fall of the Berlin Wall, history proved capitalism to be the superior system – one to be celebrated and jealously guarded. Humankind therefore continue to live in a capitalist world. To know what capitalism is – maybe I should start with what I think capitalism is not. Capitalism is not a hunter-gatherer socio-economic system – although in the capitalist system huge profits are made from hunting and gathering of animals and natural resources. It is why wild markets are big in countries like China. It's why some businesses in Sweden take people from rural villages in Thailand to gather berries two months in a year in Sweden.

Capitalism is not a slave system – although hundreds of millions of workers are known to work in slave-like conditions under capitalism. Capitalism is not a feudal system – although there exist many landlords extracting large amounts of rent for land and housing under capitalism. Capitalism is not a socialist system where crucial needs like health care, education, housing, food, etc. are guaranteed by the state – although health care, education, housing, etc. is on offer under capitalism – but at a premium price – which only the well-off can afford. Many who could not afford oxygen, ambulances, and hospital beds in India perished as a destitute people in the time of COVID-19. Their loved ones – and the world – will not forget how they died – and the painful manner in which their last rites were conducted.

Capitalism is not a system that cares for people – even when they are dying and dead. Capitalism is not a socio-economic system whereby property is under common ownership – although under capitalism it is common for a few capitalists to own huge amounts of private property. Capitalism is not a system in which there is democracy in the workplaces – although workplaces thrive in democratic societies like the US, UK, South Africa, Japan, India, etc. Capitalism is not a system that advocates for strong state intervention in the economy – although capitalism depends on strong states for its existence and sustainability. Economic policies and plans favour the capitalist class.

Capitalism is not a system that thrives on social and political instability – although huge profits are made from continued wars and conflict in many parts of the world. There are lots of monies to be made – from making bombs and then dropping them in far-away countries. Businesses from Western countries got huge contracts to rebuild Iraq – after the bombing of Iraq. Capitalism is not a system that emphasises cooperation and collaboration – although big businesses like banks are known to collaborate and collude on price-fixing. Capitalism is not a system that depends on the taxpayer for its profits – although taxpayers' monies are known to be given lock, stock and barrel to private companies – especially when capitalism undergoes a crisis. Capitalist market ideologues will forever be reminded of how mountains of taxpayers' monies were used to bail out banks and big corporations during the 2008 Great Crisis.

Capitalism is not a system that shuns technological innovation – although capitalism is known to stick to labour as a source of skill and not innovate – when such labour is dirt-cheap. Capitalist society does not have slave markets in the way that slave society did – although people do sell themselves on a daily, weekly and monthly basis to capitalists. Your labour – that comes with you – belongs to the capitalist during the working day. Slave masters may have disappeared, but labour brokers are excellent at facilitating the buying and selling of labour in the labour market. Capitalism is not a system like past social systems where famine was not uncommon – although millions of people still go hungry every day in capitalist society. Famine for many is a feature of capitalist society – a society of plenty and scarcity sitting side-by-side.

Now that I have attempted to outline what I think capitalism is not, I will proceed to outline what I think capitalism is. Let me start with the experts – on the wonders of capitalism. Milton Friedman maintained that capitalism depends on "voluntary cooperation and voluntary exchange". I exchange my monies for a face mask in the commodities market and I get a face mask in return. The worker exchanges her labour with the capitalist and she gets a wage at the end of the week or at the end of the month. As to why she does not get her wage in the labour market in the way that the capitalist gets his monies in the oxygen market – this is an interesting violation of the law of exchange for the economic scientist to work out. In any event, capitalism is based on "voluntary cooperation and voluntary exchange", as the expert Milton Friedman had reminded us. You will voluntarily pay sky-high prices for oxygen – if your mom or child or dad is dying from COVID-19!

Capitalism is also "a social system based on the recognition of individual rights, including property rights, in which all property is privately owned" – as eloquently stated by Ayn Rand, another economics expert on the wonders of capitalism. The hunter-gatherers obviously were big losers – for not having the privilege of living in a capitalist society and experiencing the joys of private property. Capitalism is a system that comprises extremely wealthy people. For example, the 10 richest men in the world in 2021 – and they all happen to be men – are Jeff Bezos, Elon Musk, Bernard Arnault, Bill Gates, Mark Zuckerberg, Warren Buffett, Larry Ellison, Larry Page, Sergey Brin and Mukesh Ambani. Rich people that emerged out of the Industrial Revolution in the West – and they all happen to be men as well – were John D. Rockefeller, Andrew Carnegie, J.P. Morgan and Cornelius Vanderbilt. Communist China had done well by adopting capitalism in the 1980s – by 2021 there were 698 billionaires in China. Finally, a female billionaire was produced – Kate Wang. Women long for being equal to men in capitalist society. The ideological deficit of this approach and apparent solution is that inequality amongst women remains – as long as capitalism remains!

Since the fall of the Soviet Union, capitalist Russia produced 117 billionaires. Capitalism makes possible billionaires in a way that the hunter-gatherer society, slave society or feudal society did not. The most unequal country in the world – capitalist South Africa – also has billionaires – five of them – four white and one black. They own large quantities of private property in a country where many still have no land and live in tin shacks. Capitalist society also comprises hundreds of millions – if not billions – of poor and relatively poor people. They are in all places of the world – the inner cities, in rural areas, in the big slums, on the streets of the world, etc. We saw them come out of nowhere – and everywhere in India in the time of COVID-19. They own little or no private property to secure their livelihoods and lives. Without meaningful quantities and qualities of private property – they live precarious lives under capitalism. They have individual rights under capitalism – but they cannot eat these rights. There are no or little individual rights in China – but Chinese people are now able to eat and sleep to their heart's content. Capitalism is a system that is wonderfully designed and ordered to make loads of things – what economic scientists call products – or what Marx called commodities.

The capitalist mode of production demonstrates the unimaginable productive capacity of humans to make stuff – to produce commodities. One must surely be in awe at the colossal quantities of goods and services that the capitalist system has produced over the many centuries – since capitalism's arrival on the world's stage. One is certainly spoilt for choice under the capitalist order. Think about all the stuff that we have in our homes – and one can only marvel at the admirable productive character of the capitalist system. Think about all the stuff in the malls. Think about the many malls that adorn city and urban landscapes. Think about the many advertisements about stuff – that persistently bombard our mobile phones and computer screens when we are connected to the World Wide Web. These are stuff that are made by workers, overseen by capitalists in all parts of the world – and are brought to us by huge container ships on almost a daily basis. Thanks to capitalism! Even the containers and the container ships are made by workers and overseen by capitalists in all parts of the globe. How is that for being served by the capitalist system!

Capitalism has given us the most spectacular cities that humankind has ever imagined, experienced and lived in. Imagine living in feudal society and not having big malls to go to – to buy the latest sheep shearers, grain sickles or horseshoes! Imagine living in a slave society – and not having the freedom as an unemployed person – to look for a job on the labour market! Imagine living in a hunter-gatherer society – and not having the luxury of eating genetically modified meat and vegetables – or drinking rum in a London pub! Let us be grateful that we live in a capitalist world – a world adorned with thousands of malls, millions of labour markets, and tens of millions of food stuffs with genetically modified organisms – and other chemicals. Chemicals may be carcinogenic – but they are good for preserving foods, giving foods a good appearance and securing the bottom line.

The rich can afford to buy expensive organic or free-range chicken or meat – which the hunter-gatherer took for granted – and which was provided by nature for free. No system before capitalism could put on the table the choices of foods we currently have under capitalism. Capitalism has produced technologies beyond our wildest imaginations. It has conceptualised, shaped, and produced all wonders of the material world that our ancestors would be totally in awe of – if they were given the chance to experience life under capitalism – even if only for a day. Imagine if a hunter-gatherer appeared in New York City in 2022 – like when Crocodile Dundee appeared in the Big Apple in 1986! Even though the richest countries in the West were not able to produce PPEs for their citizens – capitalist China – managed by a communist state – was able to produce and send such PPEs by sea, land and air to about 150 countries. This would have been unthinkable in feudal society – when the Black Death struck around 1348. To think that the capitalist system is only a recent invention of humankind! Even Marx – the much-hated figure by capitalism's apologists and praise singers – praised the productive nature of capitalism in the *Communist Manifesto of 1848*:

> It [capitalism] has been the first to show what man's activity can bring about. It has accomplished wonders far surpassing Egyptian pyramids, Roman aqueducts, and Gothic cathedrals (16).

If Marx speaks about capitalism as 'accomplishing wonders' – it must mean that capitalism is grand! Capitalism is innovative. It is excellent at unleashing the motivational drive for profit. The hunter-gatherer had no such motive. The slave master comes nowhere near J.P Morgan. The wealth of the feudal lord is no match to that of Mark Zuckerberg's or Elon Musk's. Of the many attributes of capitalism – the two most sacred ideologies and value-priorities of capitalism are that of profit and economic growth: "the forward motion of the capitalist system is founded on the continued prospect of future profits and economic growth" (Heller, 2011: xi).

If one works hard and smart as a capitalist – one can make lots of money and profit. If one works hard as a worker in the capitalist system – one can get a wage as a worker in order to survive – and still the capitalist can make loads of money and profit. The workers of Henry Ford got a good wage and were able to survive – and Henry Ford became a wealthy person as well. Workers working in clothing companies in countries like Bangladesh get a wage in order to survive – and their bosses make huge profits too. Even the clothing stores in the West – that sell these clothing brands make huge profits. Capitalism makes this possible. Everybody gets a share – even if such shares may be grossly unevenly distributed and manifestly unfair, unequal, unjust and immoral. But capitalist ideologies make this legal! That's what matters!

A worker can also dream big and become a capitalist someday – although this is rare and far between. But reality is not what's important under capitalism; idealism, hope, ideology and the constant pining for utopia is what must prevail. Profit-making is an economic ideology that has taken on a religious form in contemporary society. Hence the religious fervour of all governments is that of economic growth. Any signs of the economy growing unusually slow or not growing at all – sends shivers through the entire spinal cord of the global capitalist system. Capitalism has to grow. Feudal society and slave society did not experience economic growth – in the way that capitalist society does. In the same breadth, nature was not degraded in feudal and slave societies in the way it is in capitalist society. Probably the only two grown things that the hunter-gatherer may have hoped for on their regular hunts – were grown animals and grown vegetables.

Under the hunter-gatherer society, slave society and feudal society – the Amazon rainforest was not cleared for the wonders of enterprise and economic growth. But under capitalism it is. The oceans were not dumped with plastic. Under capitalism it is. The sky was not choked with CO_2. Under capitalism it is. As a capitalist society – we have to keep growing – regardless. It is the mark of progress. Donald Trump staked his next election win on economic growth – that is until COVID-19 came along! Capitalism's bedrock foundation is that of private property. In the hunter-gatherer society, private property was miniscule – spears, bows and arrows, sparse clothing, ostrich eggshells, etc. Land and nature were never part of private property. Under slave society – women, children and men were the private property of the property-owning class. Under capitalism – capitalists are entitled to own lots of private property. Politically-connected capitalists are able to own large tracts of land – in order to mine for diamonds, gold, rare earth minerals, etc. They are assisted by the state to make this possible. Harry Oppenheimer – the richest man in South Africa – was a diamond miner.

Large and huge amounts of machinery and equipment for the extraction of oil and coal is made possible through the private property of industrialists. Not many of us own such private property. In fact, we hardly think about it; we accept things as they are under capitalism. Capitalist ideologies overpower and numb the mind and body! Capitalism is a system of the ultimate perfection in specialisation. Workers in India cannot manufacture vaccines without workers in the United States manufacturing the materials for such vaccines. A hunter-gatherer would make his own paintbrush and paint to paint graffiti on rocks. Serfs and peasants would make their own clothing under feudalism.

Milton Friedman reminded us that a worker under capitalism cannot make even a pencil on his or her own. The wood is made by a worker in one part of the world. The lead or graphite is made by a worker in another part of the world. The eraser – by a worker in Indonesia probably. The little piece of metal holding the eraser – still by a different worker. They each do not see the pencil that they finally make. This is the power of specialisation under capitalism. We are all specialist workers. Capitalism continually reduces the holistic human being to meaninglessness.

One is also at liberty to choose whatever specialised career one wishes to pursue under capitalism – whether such a career is as an app developer, a coal

miner, a wood cutter, a rubber tapper, a tin miner, a porn star, etc. In fact, it may
be more lucrative to work as a porn star – than to work at Walmart or Amazon
or as a tree cutter under capitalism. One can also choose to be unemployed
under capitalism. There are many who have given up looking for work. After
all, capitalism is a system of free choice.

Capitalism is an accumulative system. Capitalism is a world made up of
rich and poor countries – and poor countries have the freedom and choice
to become like the rich countries. For example, Bangladesh can become like
the United States – if it so wishes and follows neoliberal ideologies. Zimbabwe
can become like the United Kingdom – if it so wishes and follows neoliberal
principles. This beauty of innovation, private property and free choice – capitalism – emerged after a series of historical and social transformations. Thanks
to capitalism the UK – once a backwater feudal territory – is now one of the
leading countries in the world. It is part of what is known as the G7 countries.
Its capital – London – is also the financial capital of the world – all praise must
go to capitalism. There is and there can be nothing better than capitalism! It is
why Fukuyama referred to capitalism as The End of History! If we wish to have
more of this good thing, then it might serve us well to know where capitalism
came from.

2   The Breakdown of Feudalism, Colonial Conquests and the Making
       of Capitalism

The Industrial Revolution is usually presented as the starting point of capitalism. Capitalism did not commence with the Industrial Revolution. Capitalism
picked up speed and haste with the Industrial Revolution in England in the
17th and 18th centuries. One has to travel back in time – so as to get a bird's eye
view of the emergence and the making of capitalism in Europe in general and
in England in particular.

The gradual disintegration of the Roman Empire around 400 AD gave rise
to the feudal system in Europe. With the fall of the Roman Empire, England
became a melting pot of invaders, killings, theft, plunder, ideas, merchant trading, technological development, science, intelligence, Christianity, burning of
witches and class conflict.

Crusades to other lands resulted in lost battles – but also the bringing back
of spices, gold, and Arabic science, culture, arts and philosophy. Having been
invaded by the Romans and so many other tribes in its history – it seemed
that conquest and plunder was now etched into England's genes. England
would take this restlessness and traumatic history and unleash the capitalist

system – but not without unleashing Empire upon the world – in the way that
the Roman Empire was unleashed upon England. England would go on to
change the world forever – in the way that England was forever changed by
the Roman Empire – and subsequent invaders such as the Vikings to this small
island. Out of this turbulent history, productive but exploited workers, unimaginable wealth, rich men, magnificent cities, democratic societies, grand science and numbing capitalist ideologies would be born. The End of History had
a beginning:

> At the birth of capitalism the West was geographically, economically
> and culturally marginal in the world. In the Middle East, China, Japan
> and India, the forces of production were equally or more developed. The
> breakthrough toward capitalism in Europe was a result of a prolonged
> period of class conflict between the feudal ruling classes and peasants
> and artisans, during which the balance swung sufficiently away from the
> former to permit capitalism to emerge.
>
> HELLER, 2011: 5–6

Feudalism was the social and cultural system that existed before capitalism. Capitalism is therefore not natural – like the Himalayan Mountains, the
Amazon rainforest, the Great Barrier Reef or like the air that we breathe. It is
not even natural like the coronavirus – even though capitalism often kills as
well. Where capitalism assumed a natural presence in the world in the time of
COVID-19, more people perished. For ideologues and praise singers of capitalism – capitalism is as natural as the air we breathe – part and parcel of nature.
This is capitalist ideologues like Milton Friedman and Ayn Rand blowing hot
air and spreading around myths and fake news about capitalism. The evidence
contradicts the ideologies or fake news upheld in capitalist society thus far.
Capitalism:

> Has ceased to be as natural as the air we breathe, and can be seen instead
> as the historically rather recent phenomenon that it is.
>
> EAGLETON, 2018: xv

Capitalism is therefore man-made with history thrown into the mix – no different from racism in South Africa or antisemitism in Hitler's Germany or the
collapse of communism in the Soviet Union in 1989. Capitalism is the making
of history – a history of humans. Like COVID-19 which went global – capitalism
is now a global social, political, cultural and economic system. It emerged in
the midst of the dissolution of the feudal system. Similar to slavery before and

capitalism after – feudalism was an ordered and hierarchical system. Like capitalism – feudalism was a class system. It was a society made up of kings and queens, the church, lords, knights and serfs or peasants:

> Feudalism was a combination of the legal, economic, military, and cultural customs that flourished in Medieval Europe between the 9th and 15th centuries. Broadly defined, it was a way of structuring society around relationships that were derived from the holding of land in exchange for service or labour.
>
> WIKIPEDIA

Like capitalism – feudalism was an exchange society. The peasants and serfs exchanged their labour for 3–4 days of the week for the lord – and in turn they received a strip of land to live on and to live-off of. Protection from invaders was also secured by the powers that be in feudal society. Man must mix his labour with nature in order live. Under feudalism – man as a peasant – mixed his labour with nature in order that he, his lord, the priest and the king could live.

Under capitalism – the capitalist exchanges his money for labour. The worker in turn exchanges her labour for a wage. In this way the wage worker, the supervisor, the middle man, the state worker and the capitalist can live. The church was the moral authority in feudal society. But the kings were still in charge. None was more in charge than King Henry VIII. He swept aside the Catholic Church and its reigning ideologies. He was proof that man makes religion – as and when he pleases. But King Henry VIII was not just any man – he was king of England!

Many social, economic, technological, geopolitical and scientific phenomena occurred – that made possible the transition from feudalism to capitalism. The crisis of feudalism was key among them:

> The transformation from feudalism to capitalism began in Europe with the crisis of the feudal system in the fourteenth century and continued until the Industrial Revolution, 1780–1850.
>
> HELLER, 2011:1

Like COVID-19, which dealt a major blow to capitalism, the Black Death around 1348 helped change the course of feudal society. Interestingly the concepts of feudalism and the Black Death did not escape the observer's pen in the time of COVID-19:

In societies under pre-capitalist systems such as slavery and feudalism, parallel patterns characterised their states. For considerable periods, those states also reproduced their class structures: masters and slaves in slavery and lords and serfs in feudalism.

WOLFF, 2020

Capitalist society had the Spanish Flu and COVID-19; feudalism had the Black Death. It is thought that the Black Death contributed to the demise of the feudal system: "the Black Death is widely credited with fuelling the collapse of the feudal system" (Honigsbaum, 2020). Some are more convinced that it did: "the bubonic plague ended feudalism" (Rodriguez, 2020). It is too early to tell whether COVID-19 will collapse the capitalist system. One thing for sure though – it seems nature has a way of disrupting social and economic life – when social and economic life disrupts the workings of nature. By decimating the peasants, the Black Death decimated that class which upheld the super-structure of feudal society:

The idea was that with up to 50% of the population wiped out in some regions, labour became scarce and labourers were able to secure better rights and status for themselves. But it turns out to be more complicated. In some places, the Black Death reinforced serfdom. Precisely because labour was scarce, it became more valuable to landowners who were therefore more motivated to coerce it.

SPINNEY, 2020

Under feudalism, land and livelihoods were guaranteed because the peasants were tied to the land. This was until feudalism could no longer be sustained thereby ejecting enslaved but secure man into "no man's land" and then whipping his hide and herding him into the factories that were popping up in different parts of England. Before the advent of factories:

Medieval political communities based their coherence and their success on the control of land. The reason is simple: all pre-industrial societies are based on agricultural wealth above all. There was nothing which one could call a factory in the middle ages, or for a long time afterwards.

WICKHAM, 2016: 54

A combination of factors led to the decline and final disintegration of the feudal system – labour shortages as a result of the Black Death of 1348, continued wars amongst feudal powers in Europe, increased taxation by the king and state, and class struggle between the peasants and the ruling class of feudal society.

The labouring class in class societies embark on revolutions – in order to overcome their oppression. At least this is the history of humans thus far. In just the first decade of the 21st century – revolutions took place in Tunisia and Egypt. This was unimaginable in the Arab world. It came to be known as the Arab Spring. Rebellions and revolts did feature in the US in the time of COVID-19. It appeared largely under the banner of the Black Lives Matter movement and the storming of Capitol Hill on 6 January 2021. It seemed unimaginable that this would happen in the greatest nation on earth. Rebellions and revolt played a large part in the downfall of feudalism – as it did in the downfall of slavery. The land and all that it comprises is the reason for history. More than four fifths of the population in the early middle ages were peasants working on land (Wickham, 2016).

Kings of medieval Europe constantly fought wars over land and territory. In feudal society the king was the custodian of the land but unlike capitalist society – land was made available for all to live on and to live-off of. People were allowed to hunt, collect firewood, fruit, vegetables, etc. The difference however was that a class of people – the peasants – were the ones that laboured on the land whilst the lords, nobles, clergy, etc. upheld the feudal system of pomp, pride and power for themselves through physical force and feudal ideologies. The ideology that kept the serfs and peasants in bondage for many hundreds of years was that the king was god's representative on earth. On god's earth overseen by the church – the peasants toiled from dawn until dusk, and they were also expected to work more than half the week for the lords, nobles and clergy: "in Medieval England the vast majority of the population were peasants working the land in conditions of near slavery" (Stubley, 2015: 8). So, whilst the feudal system guaranteed living and production rights to the peasants it was the central power – the king – that had ultimate power over the land and his subjects.

As is the case under capitalism, land ownership in feudal society was both wealth and a symbol of status. Like in capitalist society – all was not well in feudal society. It seems that the rich in feudal society were treated similarly to the rich in capitalist society – they paid a meagre amount of tax. It is said that Donald Trump – the former president of the USA and a powerful and wealthy capitalist – paid a measly 750 dollars in tax in 2017. Many questioned this gross injustice and unfairness of there being one set of rules for the rich and one set of rules for the rest in capitalist society. Feudal society was no different in terms of the injustices felt and injustices questioned – as depicted by William Fitz Osbert – also known as Longbeard – in London in 1196:

Why should the poor shopkeeper in his wooden house pay the same as the rich merchant in his stone fortress? Should not every man pay a proportion of what he can afford?

STUBLEY, 2015: 17

With such questioning it seemed that like slavery, feudalism was doomed from the very beginning. But like Rosa Luxemburg, who in her time questioned the injustices of the capitalist system and was bludgeoned to death – Longbeard was executed feudal style. There is a heavy price to pay for questioning reigning ideologies. Ask Edward Snowden and Julian Assange – who dared to expose the real and dominant ideologies of the Western world in general and of the US in particular. Transparency and democracy function within forceful and rigid ideological boundaries in the Western world. There are concealed limits to these cherished Western values!

There have been many hundreds of revolts during feudalism. Cohn (2008: 27) writes of "1,112 revolts in Italy, France, and Flanders between 1200 and 1425". Cohn (2008: 27) continues: "the tax revolt reflected discontent with the state. The result was economic exhaustion, flight from the land and peasant rebellion".

COVID-19 is said to have killed about 15 million people or more. Scholars put the death toll from the Spanish Flu anywhere between 50–100 million people. The Black Death of 1348 is said to have killed off 50% of England's population. The labour shortage that resulted from the deaths of about 50% of England's population gave the peasants that were spared from the Black Death a bargaining opportunity with regards to working conditions and subsequent wages. This did not go down well with the ruling class. The Peasant Revolt of 1381 is the quintessence of the class struggle in feudal society:

Nicholas Hereford, a follower of Wyclif at Oxford University, preached a public sermon in English in St Frideswide's churchyard on 15 May 1382 in which he called on all faithful Christians to put their hands to the wheel, seize the property of the friars, monks and canons who lived off the labour of others, and set them all to manual work. If this were done, he argued, there would be no need to tax the poor commons.

BARKER, 2014: 170

John Balle was another troublemaker in feudal society – similar to Yanis Varoufakis in capitalist society. Balle asked difficult philosophical questions in the form of riddles: "when Adam delved, and Eve span, who was then a gentleman?" Capitalist ideologies were unravelled in the time of COVID-19.

Feudal ideologies were also gradually questioned and unravelled in the time of feudalism:

> And continuing his sermon, he [Balle] tried to prove by the words of the proverb that he had taken for his text, that from the beginning all men were created equal by nature, and that servitude had been introduced by the unjust and evil oppression of men, against the will of God, who, if it had pleased Him to create serfs, surely in the beginning of the world would have appointed who should be a serf and who a lord.
>
> BARKER, 2014: 214

Who would have thought that peasants and serfs – stupid, filthy, stinking idiots – would one fine morning get up, philosophically question the status quo and revolt against the state of affairs. During the Peasants Revolt of 1381, the peasant class seized the many ideological documents that served to uphold feudal society and publicly burned them (Barker, 2014). Whilst John Balle was the theorist for revolution, it was Wat Tyler who was the revolutionary – the Che Guevara of his time. The leader of the Peasant Revolt of 1381 – Wat Tyler – was subsequently slaughtered in front of the 14-year-old boy King Richard II of England. If they took-off the heads of the oppressors in France with the guillotine during the French Revolution of 1789 – then in England they took-off the oppressors' heads with swords and machetes during the Peasants Revolt of 1381:

> Their heads, however, were stuck on poles by the rebels and then displayed on London Bridge, just like the heads and quartered limbs of those whom the state had sentenced to death.
>
> BARKER, 2014: 263

Feudalism as a class society was coming undone. Constant wars amongst Europeans for more land, power and resources contributed further to the decline of the feudal system:

> Over-exploitation and stagnant productivity resulted in a decline in population after 1300. Subsequent labour shortages, peasant resistance or threat of flight led to widespread commutation of labour to money rent. The manorial system was further weakened by the thinning of the ranks of the nobility through war, the growing practice of leasing demesne, the emergence of a stratum of rich and middling peasants differentiated from the mass of peasant poor, and the growing use of wage labour. By

the end of the fifteenth century the economic basis of the feudal system
had disintegrated.

HELLER, 2011: 26

Transformation of persons and roles are integral to a transforming society. The
rebels and revolutionaries of England's civil war (The American Revolution or
US War of Independence) transformed themselves into the rulers of the US
in 1776. In South Africa Mandela the terrorist was transformed into Mandela
the statesman in 1994. Comrades and unionists were transformed into wealthy
capitalists in suits and ties – when South Africa transformed from apartheid
into non-racial capitalism. Whilst peasants under feudalism initiated a series
of revolutions against the ruling class – they would finally be defeated and
transformed into wage labourers. In this gradual transformation, the grand
transformation from feudalism to capitalism occurred side by side with the
transformation of the peasant worker into a wage labourer.

The lords and other privileged persons of feudal society transformed themselves to capitalists – they found a more sophisticated, organised, and efficient way of extracting labour-power or human-energy from the lower classes.
Capitalism is feudalism with all of the trappings of modernity, science, technology, sophistication and planning. But all of these are insufficient factors for
a country to become as wealthy as England did. We therefore must tread elsewhere to look for England's richest blessings in the modern age.

Conquests and colonisation of distant shores and lands were chief architects in the making of English capitalism – in the similar manner that Roman
conquests and colonisation were chief architects in the making of the Roman
Empire. If the Roman Empire gave the world Jesus Christ – capitalism gave
the world Che Guevara. The Spanish pillaged gold and silver from Mexico and
Peru. The Portuguese were sailing the world's oceans – encountering lands,
people and commodities that aroused their appetite. Conquests were a big
part of the encounters. Merchant trading was also a large part of cultural life
in the time of feudalism – and more so during its dying days. Whilst the kings
ruled, and the peasants and workers toiled on enclosed lands – the merchant
class explored distant lands for wealth accumulation. When the Dutch, French
and English came to know about the wealth in other parts of the world – they
packed their ships with raiders and ammunition. Countries in other parts of
the world were already producing before capitalism – and Europe wanted as
much of the world's wealth as it could get its hands on. The wealth in other
parts of the world was ready for the taking.

Whilst the waged peasants of Europe toiled the land and the nobility wined
and dined, the kings' and queens' stealers were sailing the world's oceans – on

the lookout for loot. Deadly competition and conflict were part of this historical mix. Europe's hunger for wealth in Asia, Africa, the Americas and the Middle East was limitless. Ships poured out of Europe – and wealth in the form of gold, silver, copper, spices, silk, sugar, diamonds, wine, timber, tobacco, coal, coffee, tea, slaves etc. poured back into Europe. If the Spanish stole from the world – the Dutch, English and French stole from the Spanish. When the Dutch became the forerunners of the seas and trade through the Dutch East India Company (DEIC) – the English and the French stole from the Dutch. We are reminded that violence was key to wealth distribution in the dying days of feudalism and the beginning days of capitalism: "evidently in the minds of European rivals what could not be gained through competition might yield to violence" (Appleby, 2010: 52).

History and the men that ruled Europe in the time of feudalism – were seeing to it that their respective countries in Europe became wealthy. The downtrodden class that indirectly financed these conquests in the main were the peasants and workers of mainly agricultural Europe. They were worked and taxed to death! If wealth was continually extracted from the peasants and the serfs back home – it was just as well extracted from faraway lands – conquered and colonised by countries from Europe. Conquer, conquest, merchant trading and the exploitation of the toiling classes made the ruling elite wealthy in much of Europe. Feudal society was fast changing – and conquer, conquest, merchant trading and exploitation was part of the mix of this historical change: "In the 1700s many nobles and merchants made money by investing in British overseas trade in slaves, wool and other goods" (Smart, 1996: 99). Merchant capital was beginning to accumulate in Britain. The old society was dying and a new one was being born. Nobody knew the name of the new society that was slowly but surely taking shape and form. Only much later would it be called capitalism – the social system that we have made for ourselves and live with today. Feudalism and the violence and oppression that accompanied it, conquest, plunder and European rivalry – were the mid-wives of the system we know today as capitalism:

> The Seven Years War (1756–1763) was a conflict fought worldwide. It was fought between Britain and France for colonial possessions in America and India; and between Prussia, supported by Britain and Hanover, against an alliance of Austria, France, Russia and Sweden in Europe. Spain became involved as an ally of France.
>
> SMART, 1996: 102

England is a relatively small spot on the world map – when compared to the
gigantic countries and continents of the world such as China, India, Africa,
Australia, etc. Even Kazakhstan – the home-country of Borat – looks much
bigger than England on the world map. A world existed outside of England –
China, Africa, Australia, India, etc. – these lands were rich with people, animals, plants, vegetation, rivers, lakes, gold, diamonds, tea, spices, copper, coffee, technology, science, arts, philosophy, culture, etc. England also had people
and natural resources like coal – but nothing compared to the other rich lands
of the world. To get a glimpse of the state of England in comparison to India,
for example, it might help to turn to – among others – Alex von Tunzelmann
(2012: 1):

> In the beginning there were two nations. One was a vast, mighty and
> magnificent empire, brilliantly organized and culturally unified, which
> dominated a massive swathe of the earth. The other was an undeveloped,
> semi-feudal realm, riven by religious factionalism and barely able to feed
> its illiterate, diseased and stinking masses. The first nation was India. The
> second was England.

History and the men – and sometimes women – that wielded power – would
in time go on to transform this "undeveloped, semi-feudal realm" of "diseased
and stinking masses" called England – into a world superpower. One of the
ways was to form the British East India Company in the year 1600 – when
the old – feudalism – was dying and the new – capitalism – was being born.
India was already visited by the Portuguese Vasco da Gama in 1498. The Dutch
landed in 1595, the English in 1608. The French arrived late on the scene – in
1664. But history chose England as the birthplace of capitalism. And India was
"The Jewel in the Crown". The state in its late feudal form then – was intimately
involved in the economy. Queen Elizabeth I awarded the British East India
Company a charter – a legislative document granting permission to trade. This
is not dissimilar to states in capitalist society awarding capitalists licenses to
make and sell guns and ammunition for purposes of war, for example. The
state shapes the economy, and the economy shapes the state.

In any event, the markets and demand for overseas commodities were fast
developing in Europe in general and in England in particular. Indians – well
versed in supply and demand economics and ever-ready to make a quick
buck – raised the prices of goods when well-off Europeans demanded more of
Indian commodities. If China is the workshop of the world now – India was
the workshop of the world then – when kings and queens fought and killed
each other in Europe. Nowadays competition is eliminated by price-fixing. In

the time of merchant trading – European countries resorted to sinking each other's ships and fortifying trading posts in order to eliminate competition for commodities from the East. The birth of England's cotton industry was intimately tied to the death of India's well-established cotton industry. As India's cotton industry was deindustrialised – England's was fast industrialising. Marx (1853) reminds us: "it was the British intruder who broke up the Indian hand-loom and destroyed the spinning-wheel". The development of English capitalism – would be intimately tied to India for the next 350 years. As Marx annoyingly reminds the history ideologues of English capitalism in the New York Tribune:

> England began with driving the Indian cottons from the European market; it then introduced twist into Hindostan and in the end inundated the very mother country of cotton with cottons.
>
> MARX, 1853

India gained political independence from British colonialism in 1947. Capitalism and cricket stayed in India when the British left. The world witnessed the mess of Indian capitalism in the time of COVID-19. Even the lucrative Indian Premier League (IPL) of cricket chose to focus on profit-making – the bedrock of capitalism – in the midst of India's dying and burning bodies. Nothing much had changed. The people perished under British rule – and the people were perishing under Indian rule – as witnessed in the time of COVID-19. Indian independence was simply the rich and powerful in India fighting for the independence – to themselves exploit and oppress the Indian masses. Like eating juicy beef and a menstruating woman still wanting to visit the house of gods – competition to not exploit seemed taboo in Mother India. The forces of history made England the birthplace of capitalism – in a similar manner that the forces of history made England the colonial empire of the world – or made England's subjects breakaway and form the United States of America. History matters! But Marx in *The Eighteenth Brumaire of Louis Bonaparte* (1972[1852]: 9) reminds us that:

> Men make their own history, but they do not make it as they please; they do not make it under self-selected circumstances, but under circumstances existing already, given and transmitted from the past.

So much for freedom of choice under capitalism! For Marx (1848: 14) the fault line for conflict and violence in capitalist society is the class system. Under the capitalist system, the two major contending classes are the capitalist class – the owners of the means of production and the working class – the owners of their only commodity or property – labour power or human-energy. The cap-italist class stands on the backs of the working class in capitalist society – in a similar manner that the lords and barons stood on the backs of serfs and peas-ants in feudal society – or the masters who stood on the backs of slaves in slave society. As to how one set of the human race became owners of the means of production – and another the sellers of labour-power or human-energy – with no means of production – is indeed a mystery buried deep beneath the ideol-ogy of capitalist-biased economic science. Marx – in the *Communist Manifesto of 1848* – gives us a clue when he states that the workers "are reduced to selling their labour power in order to live" (1848: 14).

The question for all thinking people is: if nature makes all women and men equal – then how is it that a human being becomes reduced in a particular type of society? Homo sapiens were reduced to slaves in slave society. They were reduced to peasants in feudal society. They were reduced to animals – hunted and killed – in Nazi society. Homo sapiens were reduced to inferior beings in apartheid society. They are reduced to prisoners in their own land in Palestine. Homo sapiens are reduced to primarily workers in capitalist society. They were reduced to expendables in the Western world in the time of COVID-19.

3   The Violent-Making of Private Property: The Foundation for the Development of Capitalism

Man – like the ape, the deer, the sheep, the eagle, etc. is born into a piece of land on planet earth. But unlike the ape, the deer, the sheep, the eagle, etc. the land is no longer his property to live on and to live-off of. Had he been born into a hunter-gatherer society, he would have had the same access to land and its produce as the ape, the deer, the sheep, the eagle, etc. Times and property relations have changed over the millennia. Man is born into a capitalist soci-ety – and he must therefore spend his entire life trying to acquire what nature made easily accessible for all creatures in the first place – man included. The proviso being that he must now expend his human-energy or labour-power and time – in order to acquire what nature has on offer. If he is fortunate – he will be able to do so through the capitalist market. For many hundreds of millions of people – it is not possible – they are excluded from the capitalist market. They do not get what nature has free to offer and what the capitalist economy produces in abundance. For the lucky worker – he will acquire some private property in her or his lifetime.

The rich are extremely lucky – they own lots of private property – more than they ever need in their lifetime. For many, owning just a simple home as private property is an almost impossible task. Private property is key to survival and the good life. Ask a beggar who relies on the private property of others. For those who have private property, their survival is ensured. The more private property they have – the better is their standard of living. One's mobile phone is one's private property. So is one's car or home or the land on which his or her home is built. A piece of rotting wood can be private property – for example, in Marx's time the law made the collection of fallen branches for firewood illegal and prosecutable by the forest owners. The poor suffered because of this law. The so-called barbarian in the hunter-gatherer society was free to gather wood – not the poor of civilising Europe. The violence of the state against the poor – ensured that ordinary rotting wood remained the private property of the ruling class.

Private property is sacred and jealously guarded in capitalist society – even if such wood would provide the meagre energy needed to boil a pot of broth or to mend a collapsing home. A man's clothing is his private property. A vagabond's clothing is usually ragged and tattered – but it is still his private property. Even ideas and information have transformed into private property under capitalism. Countries and especially poorer countries were not allowed to use available information for vaccine production – even though the setting aside of private property laws would have saved hundreds of thousands or millions of lives in the time of COVID-19. Just like the privatisation of rotting wood in Europe that eventually killed – the privatisation of intellectual property killed in the time of COVID-19. Capitalism kills. Private property kills. George Floyd was killed because he dared to violate private property capitalist laws. His 20-dollar bill did not fit the description of private property in the US – even though it was his personal and private money. Private property in the form of businesses is scarce amongst black people in the US. Whites own most of the private property in the US. Come to think of it – whites once owned black people as private property!

Seven billion people and counting have to secure private property in order to make it through in life under capitalism. We live in a world where few own large tracts of land and nature. Donald Trump owns many golf courses and buildings as private property. There are others like him in capitalist society – they go by the label of "the 1%". Planet earth has become privatised. A few also own the means of producing private property. It takes a lifetime to accumulate a handful of private property. One's children are better off – after they inherit the private property that their parents have worked tirelessly for through much of their lives. They will in turn accumulate more private property – and pass it on to their children. We live to accumulate under capitalism. Bill Gates' children are lucky – and so are their children and their children and their children's children.

The children of the migrant workers of India will most probably end up being migrant workers themselves. They will have little or no private property – except their labour to exchange on India's ruthless labour market. They will most probably die in their large numbers again – if or when the next pandemic comes along – and if capitalism is still around. Capitalism reproduces itself – for as long as it can. It takes hard work and many years to secure private property such as a piece of land, a home, a car, a good phone with which to take selfies, etc. Being in debt for all these wonderful things produced by capitalism – makes it even harder. It's even harder when education and health care are privatised. It is not possible for one to own big tech companies as private property – by just using one's own time and energy. Imagine a single hunter-gatherer, or a single feudal lord owning Tesla. It is why big companies have swarms of workers working for them. It is not possible to own big people movement companies like Uber as private property; it's why Uber has millions of workers in all parts of the world working for it. The courts in the UK declared in 2021 that Uber drivers are not self-contracted; they are workers.

Many hundreds of millions of people work hard to attain private property – if and when they can. Hundreds of millions of people in all parts of the world work hard in order to secure the private property that they own – even against the many odds under capitalism. They do this by exchanging the private property that nature has endowed them with – their labour-power or human-energy. Anything has the potential to become private property – even humans. One human can be the private property of another human – in the same way that a washing machine or a soccer ball is the private property of its owner. A dog is not viewed as private property – even though he has an owner. He is regarded as a pet. Masters may have had pet slaves – but only a few may have shared the same space as their masters.

England acquired much of its private property through conquests and colonisation. It ended up owning land and nature in other parts of the world. Even Hong Kong was once the private property of England! England still believes that Hong Kong is somehow its private property. The rulers of England seem to have nostalgia for Hong Kong. They pine for the good old days of Empire. They do it through the ideological lens of Western-styled democracy and human rights.

Ayn Rand – one of the leading ideologues of capitalism notes that the institution of private property is a unique feature of capitalism:

> But a nobleman was as much chattel of the tribe as a serf; his life and property belonged to the king. It must be remembered that the institution of private property, in the full, legal meaning of the term, was brought into existence only by capitalism. In the pre-capitalist eras, private property

existed de facto, but not de jure, i.e., by custom and sufferance, not by right or by law. In law and in principle, all property belonged to the head of the tribe, the king, and was held only by his permission, which could be revoked at any time, at his pleasure. (The king could and did expropriate the estates of recalcitrant noblemen throughout the course of Europe's history.).

RAND, 1966: 15–16

Adler (2009:120) raises an interesting point about the nature of wealth and private property under capitalism:

> Adam Smith's *The Wealth of Nations*, published in 1776, is perhaps the most important economics book of all time, though a more accurate title would have included a subtitle, "The Wealth of Nations: How Did It End Up in the Hands of So Few?" According to Smith, workers in the "original state" owned all that they produced: "the produce of labour constitutes the natural recompense or wages of labour. In that original state of things which precedes both the appropriation of land and the accumulation of stock, the whole produce of labour belongs to the labourer. He has neither landlord nor master to share with him."

So, we now find ourselves in a situation whereby billions are excluded from nature's economy – and a few hundred thousand own planet earth – which the billions indirectly depend upon for life and livelihood. Such ownership patterns are protected by powerful states with powerful militaries and police forces – underpinned by the ideology of capitalist private property laws.

The question that now confronts man – the intelligent ape – is: if nature birthed man into the Garden of Eden – then how has it come to be that man has been ejected from the Garden of Eden? He now finds himself having to claw his way back into the Garden of Eden with much trials and tribulations through the capitalist market – a capitalist market that he was no part of and which was not of his choosing – but which now is the god of his fate and lot in life.

If man was part of nature – then his incremental and gradual separation from nature began with the theft of his land. Where he was part and parcel of the land – as under feudalism – man was ejected from the land. This is the prerequisite for the establishment of capitalism as a historical system. Nature sits on land. Under capitalism – nature is also wealth untransformed. Under capitalism – nature is there for the taking. Under capitalism – nature is merely a resource, a raw material, money, profit and wealth accumulation in waiting. If land was violently stolen from the First Americans – it was owing to its natural treasures – and apparently its' potential for capitalist development:

> The United States of America is capitalism's land of promise. All conditions needed for its complete and pure development were first fulfilled here. In no other country and among no other people was capitalism favoured with circumstances that permitted it to develop to the most advanced state. In no other country is it possible to accumulate capital so rapidly. There are several reasons for this. The United States is rich in precious metals. North America produces a third of all the silver and a quarter of all the gold in the world. It is rich in fertile soils: the Mississippi Plain comprises about five times as much as the best humus soil as do the black earth districts of southern Russia and Hungary together. It is rich in abundant deposits of useful minerals that today give three times as much output as any European deposits. The United States is more suited than any other country for capitalist expansion. The Mississippi Plain is ideally positioned for economically viable agriculture and for the unlimited growth of transportation: it is an area of 3.8 million square kilometres, therefore approximately seven times the size of the German Empire without any barrier to communication and, by way of a bonus, it is already provided with several natural means of transportation. On the Atlantic coast there are fifty-five good harbours that have waited thousands of years for capitalist exploitation. The striving after endless expansion, so fundamental to every capitalist economy, can be freely fulfilled for the first time in these North American expanses that stretch far beyond where the eye can see.
>
> SOMBART, 1976: 3

But people once lived on this rich land now called the United States of America. What was the common property of the Native Americans, became the private property of Britain's rebels. America and the United Kingdom are now allies – even though they killed each other in days gone by. In actual fact they killed themselves over other people's land – and killed off the inhabitants of the land as well! Capitalism now binds both countries at the military hips and ideological heads. Like its earlier history – capitalism never fails to unleash violence on nature and the people that occupy such nature.

In South America – the Amazon rainforest is known as the green lungs of the world. Yet capitalism has planted its accumulation flag on this natural wonder. But the history of capitalism is one of wiping out the indigenous peoples – the people who were closest to nature – in whichever continent capitalism was exported to during the reign of the British Empire:

> Within Western countries, dispossession of producers from the means of production and the increase and intensification of work – in other words, primitive accumulation and absolute surplus value, both backed by the state – played their part in capitalism's development as much as markets and technical improvements.
>
> HELLER, 2011: 6

About 100 years before Marx, the economic scientist Adam Smith stated in his *The Wealth of Nations* (1776):

> As soon as the land of any country has all become private property, the landlords, like all other men, love to reap where they never sowed, and demand a rent even for its natural produce. The wood of the forest, the grass of the field, and all the natural fruits of the earth, which, when land was in common, cost the labourer only the trouble of gathering them, come, even to him, to have an additional price fixed upon them.
>
> SMITH, 1776: 76

Marx (867: 508) points to the theft of land in Scotland for capitalism's development:

> As an example of the method obtaining in the 19th century, the "clearing" made by the Duchess of Sutherland will suffice here. This person, well instructed in economy, resolved, on entering upon her government, to effect a radical cure, and to turn the whole country, whose population had already been, by earlier processes of the like kind, reduced to 15,000, into a sheep-walk. From 1814 to 1820 these 15,000 inhabitants, about 3,000 families, were systematically hunted and rooted out. All their villages were destroyed and burnt, all their fields turned into pasturage. British soldiers enforced this eviction, and came to blows with the inhabitants. One old woman was burnt to death in the flames of the hut, which she refused to leave. Thus this fine lady [the Duchess of Sutherland] appropriated 794,000 acres of land that had from time immemorial belonged to the clan. She assigned to the expelled inhabitants about 6,000 acres on the sea-shore – 2 acres per family. The 6,000 acres had until this time lain waste, and brought in no income to their owners. The Duchess, in the nobility of her heart, actually went so far as to let these at an average rent of 2s. 6d. per acre to the clansmen, who for centuries had shed their

blood for her family. The whole of the stolen clan land she divided into 29 great sheep farms, each inhabited by a single family, for the most part imported English farm-servants. In the year 1835 the 15,000 Gaels were already replaced by 131,000 sheep. The remnant of the aborigines flung on the sea-shore tried to live by catching fish. They became amphibious and lived, as an English author says, half on land and half on water, and withal only half on both.

Marx continues:

> The spoliation of the church's property, the fraudulent alienation of the state domains, the robbery of the common lands, the usurpation of feudal and clan property, and its transformation into modern private property under circumstances of reckless terrorism, were just so many idyllic methods of primitive accumulation. They conquered the field for capitalistic agriculture, made the soil part and parcel of capital, and created for the town industries the necessary supply of a "free" and outlawed proletariat.
>
> MARX, 1867: 509

Everywhere – from Europe to Africa to the Americas to Australia – the birth of capitalism was dependent on stolen lands. The foundation of capitalist private property is founded on unimaginable and untold violence. The free market for private property such as land came much later. One can now buy land in South Africa on the property market. But land had to first be stolen in South Africa – as was the case for the rest of the world – in order for land to be sold on the free market under the ideology of demand and supply. The history of capitalism is drenched in blood and tears of the murdered and the dispossessed!

4   The Violent-Making of the Wage Labourer, the Labour Market and Capitalism

If nature once owned and contained man, how come the worker is no longer a creature of land and nature – but now finds himself existing as an economic-unit in the labour market – or as an economic-unit in the factory, firm or office? If man once hunted beavers and deer with bows, arrows, spears, fire, etc. – it means that man had free access to land, equipment, tools, energy, etc., the means of production. How come he no longer owns the means for making a livelihood and a life? Did he or she freely exchange all of these means of production in the capitalist market? If yes – for what and why? All they have left is their only life and livelihood commodity – their labour with which to attempt an existence in a planet of plenty – but a planet which is under the dictatorship of capitalism. We are all workers now. Billions of us must sell our labour on the capitalist labour market in order to make a life and a livelihood. We must work for our living. Whereas as hunter-gatherers we worked for ourselves, our families and our tribes – in capitalist society we work firstly for the owners of capital – owners of the means of production – and secondly for ourselves and our families. In *Capital*, Marx (1867:118) posed the conundrum:

> The question why this free labourer confronts him in the market, has no interest for the owner of money, who regards the labour-market as a branch of the general market for commodities. One thing, however, is clear – nature does not produce on the one side owners of money or commodities, and on the other men possessing nothing but their own labour-power. This relation has no natural basis, neither is its social basis one that is common to all historical periods. It is clearly the result of a past historical development, the product of many economic revolutions, of the extinction of a whole series of older forms of social production.

It seems history makes us – in the same way that it made masters and slaves, lords and serfs. We are now capitalists and workers – and sometimes in between – thanks to history. If Fukuyama is right – as pronounced in his best seller – *The End of History and the Last Man* – then we must contend with being capitalists, workers and sometimes in between. It is the same as saying that we should accept our fate as masters and slaves under slave society, or as lords and serfs in feudal society. According to Perelman in his *The Invention of Capitalism* (2000) – in order for capitalism to gain traction – the biological family has to be transformed into a commercial family:

> The establishment of this "great commercial family" required that the relatively autarkic economic structure of the independent household be broken down in order that it would become doubly dependent. First, it was to become dependent on commodities that were, in general, produced with wage labor. Second, to acquire these commodities, members of the household would have to supply the market with wage labor.
>
> PERELMAN, 2000

If there weren't scholars like Marx, we would go on believing that god and nature made capitalists and workers as separate economic species. But Marx sees through economic science myths and ideologies that have thus far pre-vailed. He reminds us how ruthless, naked and untold violence was used to make the worker in order for capitalism to emerge victorious:

> In actual history it is notorious that conquest, enslavement, robbery, murder, briefly force, play the great part. In the tender annals of Political Economy, the idyllic reigns from time immemorial. Right and labour were from all time the sole means of enrichment, the present year of course always excepted. As a matter of fact, the methods of primitive accumulation are anything but idyllic.
>
> MARX, 1867: 500

If you lived and worked on the land – then you have to be removed from the land so that you can now work for the capitalist who now owns the land:

> Thus were the agricultural people, first forcibly expropriated from the soil, driven from their homes, turned into vagabonds, and then whipped, branded, tortured by laws grotesquely terrible, into the discipline necessary for the wage system.
>
> MARX, 1867: 516

Whilst feudalism was failing as a historical system, it was also made to fail by the powers that be. The transforming system resorted to new ways of extracting surplus value – by violently disciplining the men and women thrown off the land. The state was intimately involved in the economy in general and in the making of the labour market in particular:

> For example, beginning with the Tudors, England enacted a series of stern measures to prevent peasants from drifting into vagrancy or falling back onto welfare systems. According to a 1572 statute, beggars over the age of fourteen were to be severely flogged and branded with a red-hot iron on the left ear unless someone was willing to take them into service for two years. Repeat offenders over eighteen were to be executed unless someone would take them into service. Third offenses automatically resulted in execution (Marx 1977, 896 ff.; Marx 1974, 736; Mantoux 1961, 432). Similar statutes appeared almost simultaneously during the early sixteenth century in England, the Low Countries, and Zurich (LeRoy Ladurie 1974, 137). Eventually, the majority of workers, lacking any alternative, had little choice but to work for wages at something close to subsistence level (24–25).

Wherever capitalism wanted to sink its accumulation roots, it was met with the obstacles of plenty for the inhabitants. Nature's economy already provided for man – and nature had to be seized by force. The foundation of the capitalist wage-labour system has been secured through extreme forms of violence. Man must now continually give off of himself for the endless accumulation of capital:

> These labourers, who must sell themselves piecemeal, are a commodity, like every other article of commerce, and are consequently exposed to all the vicissitudes of competition, to all the fluctuations of the market.
> MARX, 1848: 18

If nature made humans, then capitalism made sure that the vast majority of humans are converted into workers – working for a minority of other humans. If humans can now sell their labour-power on the labour market – it is because humans were cast out of The Garden of Eden through unbelievable levels of violence in the first instance. If capitalism robbed man of his land and his means of production – it also robbed man of his freedom to decide on how he would like to make a life and a livelihood. Capitalism now decides for him.

5   Failed and F/Ailing Capitalism

Those in feudal society probably thought that that's the way the world always was – and always will be. But we know that feudal society finally disintegrated. I'm sure slave owners were happy with slave society – and also believed that that's the way the world works. It's why slave owners and ideologists of slavery fought in the US Civil War to maintain the status quo. But like feudal society – we are all too aware that slave society was done away with. It now leaves us with the conundrum of capitalist society. Will it go – or will it stay? Should it go – or should it stay? Who or what will decide the fate of capitalism – only time will tell.

Marx praised the productive nature of capitalism – but he also exposed the many evils of capitalism. Eight hundred and fifty million Chinese were lifted out of poverty through capitalist means under a communist state – after the role colonialism played in the systemic impoverishment of the Chinese. Capitalism had outdone feudalism. But capitalism seems to have outdone itself. To continue with the capitalist system – is akin to flogging a dying horse. But this will not stop states, capitalists and neoliberal economic scientists from trying. It's why the world is at a breaking point.

Since its inception capitalism has failed large swathes of humankind. It has failed the inhabitants in all parts of the world – whose land and means of production were violently stolen from them for the green shoots of capitalism to sprout. Marx referred to this stage of capitalist development as primitive accumulation. Capitalism failed the many millions of men, women and children – who were ejected from their lands and violently converted into wage labourers. The men, women and children of the Industrial Revolution come to mind. Capitalism failed the millions of men, women and children who toiled until their early deaths – so that the Industrial Revolution could go on to become England's pride and joy.

The ideology of progress successfully masks the evils generated by the Industrial Revolution. The Victorian brand of violent capitalism was unleashed on an unsuspecting and innocent people. Capitalism is an inherently conflictual system – with violence being its extreme form. The violence that enabled capitalism to emerge from feudal society has not dissipated with the growth and strengthening of capitalism – it is merely buried under layers of capitalist ideologies. We experience it every day. The human race is forced to cower to capitalism – in order to make a life and a livelihood. Even capitalists have to cower to capitalism – or else they too would be destroyed by the logic of capitalism for ever-more profit.

Look around and we see violence everywhere. Under capitalism, violence has become civilisation's cultural norm – part and parcel of the new world order. Mass shootings in the world's most capitalistic country is just another American occurrence. Gun possession is protected by the 2nd amendment – and therefore mass shootings become legitimised. Nowhere else in the world does such ideological insanity exist but in the United States of America – the epitome of capitalism. Instead of pragmatically repealing gun laws – the powers that be invoke the ideology of god and religion to pacify the hurt, the angry, the lost and the confused. A call to prayer is always made after a mass shooting. With so many gods competing for our attention, which one of the many can save American lives from another mass shooting!? The country that is famous for giving the world Eat Pray Love – is also known the world over – for Shoot Pray Shoot!

Capitalism is a cultural system that also depends on god, religion and prayer as its ideological allies – to distract the masses from identifying capitalism as the generator and source of such violence. As Marx (1843) states:

> Religion is the sigh of the oppressed creature, the heart of a heartless world, and the soul of soulless conditions. It is the opium of the people.

Huge profits from gun sales is why Americans are sold the idea that guns are what keeps them safe. But it seems many Americans are numbed by ideology – not informed by reality. They keep buying guns – and they keep killing each other. If Americans are not killing each other – then the American elite continue to kill people in other parts of the world. America also happens to be the country with the most powerful military set-up in the world – not only within its borders – but on every continent on the planet. It is also the only country in the world to have dropped atomic bombs on the human race. America is violence. Violence is America. And raw and ruthless capitalism is at the heart of this violence.

On the other side of planet earth, South Africa – a country and not a continent – violence sits next to almost all other aspects of life, in schools, in homes, in the townships, in parliament, in nature reserves supposedly protecting rhinos, etc. Situated in a continent with vast expanses of richness in terms of natural resources, but impoverished through colonialism, apartheid-capitalism and non-racial capitalism, South Africa also once possessed nuclear weapons – but that made an exit with the ejection of the racist white authoritarian regime in 1994. Rather an authoritarian, racist and capitalist white state be the gatekeepers of nuclear weapons – than a black democratic one pretending to be socialist in orientation. Who would have thought that a country in Africa once possessed nuclear weapons!

How is it that the richest country on the African continent– and was once able to produce and keep nuclear weapons – had the highest number of infections and deaths in the time of COVID-19? How is this for political and ideological will by a state on the "Dark Continent"! And like America, South Africa also happens to be a capitalist country – but more Victorian in shape and form than the capitalisms of the US and other capitalist countries on the globe. Like sport, the BIG 5, Nelson Mandela, Table Mountain, marijuana and monopoly capitalism – violence is part and parcel of South African life.

Whilst writing, I received news from my sister that her domestic worker's son was stabbed to death – because he refused to hand over his hard-earned week's wages to robbers. His two children are now without a father, his wife is without a husband and his mom is without a son. My youngest sister's text message on that sad day read: "incidents like this will be a common occurrence – the poor will rob the poor and the not-so-poor in the light of COVID-19" (Noelene Govender, 2020). This is in the new South Africa. This is the story of failed capitalism for South Africa's desperate majority.

Capitalism was allowed to stay – when apartheid was shown the door in the early 1990s. The entire capitalist world is one of violence on a massive scale: continued wars, killings, murders, rapes, abuses, assaults, bullying, deaths by design, child kidnapping, forced labour, gender-based violence, etc. Violence has globalised capitalism since its beginnings – and capitalism has globalised violence ever since. Capitalist violence has failed the millions of soldiers – who were used as cannon fodder in so many wars – for capitalism's grand pursuit of resource and wealth accumulation – as well as for Western ideological supremacy.

Even when it had the chance to prove how successful it could be in the time of COVID-19, when the world needed its productive capacity the most – capitalism instead chose to leave strewn bodies on its path. Death and destruction were the highest and most severe in the capitalist countries of the world. All the grandeur, wealth, technology and successes of capitalism built up over the many centuries were not effectively, efficiently and timeously unleashed to save the millions that needed hospital beds, ventilators, vaccines, oxygen, medicines, etc. Capitalism failed 21st century society. Capitalism failed the Western world. Capitalism failed modern civilisation. Capitalism failed Homo sapiens. Capitalism failed the dead granny who did not get a vaccine on time. Capitalism failed the mother who died – because she did not have access to a hospital bed. Capitalism failed!

Capitalism failed the brother who died on the roadside of India – because oxygen was in short supply. Capitalism failed black Americans. Capitalism is a system of tyranny and dictatorship in the workplace. It fails the test of democracy. All men are created equal but capitalism ensures that all men are recreated as unequals in society in general and in the workplace in particular – many are workers like peasants, others are supervisors and managers like lords and barons, and a few are wealthy owners of private property – like kings and queens. A few earn lots of money – and the many just a little.

In capitalist society there is so much inequality amongst Homo sapiens – that many don't earn a wage at all. Capitalism continues to fail the unemployed masses in many parts of the world. In the time of COVID-19, workers had no choice but to get back to work whilst under continued attack by an invisible enemy. Whilst the kings and queens of the middle ages used violence to force people to work as wage labourers to discipline them for the emerging factories, the states in the capitalist world used different forms of coercion to get people back to work during a global pandemic.

Hundreds of millions of workers in all parts of the world do not own the means of production – and without a surplus reserve fund to help them wait out the pandemic – they had no choice but to put themselves out in the labour market to continue to sell the only commodity or private property that they own – their labour. Capitalism failed the workers. Workers do not own land, nature, factories, equipment, energy, etc. These are owned by a minority of people in global capitalist society. Capitalism is a system that is comprised of the working class – the owners of labour-power and the capitalist class – the owners of the resources for production. But capitalism is also made up of lawyers, teachers, doctors, academics, etc. This layer of society makes up the middle class in capitalist society and helps to stabilise capitalist society. For those that do own private property such as homes, cars, clothing, etc. such commodities are on loan to them – until and unless they are able to pay off the debt on such private property. By the time they pay off their debt on their private property– if they are fortunate to do so – they are physically and emotionally drained and are usually at the end of their lives.

Under capitalism – you can shop until you drop – and the banks will happily back you up with credit facilities. For example, in the time of COVID-19, I received emails and short text messages with the following subject heading: "you have been approved for a credit limit increase". I have learnt from my family's painful experiences of the horrors of being in debt – and refused to be coerced into accepting the debt-carrot that was dangled before me by the capitalist market. There are many hundreds of millions of people in all parts of the world who don't have much choice but to accept the credit carrot offered by the capitalist market – and to live a life of debt under capitalism. Capitalism has converted hundreds of millions into debt-slaves. In fact, states themselves are neck-deep in debt under capitalism. States themselves have become slaves to capitalism. This is demonstrable of capitalism as a failed socio-economic system for Homo sapiens.

Capitalism is a system of massive amounts of poor and unemployed people. Capitalism is an economic, political and social system engineered to generate inequalities. Equality was not, is not, and will not be the hallmark of capitalism – precisely because under capitalism the poor make the rich – and the rich make the poor. Capitalism is a pyramid scheme – a Ponzi scheme – designed to siphon-off value from the hordes of workers and nature – with the implicit and explicit aim of directing such value to the apex of the pyramid of capitalist society. Capitalism has produced and continues to reproduce the 1% of wealthy individuals and the 99% that are in constant competition with each other – to both survive and to make it up the economic ladder – if at all possible. Under capitalism the rich gets preferential treatment. To use the familiar adage – the rich get richer and the poor get poorer.

Observers of the capitalist system have and are pronouncing that capitalism as a socio-economic and cultural system is also a failed or failing system. COVID-19 has revealed that capitalism is a broken system:

Capitalism, the greatest engine for prosperity and innovation ever created, was already under strain before the coronavirus pandemic. Despite
a decade of impressive economic growth and job creation, a plurality of
Americans still reported feeling as though the system was rigged, that
hard work and playing by the rules no longer ensured success.

LANE, 2020

Back home, we are reminded that "South Africa was bankrupt even before the
pandemic" (Sartorius, 2020: 16). Capitalism was already in trouble in South
Africa before COVID-19. The rating agencies relegated the capitalist economy to almost junk status. The entire global capitalist economy was on its
knees before COVID-19: "much of the world economy was already in chronic
slowdown when the COVID-19 shock pushed it into an unprecedented crisis"
(Deepak, 2020). A decade ago we were told that capitalism is huffing and puff-
ing along:

> In the early years of the twenty-first century the sense of capitalism in
> crisis has deepened. Yet the way ahead is obstructed by many difficulties:
> low rates of profit and over-accumulation of capital; under-consumption
> and insufficient demand; the breakdown of the system of global finance;
> the prospect of energy shortage and acute symptoms of environmental
> crisis; and a crisis of world governability. Weighed down by these seri-
> ous problems, the production of profits and growth in the future within
> the existing system has been thrown into doubt. The multiplicity and
> depth of the difficulties burdening contemporary capitalism poses the
> question of whether the system can stabilise and continue to reproduce
> itself, whether humanity is on the threshold of a momentous transition
> to socialism, or whether we face an unending stagnation and even a
> descent into ruin.
>
> HELLER, 2011: xi

Insight after insight has pointed to the failed and failing capitalist system:

> Capitalism has created more prosperity than history has ever witnessed,
> but the cost—not least in the near-destitution of billions—has been
> astronomical. According to the World Bank, 2.74 billion people in 2001
> lived on less than two dollars a day. We face a probable future of nuclear-
> armed states warring over a scarcity of resources; and that scarcity is
> largely the consequence of capitalism itself.
>
> EAGLETON, 2018: 9

When capitalism does not know any longer whether it is capitalism and free market functioning for the entire of society or socialism for the rich – then it should be construed as a failed or failing system:

> Many people became disillusioned with the workings of their political systems—particularly when governments bailed out bankers with tax-payers' money and then stood by impotently as financiers continued to pay themselves huge bonuses. The crisis turned the Washington consensus into a term of reproach across the emerging world.
>
> DELAIBATIKI, 2021

Under capitalism the climate has not healed. The unemployed have not been guaranteed work. The wars have not stopped. The migrations across the seas and lands have not halted. Border walls have not stopped going up. The wall imprisoning Palestinians has not fallen – like the Berlin Wall had done. No US president stands in front of the apartheid wall – and cries out to the Israeli president to "tear down the wall" – in the way that Ronald Reagan had done when Gorbachev was president of the Soviet Union. But US presidents are still on the lookout and hunt for more natural resources, more energy and more markets for American-styled capitalism.

The use of fossil fuels the world over and especially in the developed world has not stabilised or decreased. Mental illnesses have not subsided. The Middle East has not yet found peace. Black Lives still do not matter. Many more blacks were killed and are still being killed in the US after George Floyd. Women and girls are still subservient to men and boys. The black majority still do not own much land in South Africa. The elite in the state apparatus have not stopped stealing from the poor. The rich are still not paying their fair share of taxes. Surely, all of these crucial benchmarks must relegate capitalism to a failing if not a failed historical system.

Big Pharma refused to waver patent rights for vaccine development claiming that it will dull innovation in the time of COVID-19. If private property laws leave hundreds of millions destitute under capitalism – then intellectual property laws condemn them to sicknesses and death. The government waivered all free market rules when it came to handing out trillions of tax dollars to the private sector during the 2008 Great Crisis. Capitalism is failing and socialism for the rich is succeeding – as it always does under capitalism.

COVID-19 revealed how utterly dependent the masses are on the capitalist system – the fear economy – for our material security and mental health. Man – an animal that has evolved and survived for millennia on planet earth – found himself at the mercy of a brutal and harsh historical system – that was ill-prepared to help him when he needed it most. Man, who had once discovered fire – felt helpless, lonely, anxious, depressed and fearful in capitalist society in the time of COVID-19. Man, who once tamed nature and gave us the agricultural revolution – found himself without food under free market capitalism. A tool-making animal – technological man could not access the necessary technologies in order to give him a chance at life. Man, who discovered and perfected medicine – was not able to access vaccines timeously and without capitalist market barriers and Western-imposed ideologies such as patents. Man died – as money, profit and all of his other inventions – lived on around him. Pragmatic man died as ideological man ballooned and sought to ruthlessly dominate the world in the time of a global pandemic. Leaders are meant to save their 'followers'. Instead, we found out that leaders of capitalist countries allowed their 'followers' to perish in the time of COVID-19. Almost two decades before COVID-19, Friedman (2003: 35) wrote:

> As one would expect of a system in which the bottom line is the ultimate measure, the conflict of interest between profits and health is routinely decided in favor of profits. Profits outweigh even lives.

I have quite a few self-help books in my home such as *The Power of Now*, *The Monk who Sold his Ferrari*, etc. I'm sure millions of others the world over also have many of such books. The proliferation of such books points to the spiritual, emotional and psychological deficit of capitalist society. Such books point to the constant and continuous searching of humans in capitalist society for happiness, well-being, and peace of mind – and just when we believe we may have found such happiness, we look for other such books – with the aim of trying to fulfil the spiritual, emotional and psychological void that is constantly and continuously generated in capitalist society.

Such books' focus is always on individualistic change. The problem is not the individual or the individual's mind per se – but capitalism itself. Capitalism is failing humankind spiritually, emotionally and psychologically. We can now click on the YouTube icon to access the many millions of videos instructing us on how to be happy Homo sapiens. Even after we have accomplishment our material goals, there is still that feeling of being incomplete and unfulfilled in capitalist society. We are on a continuous search for meaning in our lives. COVID-19 has shone the light on those challenges of life that Homo sapiens are yet to overcome.

Many of the social and mental illnesses that were experienced were not totally the result of COVID-19. COVID-19 has merely amplified much of what has been concealed in capitalist society for so long. Even before COVID-19 – communal and social man has always felt out of place in capitalist society. He either looks back to his younger days with nostalgia – or continually looks forward to a hopeful future of happiness, well-being and peace of mind. He is never satisfied with his present state of affairs and mind-set, no matter what or how much he has attained in his life. Now has no power under capitalism – because happy time under capitalism is always about the past or an imagined future. The good life of happiness and satisfaction is almost always elusive in capitalist society. Capitalism has transformed social man into an ideological singular unit and the results are evident – if one has time to notice:

> The world has been splintered into countless fragments of atomised individuals and groups. The disruption in the wholeness of individual experience corresponds to the disintegration in culture and group solidarity. When the bases of unified collective action begin to weaken, the social structure tends to break and to produce a condition which Emile Durkheim has termed anomie, by which he means a situation which might be described as a-sort of social emptiness or void. Under such conditions suicide, crime, and disorder are phenomena to be expected because individual existence no longer is rooted in a stable and integrated social milieu and much of life's activity loses its sense and meaning.
>
> MANNHEIM, 1953: XXV

Scholars have called out capitalism for weakening men and women in all manner of speaking:

> As career patterns, housing patterns, mortality patterns, and social policies follow the lead of global capitalism, much of the world seems determined to adopt a lifestyle that will compound and reinforce the chronic sense of isolation that millions of individuals already feel, even when they are surrounded by well-meaning friends and family. The contradiction is that we have radically changed our environment, and yet our physiology has remained the same. However wealthy and technologically adept our societies have become, beneath the surface we are the same vulnerable creatures who huddled together against the terrors of thunderstorms sixty thousand years ago.
>
> CACIOPPO and PATRICK, 2008: 72

The source of unhappiness in capitalist society – is capitalism itself:

Alienation, the commodification of social life, a culture of greed, aggression, mindless hedonism and growing nihilism, the steady haemorrhage of meaning and value from human existence: it is hard to find an intelligent discussion of these questions that is not seriously indebted to the Marxist tradition.

EAGLETON, 2018: xvi

The sorry state of frightened humans in capitalist society are well documented:

The messages addressed from the sites of political power to the resourceful and the hapless alike present 'more flexibility' as the sole cure for an already unbearable insecurity – and so paint the prospect of yet more uncertainty, yet more privatisation of troubles, yet more loneliness and impotence, and indeed more uncertainty still. They preclude the possibility of existential security which rests on collective foundations and so offer no inducement to solidary actions; instead, they encourage their listeners to focus on their individual survival in the style of 'everyone for himself, and the devil take the hindmost' – in an incurably fragmented and atomised, and so increasingly uncertain and unpredictable world.

BAUMAN, 2007: 14

Like those that bought into Nazi or apartheid ideology – many amongst us have bought into the ideology of the neoliberal economists of our time. If communism failed the Soviet-Union then – then it seems that capitalism is failing the Russian people now:

Despite aid and investment from other industrialised countries, the rapid Russian transition from communism to free market capitalism was a disaster. It more deeply impoverished the majority of its people. It reduced most of the country outside the major cities to a meagre subsistence exacerbated by the collapse of communications, health care and law enforcement. This led to a decline in life expectancy. It strengthened a powerful underworld that has little allegiance to the country itself or to the quality of life of its citizens.

FRIEDMAN, 2003: 16

By printing more money or borrowing more money or lowering interest rates – states are merely papering over the contradictions generated by failing capitalism and not really resolving the two core problems of capitalism – the exploitation of the worker and the exploitation of the natural environment.

That capitalism was a failed system for intelligent Homo sapiens and the natural environment – was observed when capitalism was only just taking-off many centuries ago. The following is but just one stanza of Oliver Goldsmith's long poem –*The Deserted Village* – written in 1770 – six years before Adam Smith's *The Wealth of Nations* (1776). It was the time when capitalism was picking up speed in England. It was a time when the destructive ideologies of capitalism were beginning to be observed:

Far, far away, thy children leave the land.
Ill fares the land, to hastening ills a prey,
Where wealth accumulates, and men decay:
Princes and lords may flourish, or may fade;
A breath can make them, as a breath has made;
But a bold peasantry, their country's pride,
When once destroyed, can never be supplied.
A time there was, ere England's griefs began,
When every rood of ground maintained its man;
For him light labour spread her wholesome store,
Just gave what life required, but gave no more:
His best companions, innocence and health;
And his best riches, ignorance of wealth.
But times are altered; trade's unfeeling train
Usurp the land and dispossess the swain;
Along the lawn, where scattered hamlets rose,
Unwieldy wealth and cumbrous pomp repose;
And every want to opulence allied,
And every pang that folly pays to pride.
Those gentle hours that plenty bade to bloom,
Those calm desires that asked but little room,
Those healthful sports that graced the peaceful scene,
Lived in each look, and brightened all the green;
These, far departing seek a kinder shore,
And rural mirth and manners are no more.

The Deserted Village – OLIVER GOLDSMITH

CHAPTER 11

Conclusion to Volume I

They say COVID is spread by mouths and noses, but scientists are now saying the greatest risk is assholes.

SHELLEN LUBIN

• • •

The secret of change is to focus all of your energy, not on fighting the old, but on building the new.

SOCRATES

⸫

Volume I viz. *F/Ailing Capitalism and the Challenge of COVID-19* has sought to explain the workings of the capitalist system through the lens of COVID-19. It has also sought to explain and understand COVID-19 through the ideological framework of capitalism. Volume I deals with the failure of capitalist countries in the main to respond timeously and effectively to COVID-19. The intention behind *F/Ailing Capitalism and the Challenge of COVID-19* is to expose the many ideologies that uphold the capitalist system, a 500-year-old system that is proving to be unsustainable on many levels and in so many spheres of life.

Due to the large amounts of data that was made available by the COVID-19 phenomenon, it was decided to compile the workings of different parts of the world in dealing with COVID-19 in two volumes. Volume II is titled *COVID-19 and Capitalism: Time to Make a Democratic New World Order.* Volume II engages with the themes of nature and climate change, discrimination, gender-based violence, ideological awakening, science, etc. in the time of COVID-19. In the final analysis, Volume II argues for the democratic remaking of the current world order by exploring ideas and spheres of influence for a post-capitalist world. *COVID-19 and Capitalism: Time to Make a Democratic New World Order* proposes the deepening and consolidation of freedom, democracy, human rights and privacy in a post-capitalist world. It suggests that humans should be 'placed back in nature' and nature back in humans, and argues for a global environmental movement. Volume II explores the idea of an o-shaped or use-value economy and society – and maintains that the free market should serve people and planet – instead of people and planet serving the free market. It motivates for deepening, strengthening, consolidating and trusting the state in leading the transition to a post-capitalist world. Making a democratic new world order should entail declaring war on global enemies such as gender-based violence, gun violence, poverty, racism, inequality, unemployment, classism, etc. and flattening their curves. A post-capitalist society should be one whereby planetary and peoples' well-being sit side by side with economic well-being. Transitioning to a post-capitalist society requires that economic science in its current ideological form be revisited in order to provide a more scientific understanding and analysis of the world economy. Exiting capitalism requires the unity of workers of all countries and the formation of a global workers movement. Ideally the transition to a post-capitalist society should be peacefully assisted and guided – instead of leaving socio-economic conditions unchanged – thereby increasing the risk of violence to enforce change for a better world. Volume II – *COVID-19 and Capitalism: Time to Make a Democratic New World Order* calls for reimagining and recreating the best of all possible worlds for present and future generations. In the final analysis, Volume II both predicts and maintains that *capitalism too shall pass*!

Bibliography

Abbott, T., 2020. We need a strong economy, but people come first. The path ahead should be about a better society rather than just dollars and cents. *The Australian.* 24 April 2020.

Addley, E., 2020. "I feel as if I'm part of a village" – How COVID-19 has transformed neighbours into communities. *The Guardian.* 6 June 2020.

Adler, M., 2009. *Economics for the rest of us – debunking the science that makes life dismal.* London: The New Press.

AFP, 2020. Help! British stars say virus is killing off live music. *Sunday Times*, South Africa. 5 July 2020.

Al Basam, D., 2020. Behind the veil of the coronavirus. Sociology of the precariat dilemma. *Gulf Times.* 17 May 2020.

Al Jazeera Television Network. 2020. COVID-19 coverage. *Al Jazeera.*

Alden, T., 2020. Why nobody can agree on anything. *The Malta Independent on Sunday.* 7 June 2020.

Anderson, G., 2020. The Black Lives Matter upheaval follows a well-worn path and is going downhill precipitously. *The Washington Times Daily.* 30 July 2020.

Anderson, R.D., 2020. Defining socialism and communism. *The Union Democrat.* 8 August 2020.

Ang, Y.Y., 2016. *How China escaped the poverty trap.* London: Cornell University Press.

AP, 2020. Chaos hits Japan as infections surge. *The Manila Times.* 19 April 2020.

Appleby, J., 2010. *The relentless revolution – a history of capitalism.* New York: W.W. Norton and Company.

Arvas, T.M., 2020. Whiplash from investing? Here's how to trade it. *Daily Sabah* (Turkey). 18 June 2020.

Augustin, E., 2020. How the communists took on coronavirus. *The Guardian.* 8 June 2020 – 25.

Bandyopadhyay, G., and Meltzer, A., 2020. Let us unite against COVID-19 – a New Zealand perspective. *Irish Journal of Psychological Medicine*, (2020), 37, 218–221.

Barker, J., 2014. *1381 –The year of the peasants' revolt.* UK: The Belknap Press of Harvard University Press.

Bauman, Z., 2007. *Liquid times: Living in an age of uncertainty.* UK: Polity Press.

BBC 23 May 2020. Coverage on COVID-19. *BBC.*

Beard, M., 2020. Those talking about a fast end to social distancing should consider the cost paid in human lives. *The Guardian Australia.* 17 April 2020 – 23.

Bergman, G., 2021. Peace prize should go to Gift of Givers. *The Citizen (KZN).* 15 February 2021.

Berkert, K., 2020. Anti-guns is anti-U.S. *The Washington Times.* Sunday, May 3, 2020.

Bohn, A., and Berntsen, D., 2007. Pleasantness bias in flashbulb memories: Positive and negative flashbulb memories of the fall of the Berlin Wall among east and west Germans. *Memory & Cognition*, 35 (3), 565–577.

Booth, W., and Adam, K., 2020. A plea for pickers: Prince Charles says farms need Brits' help. *The Washington Post*. 22 May 2020.

Brennan, T., 1993. *History after Lacan*. London: Routledge.

Brenner, T., 2020. Trump invokes defense production act for ventilator manufacturing. *Reuters*. April 2, 2020.

Cacioppo, J.T. and Patrick, W., 2008. *Loneliness – human nature and the need for social connection*. New York: W. W Norton & Company.

Caiyu, L., and Xiaojing, X., 2020. Japan's 2nd wave from west. US, Europe's failure drags world pandemic fight. *Global Times*. 30 April 2020.

Çam, T., & Kayaoğlu, M., 2015. Marx's distinction between socialism and communism. *International Journal of Human Sciences*, 12(1), 385–391.

Camber, R., 2020. 200,000 snitch on neighbours who break lockdown. *Daily Mail*. 1 May 2020–3.

Capurro, D., 2020. Why lockdown decision was tough call to make. *The Daily Telegraph*. 12 June 2020.

Carr, E.H., 1990. *A history of Soviet Russia – foundations of a planned economy: 1926 – 1929*. London: MacMillan Academic and Professional Ltd.

Carroll, R., Todo, L., Connolly, K., Jones, S., Gillet, K., 2020. Need for migrant farm workers across EU increasing tensions. *The Guardian*. 11 May 2020.

Cavazuti, L., McFadden, C., and Romo, C., 2020. CEO of ventilator maker speaks out as Trump invokes defense production act. *NBC News*. 28 March 2020.

Cerullo, M., 2019. 60 of America's biggest companies paid no federal income tax in 2018. *CBS News*. 12 April 2019.

CGTN – 20 May 2020. Coverage on COVID-19. *CGTN*.

Chabria, A., 2020. Farmworkers were hit hard. *Los Angeles Times*. 25 July 2020.

Charoensuthipan, P., 2020. Migrant workers left destitute by economic nosedive. No safety net for those hit by business closures. *Bangkok Post*. 19 May 2020.

Cheek, T., 2013. *Mao and Maoism in the Oxford handbook of the history of communism*. Edited by Stephen A. Smith. UK: Oxford University Press.

Cherian, J., 2020. A devastated world. *FrontLine*. 19 June 2020.

Chomsky, N., 2011 in Naiman, A., (Ed). *What uncle Sam really wants* in *How the world works*. New York: Soft Skull Press.

Choon, C.M., 2020. S. Korea battles new cluster. Country rushes to trace and test thousands who could be linked to nightclub cluster. *The Straits Times*. 13 May 2020.

Cohn, S. K., 2008. *Lust for liberty: the politics of social revolt in medieval Europe, 1200–1425: Italy, France, and Flanders*. London: Harvard University Press.

Creighton, A., 2020. We're paying a high price for saving not many lives. Australia was getting on top of the virus before the costlier stage three lockdowns. *The Weekend Australian*. 25 April 2020.

Cronin, J., 2020. Communist struggle continues – capitalism has proved to be resilient and 'barbaric' as seen in the profit race for COVID-19 vaccines. *Sunday Tribune*. 2 August 2020.

Curwen, T., 2020. Protesters defy O.C. beach closure. Dozens gather on the shore in opposition of the governor's order, which they see as unconstitutional. *Los Angeles Times*. 3 May 2020.

Da Silva, C., 2021. Nurse felt pressured to work despite COVID safety concerns, inquest hears. *The Independent*. 24 March 2021.

Dann, L., 2020. Ratings upgrade: What it means for NZ. *The New Zealand Herald*. 24 February 2021.

Davis, J., 2020. The world needs to start treating incel-related violence as a form of terrorism, because that's what it is. *The Globe and Mail (Ontario Edition)*. 22 May 2020.

Deepak, K., 2020. Capital's Malthusian moment. *FrontLine*. 5 June 2020.

Delaibatiki, N., 2021. Assault democracy. What kind of democracy do we want? We must guard against the rise in extremism. *Fiji Sun*. 10 January 2021.

Dennis, B., Flynn, M., and Noack, R., 2020. Crowded holiday events fuel worries about effect of unchecked behavior. *The Washington Post*. 27 May 2020.

Dewey, C., 2013. Why Nelson Mandela was on a terrorism watch list in 2008. *The Washington Post*. US. 7 December 2013.

Diacon, E., 2020. Why should I deny someone younger a hospital bed? *Daily Mail*. 17 Apr 2020.

Diamond, D., 2021. U.S. handling of Wuhan evacuees increased virus risks, watchdog finds. *The Washington Post*. 29 Jan 2021.

Diehl, J., 2020. A wasted chance to stand up to Beijing. *The Washington Post*. 3 August 2020.

Dilworth, M., 2020. 5,300 dead in six weeks. *Daily Mail*. 17th April 2020.

Dinan, S., 2020. Communist, Marxist movements in U.S. throw all their support to Biden. *The Washington Times Daily*. 4 August 2020.

Dodd, V., and Campbell, D., 2020. Experts call for criminal investigation into deaths of medics caused by lack of PPE. *The Guardian*. 9 May 2020.

Doherty, B., 2020. Australia[[[I_03739]]]'s coronavirus relief exclusions prove we are not all in this together. *The Guardian Australia*. 24 April 2020.

Dreier, P., 2016. Jesus was a socialist. *Huffpost*. https://www.huffpost.com/entry/jesus -was-a-socialist_b_13854296. Accessed on 23 May 2020.

Dudden, A. and Marks, A., 2020. South Korea took rapid, intrusive measures against COVID-19 – and they worked. *The Guardian – International Edition*. 20 March 2020.

Duncan, I., 2020. Truckers rally in D.C. over low rates. *The Washington Post*. 2 May 2020.

Dutta, M.J., Elers, C., and Jayan, P., 2020. Culture-centered processes of community organizing in COVID-19 Response: Notes from Kerala and Aotearoa New Zealand. *Frontiers in Communication. Vol. 5/article 62.* https://doi.org/10.3389/fcomm.2020.00062. Accessed in December 2020.

Eagleton, T., 2018. *Why Marx was right.* London: Yale University Press.

Edgerton, D., 2020. Where Brexit and COVID collide. *The New European.* 30 April 2020.

Editor, 2019. Will penny drop for UK banks? *Deutsche Welle (English edition).* 26 December 2019.

Editor, 2020. Cash support for fossil fuels amid call to ease control. *The Guardian Weekly.* 17 July 2020.

Editor, 2020. Improve the world: Stop buying from China. *Santa Fe New Mexican.* 12 July 2020.

Editor, 2020. Nepal PM Oli's remarks against India. Party leader says Oli made mistake by blaming India for trying to topple his government. *Mail Today.* 1 August 2020.

Editor, 2020. New England marks a fourth with less fizzle during pandemic. *Pawtucket Times.* 6 July 2020.

Editor, 2020. New infections as Cubans relax. *Bangkok Post.* 1 August 2020.

Editor, 2020. Official: US will extend support for Venezuela's Guaidó. *Daily Observer (Jamaica).* 5 August 2020.

Editor, 2020. Pyongyang. *The Week.* 31 July 2020.

Editor, 2020. Stop the war on masks. Face it: They have helped flatten coronavirus curve & should be worn. *Philadelphia Daily News.* 1 July 2020.

Editor, 2020. Take charge, Mr President, and focus your ministers' minds on what matters. *Sunday Times.* 10 May 2020.

Editor, 2020. The coronavirus slayer! How Kerala's rock star health minister helped save it from COVID-19. *Fiji Sun.* 16 May 2020.

Editor, 2020. Two ex-green berets sentenced to 20 years for Venezuela attack. Washington vows to use all possible means to win pair's freedom. *The Atlanta Journal-Constitution.* 9 August 2020.

Editor, 2020. Vietnam records 1st death in virus rebound. *New Straits Times.* 1 August 2020.

Editor, 2020. White House directs staff to wear masks. *The Straits Times.* 13 May 2020.

Editor, 2020. No place for nanny as freedoms return. *Scottish Daily Mail.* 23 May 2020.

Editor, 2020. Outraged experts charge: Coronavirus is Chinese bioweapon. *National Enquirer.* May 11 2020.

Engels, F., 1845. *The condition of the working-class in England in 1844.* Translated by Florence Kelley Wischnewetzky. London: George Allen and Unwin Ltd.

Fadden, R. and Jones, P., 2020. Donald Trump is erecting a White House of mirrors on China and COVID-19. *The Globe and Mail (Alberta Edition).* 11 May 2020.

Farmer, G., 2020. Negativity is pointless and demoralising. *Western Daily Press.* 25 May 2020.

Fogel, B., 2020. Jair Bolsonaro: the president who 'ordered his country to die', *Mail and Guardian Online*. 4 April 2020.

Frederick, Engels', Speech at the grave of Karl Marx Highgate Cemetery, London. March 17, 1883 https://www.marxists.org/archive/marx/works/1883/death/burial .htm. Accessed on 5 April 2020.

Fresco, Al., 2020. Eight days in a COVID hospital. *Business Standard*. 4 July 2020.

Friedman, M. 2002. *Capitaism and Freedom*, USA: University of Chicago Press.

Friedman, K., S. 2003. *Myths of the capitalist market*. New York: Algora Publishing.

Fromberg, N., 2020. Nanny state or money? *Mercury (Hobart)*. 25 June 2020.

Fukuyama, F., 1992. *The end of history and the last man*. New York: The Free Press, Macmillan Inc.

Furst, J., Pons, S., and Seldon, M., (Editors). 2017. *Endgames? Late communism in global perspective, 1968 to the present. Vol III*. UK: Cambridge University Press.

Gearan, A., and Wagner, J., 2020. 'Very good people': President supports Mich. protest-ers. Demonstrators, some armed, had gathered to oppose state restrictions. *The Washington Post*. 2 May 2020.

Gearan, A., Chiu, A. and Wagner, J., 2020. Trump skips mask in plant visit, defying Ford's request and Michigan law. *The Washington Post*. 22 May 2020.

Gel'man, V., 2011. The communist party of the Russian Federation: "Paper tiger" of the opposition. *Russian Analytical Digest. No. 102*.

Gerard, L., 2020. Journalism's jeopardy. *The New European*. 30 April 2020.

Gerber, L., 2020. Focusing on plight of migrant workers. *Waterloo Region Record*. 10 June 2020.

Gerstenberger, K., and Braziel, J.E., 2011. *After the Berlin Wall – Germany and beyond*. New York: Palgrave Macmillan.

Gillits, T.B., 2020. Tweak narrative on black lives to forge racial unity. *Daily News*. 11 June 2020.

Govender, N., 2020. Social media message.

Grace, J., 2015. McDonnell's great leap forward puts Osborne one step ahead. *The Guardian*. 25 November 2015.

Graham, B.A., 2020. "Swastikas and nooses": governor slams 'racism' of Michigan lock-down protest. *The Guardian (USA)*. 5 May 2020.

Groves, J., and Ledwith, M., 2020. Ministers: Virus will be here this week. *Daily Mail*. 27 January 2020.

Gutierrez, A. M., 2020. Accredited service providers association of Pagcor reacts to Carpio: No 'invisible hand' in Pogos. *Philippine Daily Inquirer*. 29 May 2020.

Hall, C.A.S. and Klitgaard, K.A., 2018. *Energy and the wealth of nations – Understanding the biophysical economy. 2nd Edition*. New York: Springer.

Hamilton, C., and Ohlberg, M., 2020. Beijing's hidden hand: How the communist party is reshaping the world. *National Post (National Edition)*. 4 August 2020.

Hannan, E., 2020. Laundry sackings 'industrial massacre'. *The Australian*. 29 May 2020.

Harte, L., 2021. When will I ever get home to see my family? We talk to NI expats in New Zealand. *Belfast Telegraph*. 20 February 2021.

Haskens, J., 2020. Political monster. *The Washington Times Weekly*. 11 May 2020.

Heath, A., 2020. The chancellor wants to replace central control with policies that harness the power of the market. *The Daily Telegraph*. 9 July 2020.

Heller, H., 2011. *The birth of capitalism – A twenty-first-century perspective*. London: Pluto Press.

Henley, J. and Harding, L., 2020. Sweden left out as neighbours strike border control deal. *The Guardian*. 30 May 2020.

Henley, J., Jones, S., Giuffrida, A., Oltermann, P., Smith, H., and Carroll, R., 2020. UK handling of crisis gets short shrift overseas. *The Guardian*. 7 May 2020.

Hepburn, C., O'Callaghan, B., Stern, N., Stiglitz, J., and Zenghelis, D., 2020. Will COVID-19 fiscal recovery packages accelerate or retard progress on climate change? Forthcoming in the *Oxford Review of Economic Policy, 36(S1)*.

Honigsbaum, M., 2020. How do pandemics end? Just like the Black Death, influenza and smallpox, COVID-19 will affect almost every aspect of our lives – even after a vaccine turns up. *The Observer*. 18 October 2020.

Hoobler, T., and Hoobler D., 2009. *Confucianism world religions: Third edition*. New York: Chelsea House Publishing.

Hoodvaavdooh, 2019. *Does socialism work? Soviet citizens speak about their lives in the USSR (Moscow)*. https://www.youtube.com/watch?v=ui11x8vLQFI. Accessed on 23 March 2020.

Hosken, G., and Nair, N., 2020. Nightmare at hospitals as alcohol takes its toll – booze-based trauma surges in overworked ERs after ban is lifted. *Sunday Times*. 07 June 2020.

Interview on NBC-TV "The today show" with Matt Lauer. 1998. https://1997-2001 .state.gov/statements/1998/980219a.html#:~:text=It%20is%20the%20threat%20 of,here%20to%20all%20of%20us. Accessed on 10 December 2020.

Javed, A., 2020. War against the invisible enemy viz-a-viz COVID-19. *Times of India*. 30 March 2020.

Jefford, S., 2020. Bridge the gap: Solicitor general says the legislation is needed to 'bridge the gap' emerging from strict lockdown, *The Niagara Falls Review*. 8 July 2020.

Joffe, H., 2020. Growth problem is mindset, not money – ANC needs to wake to real prerequisites of post-COVID recovery. *Sunday Times*. 07 June 2020. South Africa.

Johnston, M., 2020. Time for renewables to compete on open market. *Townsville Bulletin*. 14 July 2020.

Johnstone, C., and Taylor, P., 2020. PM schools teachers: go back to class. 'Bus drivers are showing up for work'. *The Weekend Australian*. 25 April 2020.

Jonas, M., 2020. This is the moment that we need to awaken and demand an alternative future. *Sunday Times*. 07 June 2020.

Kabiling, G., 2020. No free vaccine for the rich. *Tempo*. 1 August 2020.

Kate, N.G., 2020. Sweden admits lockdown strategy was less than ideal. *The Independent*. 4 June 2020.

Kelly, P., 2020. Morrison needs to find his finest hour. Political capital built during the crisis must be spent on reform. *The Weekend Australian*. 25 April 2020.

Kelly, T., Borland, S., and Coen, S., 2020. 4,000 Feared dead in our care homes. Shocking virus death toll hugely under-reported, warn experts. *Daily Mail*. 15 April 2020.

Kelly, W.J., 2020. At the mercy of the invisible hand. *National Post (Latest Edition)*. 23 September 2008.

Klein, N., 2014. *This changes everything – capitalism versus the climate*. New York: Simon and Schuster.

Knaus, C., 2020. Australian travel companies must honour refund policies, consumer watchdog says. *The Guardian Australia*. 24 April 2020.

Kress, G., and Hodge, R., 1979. *Language as ideology*. London: Routledge and Keagan Paul.

Krishna, T.M., 2020. Chaos and insensitivity reign. Even now, migrant workers continue to be treated as irritants. *The Hindu*. 2 June 2020.

Kubicek, P., 2011. *The diminishing relevance of ostalgie 20 years after reunification* in Gerstenberger, K., and Braziel, J.E., 2011. *After the Berlin Wall – Germany and beyond*. New York: Palgrave Macmillan.

Lake, E., 2020. Maduro has reason to worry if Biden comes to power. *Gulf Today*. 8 August 2020.

Lane, R., 2020. Greater capitalism: The coronavirus pandemic is transforming the economic system day by day, hour by hour What's emerging is something better, fairer, smarter – and it's happening right now. *Forbes*. 21 June 2020.

Lange, O and Taylor, F.M., 1964. *On the economic theory of socialism*. London: McGraw-Hill Book Company.

Ledwith, M., 2020. Get us out now, demand Britons. Cry for help from virus-hit Chinese city as UK accused of dithering. *Daily Mail*. 27 January 2020.

Leopold, D., 2013. *Marxism and ideology: From Marx to Althuser* in *the history of ideology and of ideology studies*. Eds. Freeden, M., Sargant, L.T., and Stears, M., UK: Oxford University Press.

Leuenberger, C., 2011. *From the Berlin Wall to the West Bank Barrier: How material objects and psychological theories can be used to construct individual and cultural traits* in Gerstenberger, K., and Braziel, J.E., 2011. *After the Berlin Wall – Germany and beyond*. New York: Palgrave Macmillan.

Li, T.W., 2020. Why S'pore has not adopted herd immunity strategy to fight virus. *The Straits Times*.13 May 2020.

Lovett, S., 2021. Labour: Punish UK firms working with PPE suppliers accused of modern slavery. *The Independent*. 24 March 2021.

Macionis, J.J and Plummer, K., 2012. *Sociology–A global introduction. 4th edition.* London: Pearson Prentice Hall.

Malankar, A., 2020. Face of opportunism. *Business Standard.* 30 July 2020.

Malnick, E., and Donnelly, L. 2020. NHS hospitals on brink of running out of gowns to protect medics from coronavirus. *The Sunday Telegraph.* 12 April 2020.

Mangahas, M., 2020. Social Climate: Try the invisible hand. *Philippine Daily Inquirer.* 4 July 2020.

Mannheim, K., 1953. *Ideology and utopia: an introduction to the sociology of knowledge: 1893–1947.* London: Routledge and Kegan Paul Ltd.

Marshall, E., 2020. A nation adrift under a president still in denial. With his country now at the centre of the COVID-19 pandemic, Brazil's Jair Bolsonaro is in deep water. *The Daily Telegraph.* 25 May 2020.

Martain, T., 2020. Plea to leave the pokies turned off. *Mercury (Hobart).* 24 June 2020.

Martin, J., n.d. *Social solidarity in Scandinavia after the fall of finance capitalism.* Boston University. Prepared for the Boston University-Warwick workshop on finance capitalism.

Marx, K., 1845 [1998]. *The German ideology.* New York: Prometheus Books.

Marx, K., 2011 [1867]. *Capital vol 1 – A critique of political economy.* New York: Dover Publications, Inc.

Marx, K. and Engels, F., 1848. *Manifesto of the communist party.* Moscow: Progress Publishers.

Marx, K., 1843. *Works of Karl Marx 1843. A contribution to the critique of Hegel's philosophy of right.* https://www.marxists.org/archive/marx/works/1843/critique-hpr/intro.htm.

Marx, K., 1852 [1972]. *The Eighteenth Brumaire of Louis Bonaparte.* Moscow: Progress Publishers.

Marx, K., 1853. The British rule in India. *New-York Daily Tribune,* June 25, 1853. https://www.marxists.org/archive/marx/works/1853/06/25.htm. Accessed on 3 October 2020 at 4pm.

Meredith, S., 2019. CNBC. World Politics. *'Illegal colonial occupier': Mauritius condemns UK for failing to give up control of an overseas territory.* 28 November 2019.

Merritt, J.A., 2016. *Using OPEC as a villain in narratives.* For the degree of masters of public policy in public policy presented on 6 June 2016.

Milman, O., 2020. Trump ignores warning of 'death sentence' to press on with 'getting our country open'. *The Guardian.* 7 May 2020.

Moore, J., 2020. We're seeing dangerously misleading COVID-19 figures. *The Independent.* 19 April 2020.

Mordock, J., 2020. Virus patient privacy clashes with need to know. *The Washington Times* Weekly. 4 May 2020.

Morrow, A., 2020. Why is there a resurgence of COVID-19 cases across the U.S.? *The Globe and Mail (Alberta Edition)*. 11 July 2020.

Mthombothi, B., 2020. Some ministers a bit too happy to wield total control without the nuisance of a bill of rights. *Sunday Times*. 07 June 2020.

Mulcahy, S., Shah, A. and Jacobs, J., 2020. Nursing-home staffs lay lives on the line to keep working: More than four months into the outbreak, caregivers feel largely left to fend for themselves. *The Washington Post*. 4 July 2020.

Naish, J., 2020. From bat to snake to humans – it's a real-life sci-fi nightmare. *Daily Mail*. 27 Jan 2020.

Ning, Yu., 2020. US virus death toll a new stain on its human rights record and politics. *Global Times*. 29 May 2020.

Nsenduluka, M., 2020. Big brother Dan. *The Daily Telegraph (Sydney)*. 9 July 2020.

Nuki, P. and Newey S., 2020. UK patient zero? East Sussex family may have been infected with coronavirus as early as mid-January, *The Telegraph*. 25 March 2020.

Onselen, P., 2020. Denying unis a lifeline is ideological wilful ignorance. Higher education is vital to our future, and not just economically. *The Weekend Australian*. 25 April 2020.

Osama, K., 2020. What planet does Johnson live on to think our virus response has been a success? *The Independent*. 1 May 2020.

Paz, I.G., 2020. Read Bernie Sanders's full speech on ending his campaign. *New York Times*. April 8, 2020.

Perelman, M., 2000. *The invention of capitalism. Classical political economy and the secret history of primitive accumulation.* Durham & London: Duke University Press.

Petri, R., 2018. *A short history of western ideology – A critical account.* New York: Bloomsbury Academic.

Phillips, D., 2020. 'Totalitarian' government halts release of Brazil's virus figures and wipes data. *The Guardian*. 8 June 2020.

Picard, A., 2020. The coronavirus mess in the U.S. will only get worse. *The Globe and Mail (Ontario Edition)*. 4 July 2020.

Pierce, A., 2020. Corbynite lover of communist Cuba who says the first word she learned was 'strike' – Introducing intransigent schools union chief. *Daily Mail*. 15 May 2020.

Piketty, T., 2020. *Capital and ideology.* London: The Belknap Press of Harvard University Press.

Pilkington, E., 2020. Blow for Trump's image of control over virus as top doctor self-isolates. *The Guardian*. 11 May 2020.

Pollard, S., 2020. The tracing app has got lawyers howling about human rights, but what about the rights of people like me to stay alive! *Daily Mail*. 7 May 2020.

Prashad, V., 2020. The Three apartheids of our times (money, medicine, food). The sixth newsletter. *Tricontinental*: Institute for Social Research.

Prashad, V., 2020. These migrant workers did not suddenly fall from the sky. The four-teenth newsletter. *Tricontinental:* Institute for social research.

Prebble, R., 2021. Why was latest COVID lockdown the only option? *Bay of Plenty Times.* 26 February 2021.

Quinn, B., 2020. BBC stands by its PPE investigation after minister weighs in. *The Guardian.* 4 May 2020.

Quinn, B., and Parveen, N., 2020. Woman shares picture of her dying mother to 'show reality of COVID', *The Guardian.* 4 May 2020.

Radchenko, S., 2013. *Global moments in the Oxford handbook of the history of communism.* Edited by Stephen A. Smith. UK: Oxford University Press.

Rand, A., 1966. Rand, A., *Capitalism – the unknown ideal.* New York: Published by New American Library.

Reyes, J., 2020. Ex-rebel supporters denounce communism. *Daily Tribune (Philippines).* 3 August 2020.

Rodriguez, A., 2020. Deep democracy of mother earth – The profanation of the sacred mother has provoked an apocalypse. *The Taos News.* 15 October 2020.

Roemer, J.E., 1994. A future for socialism. *Politics and Society.* Vol. 2. No. 4, 451–478.

Romm, T., 2020. Return to work or risk jobless aid, states warn. *The Washington Post.* 1 May 2020.

Ross, J., 2020. Openmic. *Global Times.* 31 July 2020.

Ryan, M., 2020. *Views on COVID-19 and nature.* Executive Director, WHO Health Emergencies Programme.

Safi. M., 2020. 400,000 deaths grim global milestone as China hails its response to out-break. *The Guardian.* 8 June 2020.

Saunderson-Meyer, W., 2020. Wash your hands and stop whimpering for nanny. *Weekend Argus (Saturday Edition).*13 June 2020.

Sartorius, K., 2020. Logic demands that sugar should join the banned list. Letters to the editor. *Sunday Times.* 10th May 2020.

Schottenfeld, R., 2020. Corporate welfare is killing American capitalism. *The Trentonian (Trenton, NJ).* 17 June 2020.

Schram, S.F and Pavlovskaya, M. (Ed). 2018. *Rethinking neoliberalism – resisting the disciplinary regime.* New York: Routledge.

Schumpeter, J.A., 1950. The March into Socialism. *The American Economic Review, Vol. 40, No. 2.* Papers and proceedings of the sixty-second annual meeting of the American economic association (May, 1950), pp. 446–456.

Service, R., 2000. *Lenin – A biography.* London: MacMillan Publishers.

Shepherd, C., 2018. No regrets: Xi says Marxism still 'totally correct' for China. *Reuters.*

Shlapentokh, V., Shiraev, E. and Carroll, E., 2008. *The Soviet Union – Internal and external perspectives on soviet society.* US: Palgrave, Macmillan.

Shubin, V. G., 2008. *The hot cold war – The USSR in southern Africa.* London: Pluto Press.

Siddique, H., 2020. Doctors take legal action to demand independent inquiry. *The Guardian*. 11 May 2020.

Silke, D., 2020. SA post-COVID: more state control, or pragmatism? *Sunday Times*. 16 May 2020.

Skell, A., 2020. Reject left-wing socialist anarchy. *The Dallas Morning News*. 1 August 2020.

Smart, T., 1996. *Children's encyclopaedia of British history*. London: Kingfisher.

Smit, S., 2020. Invisible threat to workers' rights. Nearly half of all workplaces inspected by the department of labour found to be unsafe. *Mail & Guardian*. 15 May 2020.

Smith, A., 2003 [1776]. *An inquiry into the nature and causes of the wealth of nations*. New York: Bantam Dell.

Smith, K., 2019. *Does socialism work? Soviet citizens speak about their lives in the USSR* (Moscow). https://www.youtube.com/watch?v=ui11x8vLQFI. Accessed on 23 March 2020.

Smith, S.A., 2014. *Towards a global history of communism* in *The Oxford handbook of the history of communism*. UK: Oxford University Press.

Sombart, W., 1976. *Why is there no socialism in the US*. London: The Macmillan Press Ltd.

Sono, T., 2021. Mapaila exposes Barron's bias. *Sunday Times,* 24 January 2021.

Spencer, B., Groves, J., and Harris, S., 2020. Now killer virus as hunt is on in UK for 2,000 who flew in from Wuhan in last 2 weeks. *Daily Mail*. 25 January 2020.

Spinney, L., 2020. 'We must revive the social state'. Pandemics can lead to equality, suggests Piketty. *The Guardian*. 13 May 2020.

Stein, C., 2020. Give us our rights back, nanny state. *The Daily Courier*. 15 May 2020.

Stewart, C., 2020. Excuses being made for doctor just don't cut it. *Evening Times*. 7 April 2020.

Stewart, H. and Walker, P., 2021. Tens of thousands of people died who didn't need to die. *The Guardian*. 27 May 2021.

Stone, L., and Grant, T., 2020. Ford apologises for claims about migrant workers. *The Globe and Mail (Ontario Edition)*. 4 July 2020.

Stubley, P., 2015. *A pauper's history of England – 1000 years of peasants, beggars and guttersnipers*. Great Britain: Pen and Sword Books Ltd.

Summers, L.H., and Stansbury, A., 2020. U.S. workers need more power. *The Washington Post*. 30 June 2020.

Super Trini Gamer, 2019. *Does socialism work? Soviet citizens speak about their lives in the USSR (Moscow)*. https://www.youtube.com/watch?v=ui11x8vLQFI. Accessed on 23 March 2021.

Tait, C., Grant, T., Thanh, T., Kathryn, H. and Baum, B., 2020. Cargill, union at odds on plant reopening. *The Globe and Mail (Prairie Edition)*. 4 May 2020.

Taylor, G. 2020. Crisis lets Beijing get more debtors under its belt. *The Washington Times Weekly*. 11 May 2020.

Taylor, H.K., 2020. How the other half locks down. *Scottish Daily Mail*. 19 June 2020.

Tiku, N., 2020. Delivery apps: Opaque rules and poor pay await many workers. *The Washington Post*. 27 May 2020.

Vine, S., 2020. Lockdown stasi are coming for you. *Daily Mail*. UK. 15 April 2020.

von Tunzelmann, A., 2012. *Indian summer: The secret history of the end of an empire*. UK: Simon and Schuster.

Vosloo, R.R., 2015. The Bible and the justification of apartheid in reformed circles in the 1940's in South Africa: Some historical, hermeneutical and theological remarks. *Stellenbosch Theological Journal 2015*, Vol 1, No 2, 195–215.

Walker, P., 2020. 'We did not understand virus,' says Johnson, *The Guardian*. 25 July 2020.

Wattenbarger, M., 2020. Mexico factories at US border pressured to remain open despite risk. *The Guardian*. 15 May 2020.

Wearden, G., and Brignall, M., 2020. Big cities face financial pain as workers stay at home, economists warn. *The Guardian*. 3 August 2020.

Weaver, M., 2020. Privacy rights group warns over contact app 'coercion'. *The Guardian*. 27 April 2020.

Wickham, C., 2016. *Medieval Europe*. London: Yale University Press.

Wikipedia. 2020. Australia. https://en.wikipedia.org/wiki/Australia. Accessed on 20 August 2020.

Wikipedia. 2020. https://en.wikipedia.org/wiki/Brazil. Accessed on 30 August 2020.

Wikipedia. 2021. https://en.wikipedia.org/wiki/China. Accessed on 18 December 2021.

Wikipedia. 2020. https://en.wikipedia.org/wiki/Feudalism. Accessed on 14 September 2020.

Wikipedia. 2020. https://en.wikipedia.org/wiki/India. Accessed on 8 April 2020.

Wikipedia. 2020. https://en.wikipedia.org/wiki/Nanny_state Accessed on 11 April 2020.

Wikipedia. 2020. Japan. https://en.wikipedia.org/wiki/Japan. Accessed on 24 August 2020.

Wikipedia. 2022. https://en.wikipedia.org/wiki/New_Zealand. Accessed on 22 December 2022.

Wikipedia, 2022. https://en.wikipedia.org/wiki/United_Kingdom. Accessed on 22 December 2022.

Wikipedia. 2020. USA https://en.wikipedia.org/wiki/United_States. Accessed on 5 April 2020.

Wikipedia. 2020. Wuhan. https://en.wikipedia.org/wiki/Wuhan. Accessed on 14 August 2020.

Witt, G., 2020. Socialism helps Texas time to decide. *Tulsa World*. 7 August 2020.

Wolff, R.D., 2020. Fascism in capitalist states. *The Pak Banker*. 17 October 2020.

Zhao, H., Jatana, S., and Loeb, M., 2020. What history can tell us about wearing masks. *The Globe and Mail (Ontario Edition)*. 4 July 2020.

Zhou, N., 2020. Ruby Princess crew fear for their health as ship leaves Australia. *The Guardian*. 23 April 2020.

Index